you out tonight?

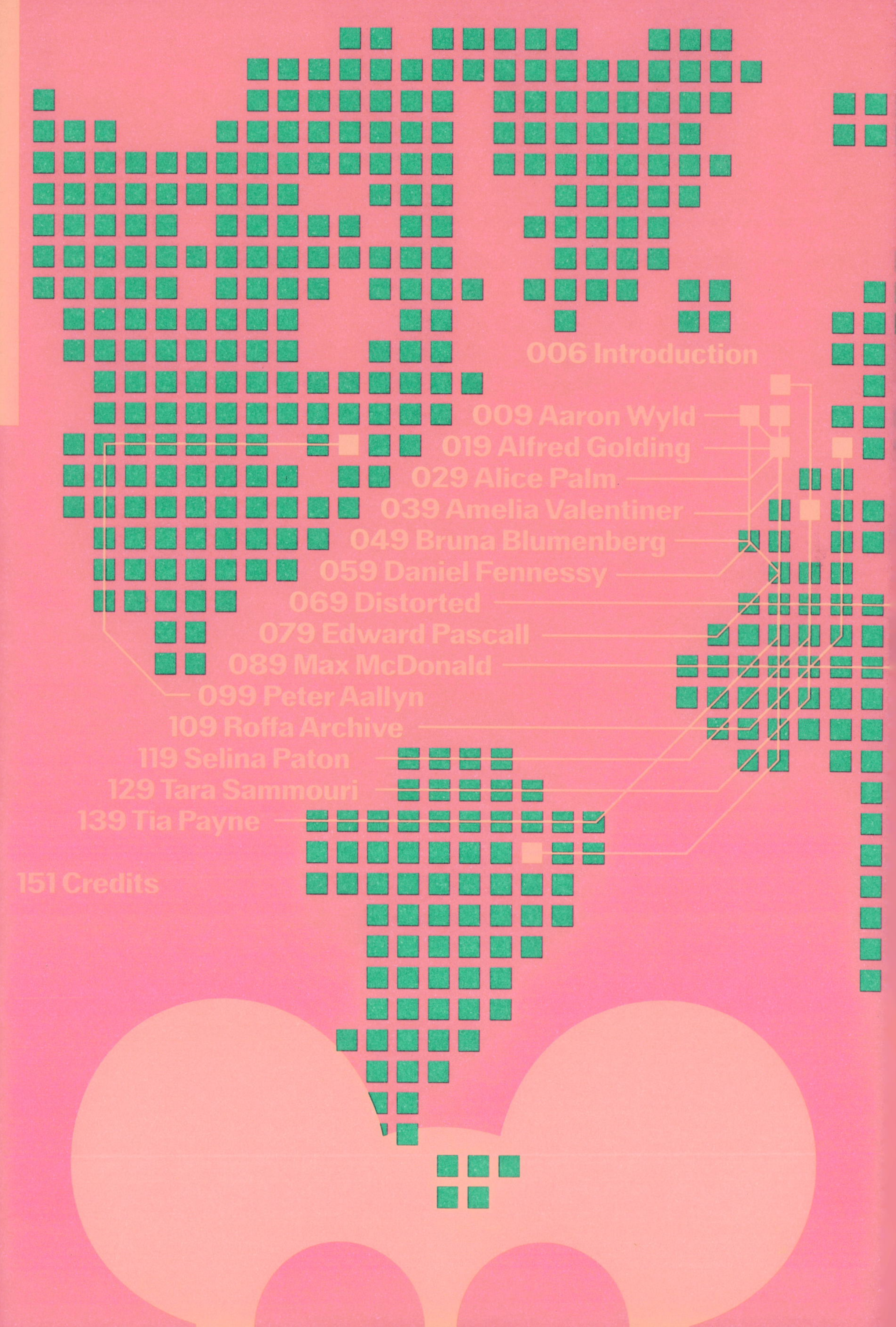

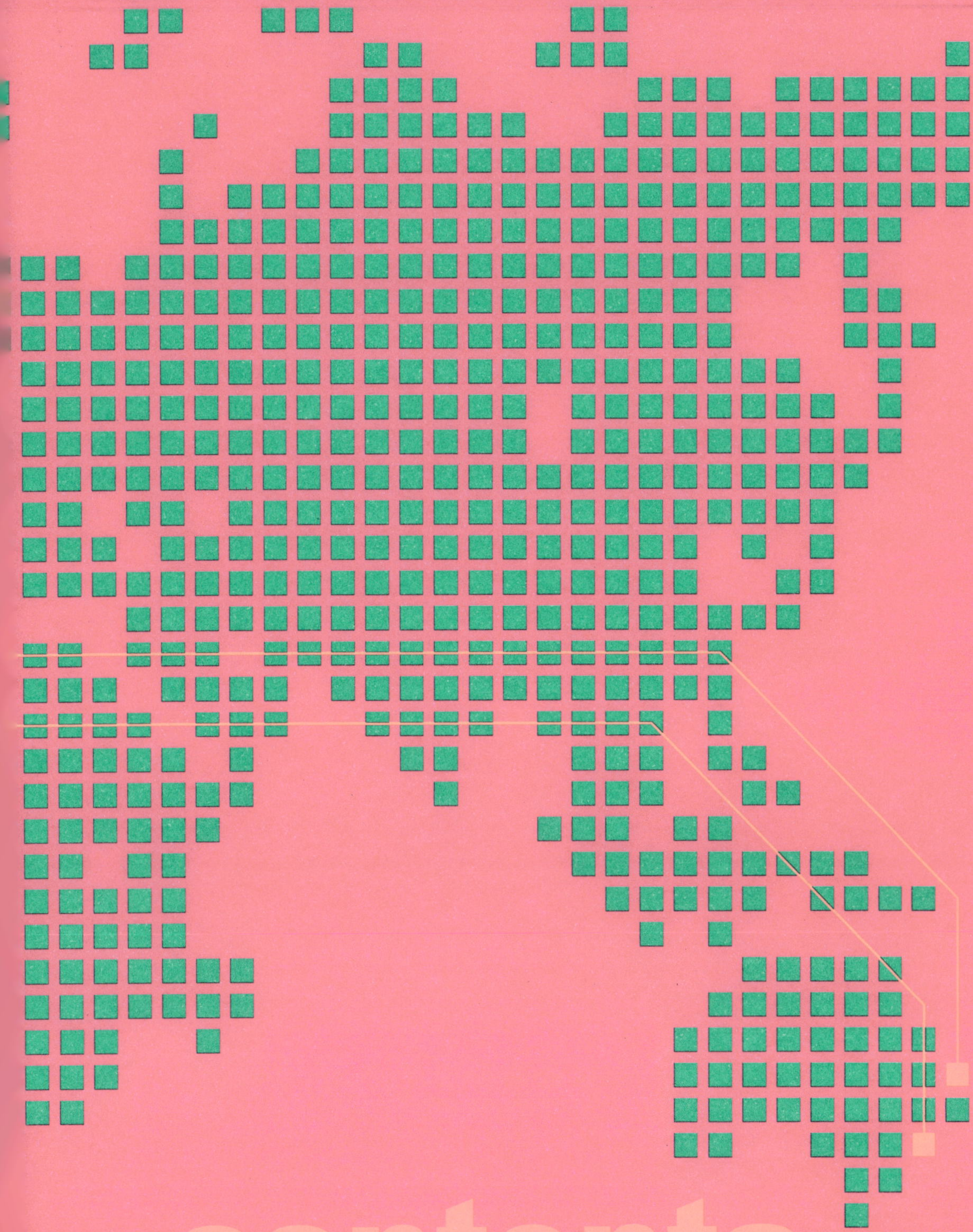

contents

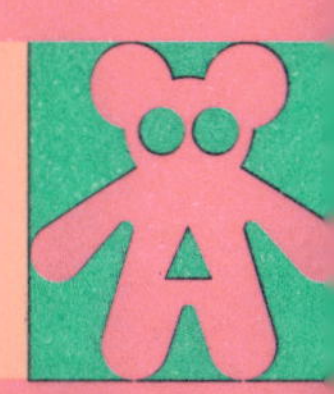

In the midst of the 2020 lockdown blues, Tough Luck started as an Instagram page as a personal archive, a collection of photos capturing the essence of the nightlife we were missing. Little did we know, it would grow into a global community, echoing the sentiments of many craving an escape through the lens of rave photography. As lovers of photography, Tough Luck began this journey by curating images that resonated with us. What ensued was a flood of contributions from extremely talented photographers from all corners of the globe—from England to Brazil, Australia, and beyond. Tough Luck evolved from a personal project to a shared passion, a testament to the universal longing for the freedom and thrills found in raves.

'You Out Tonight?', a phrase said by many, serves as more than just a title for this photography book; it's an invitation, a call for adventure. This phrase encapsulates the essence of spontaneity, the spirit of seizing the night, and the anticipation of stepping into a world where music, freedom, and creativity converge. Each image in this book captures the essence of stepping outside our comfort zones, an invitation for you to join the ultimate party.

Words by Jordan Taylor

introduction

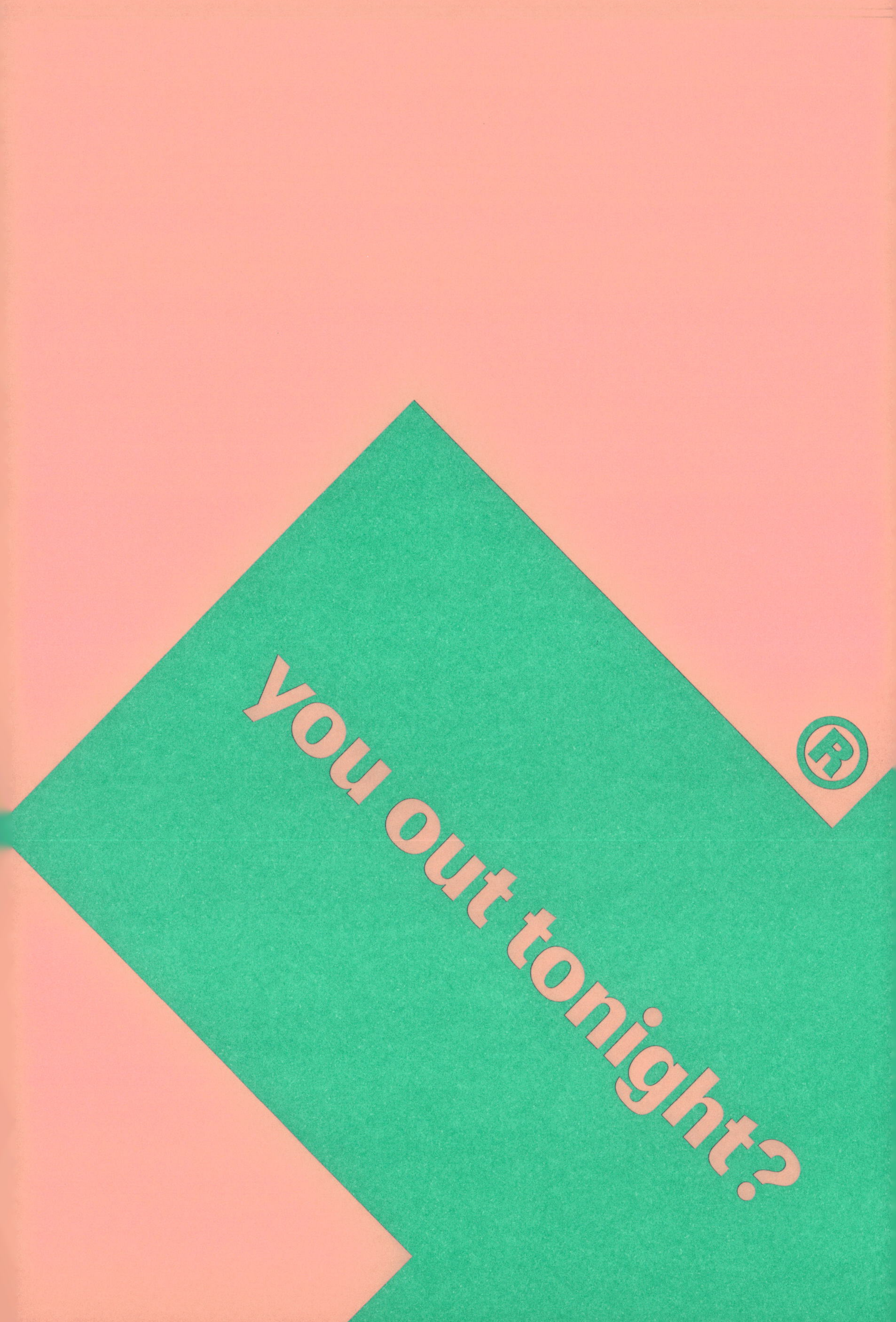

you out tonight?
®

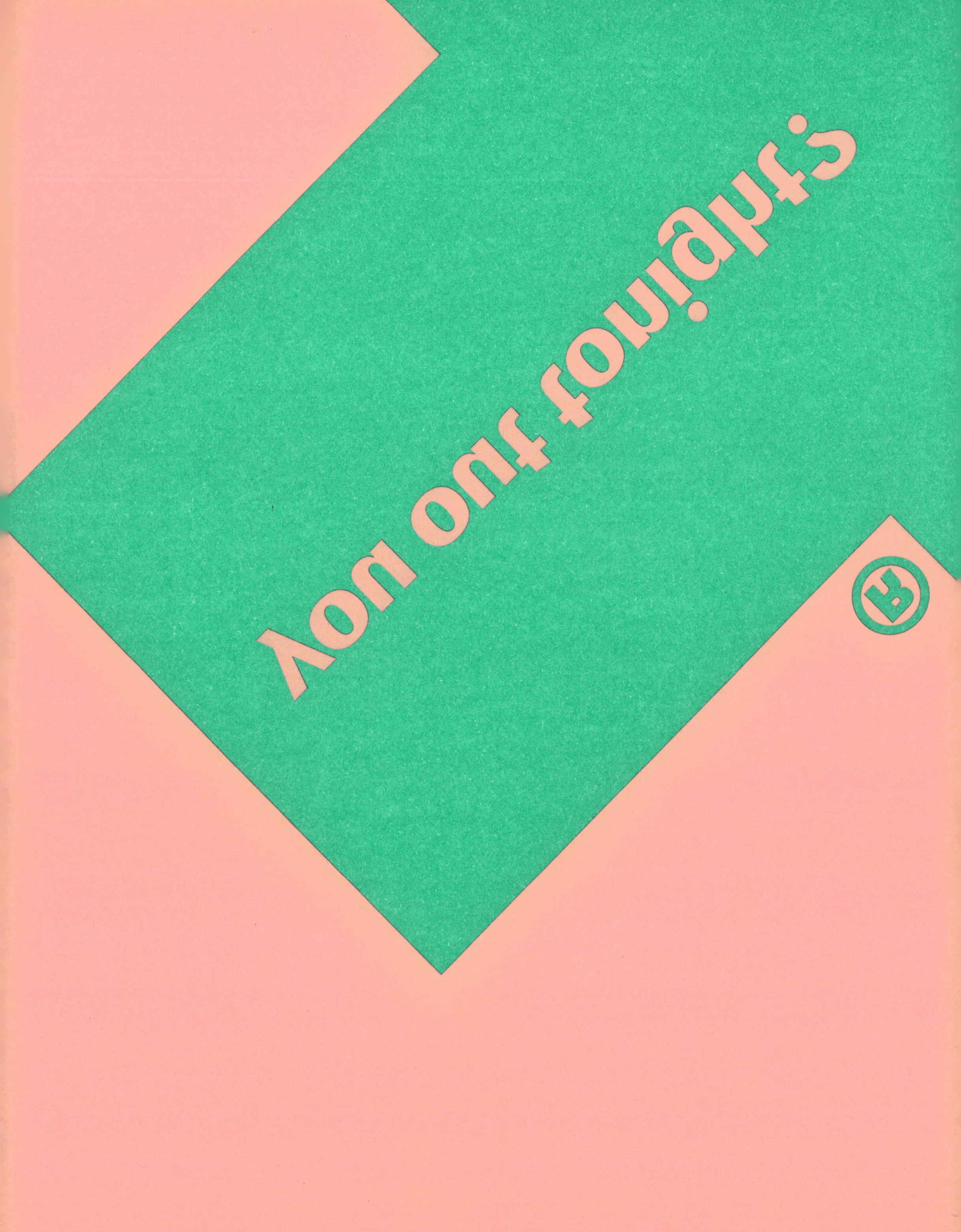

You out tonight's?

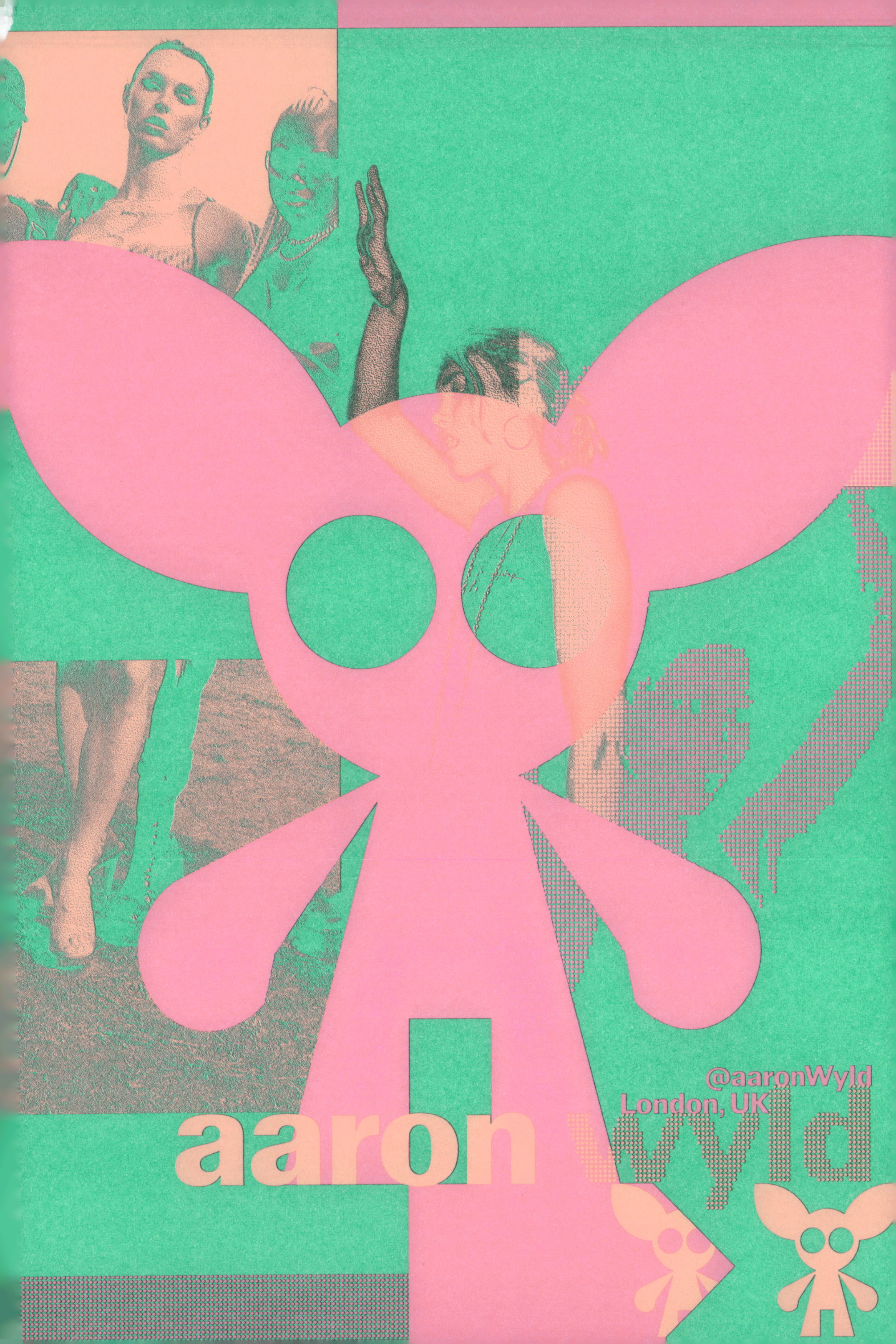

@aaronWyld
London, UK
aaron wyld

I'm Aaron, a Sheffield-born photographer now based in London. I was drawn into music photography in 2022 living in Newcastle upon Tyne through a fascination with music scenes, their audiences and fashion. By documenting club nights, festivals, and music events, along with the subcultures within them, I hope to capture those candid moments and the raw emotion and energy that music conjures in us all. It's the euphoria and escapism of music inhabiting nostalgia and freedom that I am attracted to and direct my lens towards.

Rave culture is a particular focus because it is so much more than the music. It's the crowds that raves attract, with people from every corner of society and the beauty in the self-expression, strong sense of individualism and inclusivity within. Hedonism, rebellion and adoration for underground sound are elements that are shared and echoed throughout this culture and this is why I love photographing it.

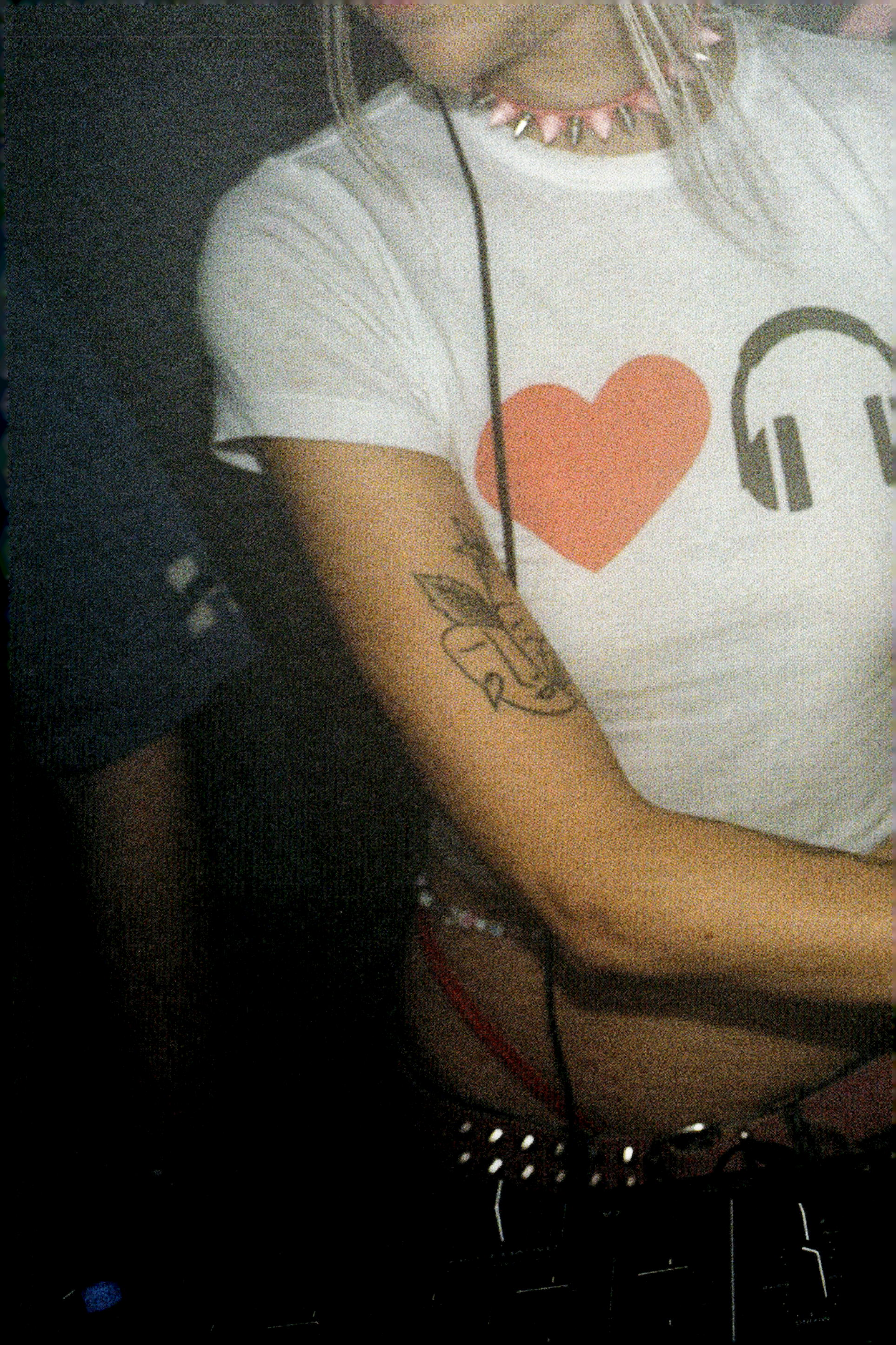

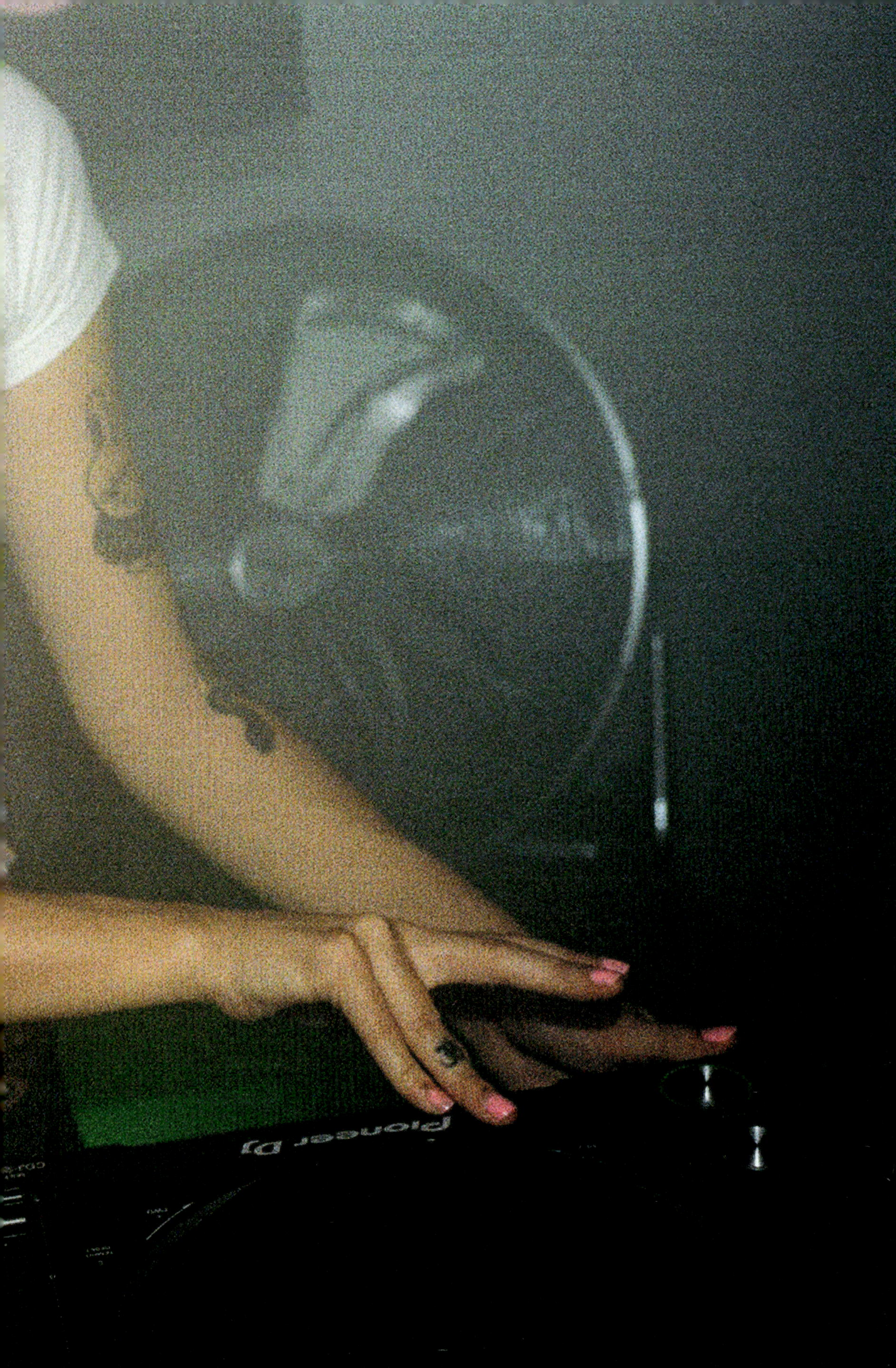

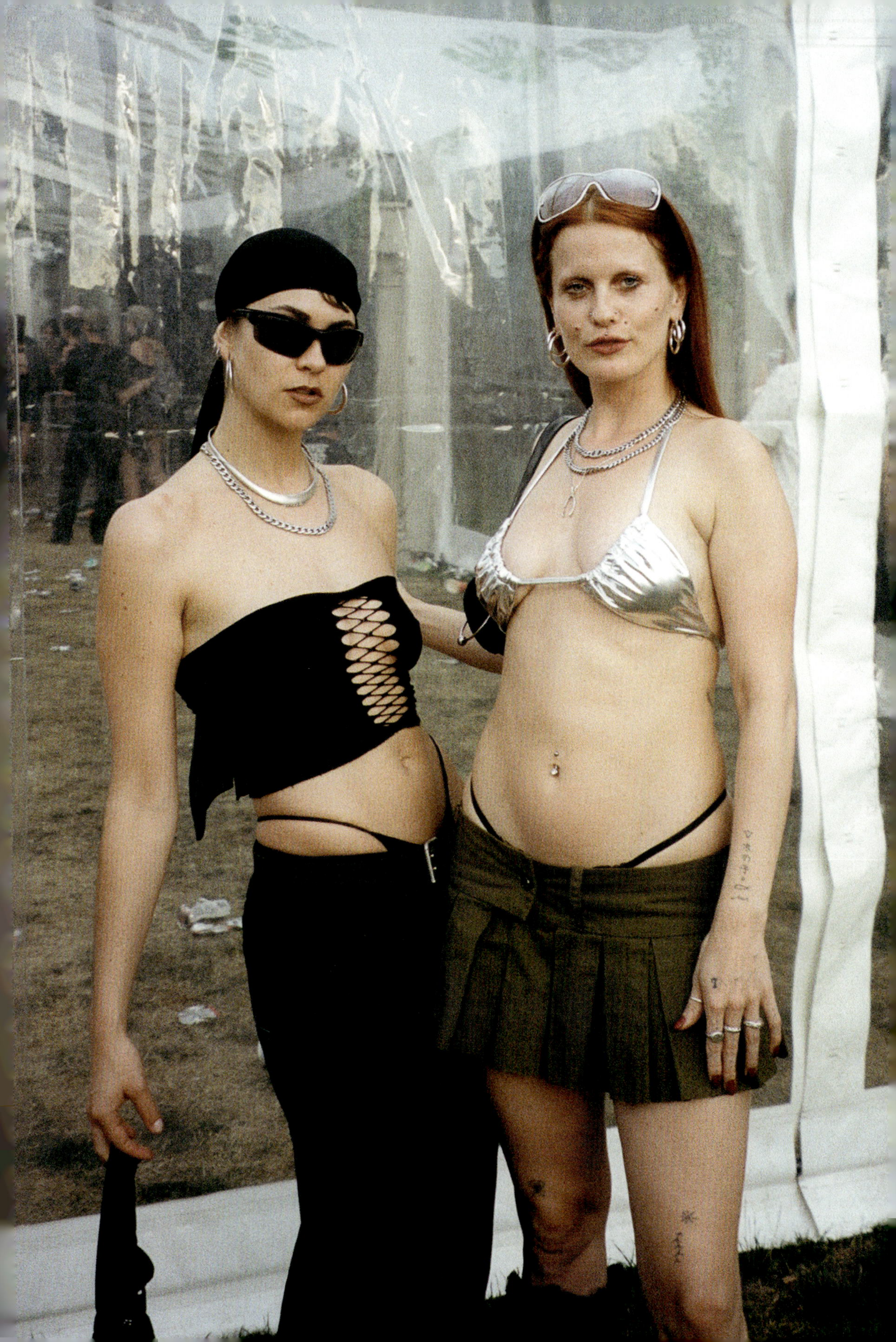

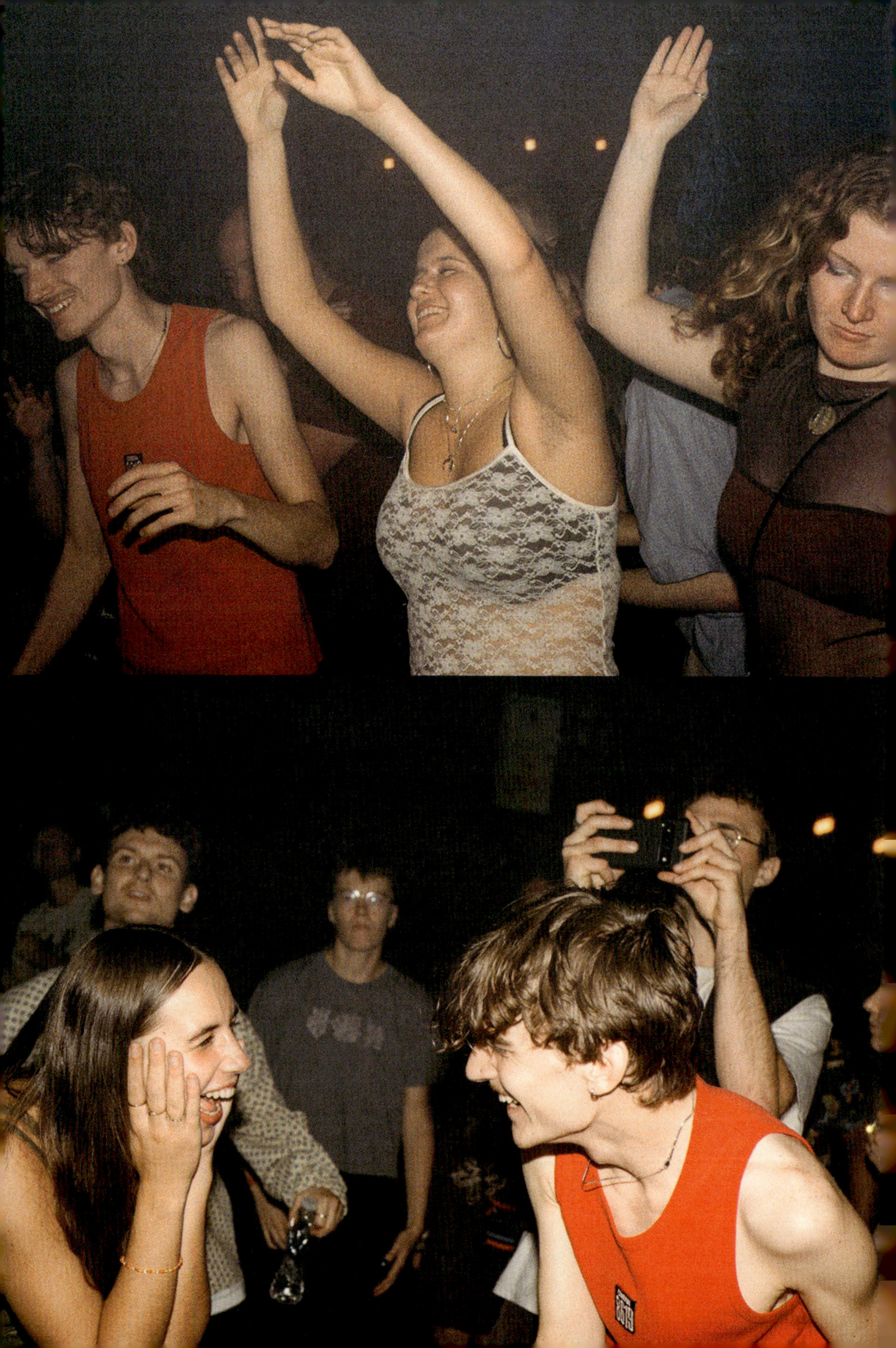

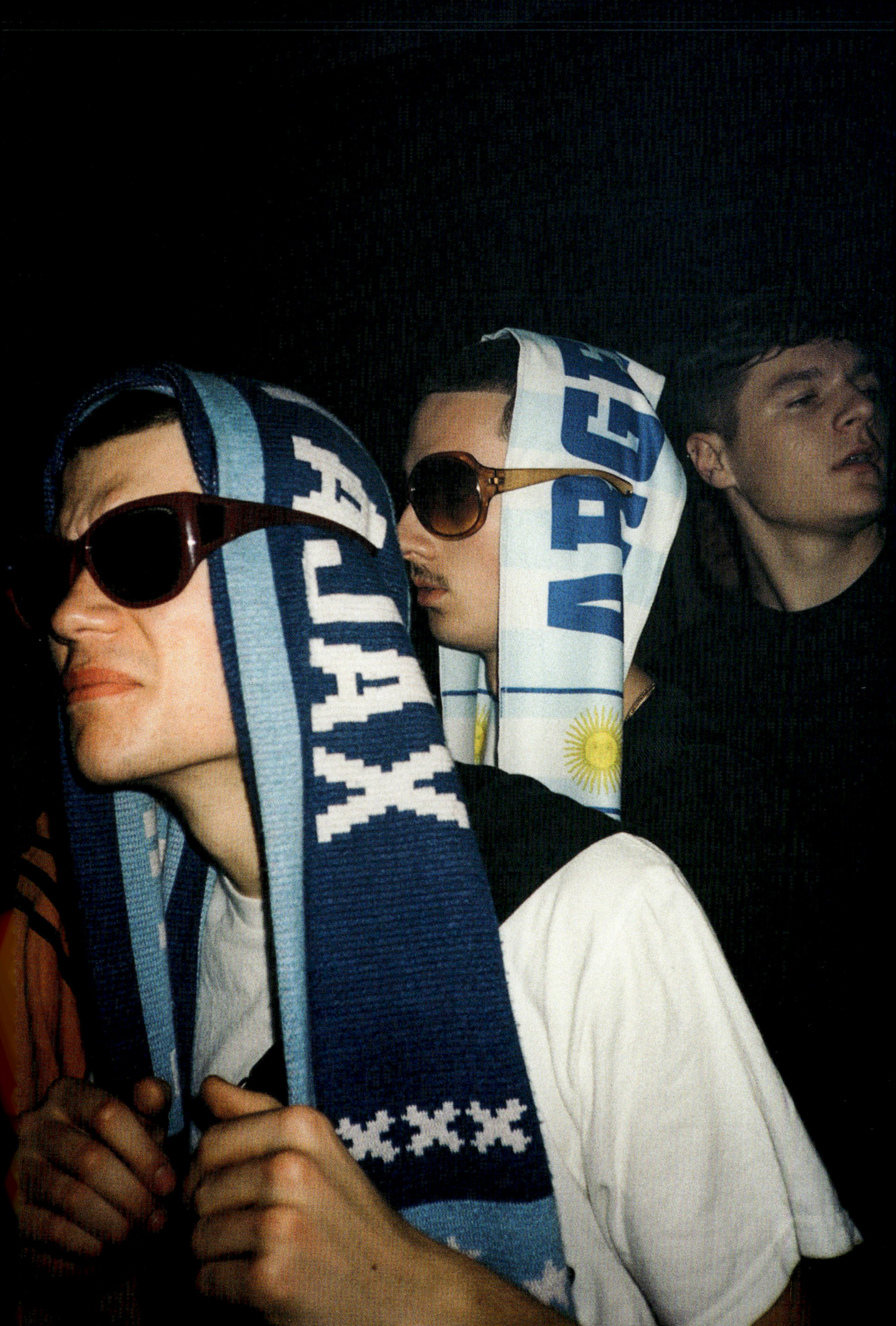
AJAX

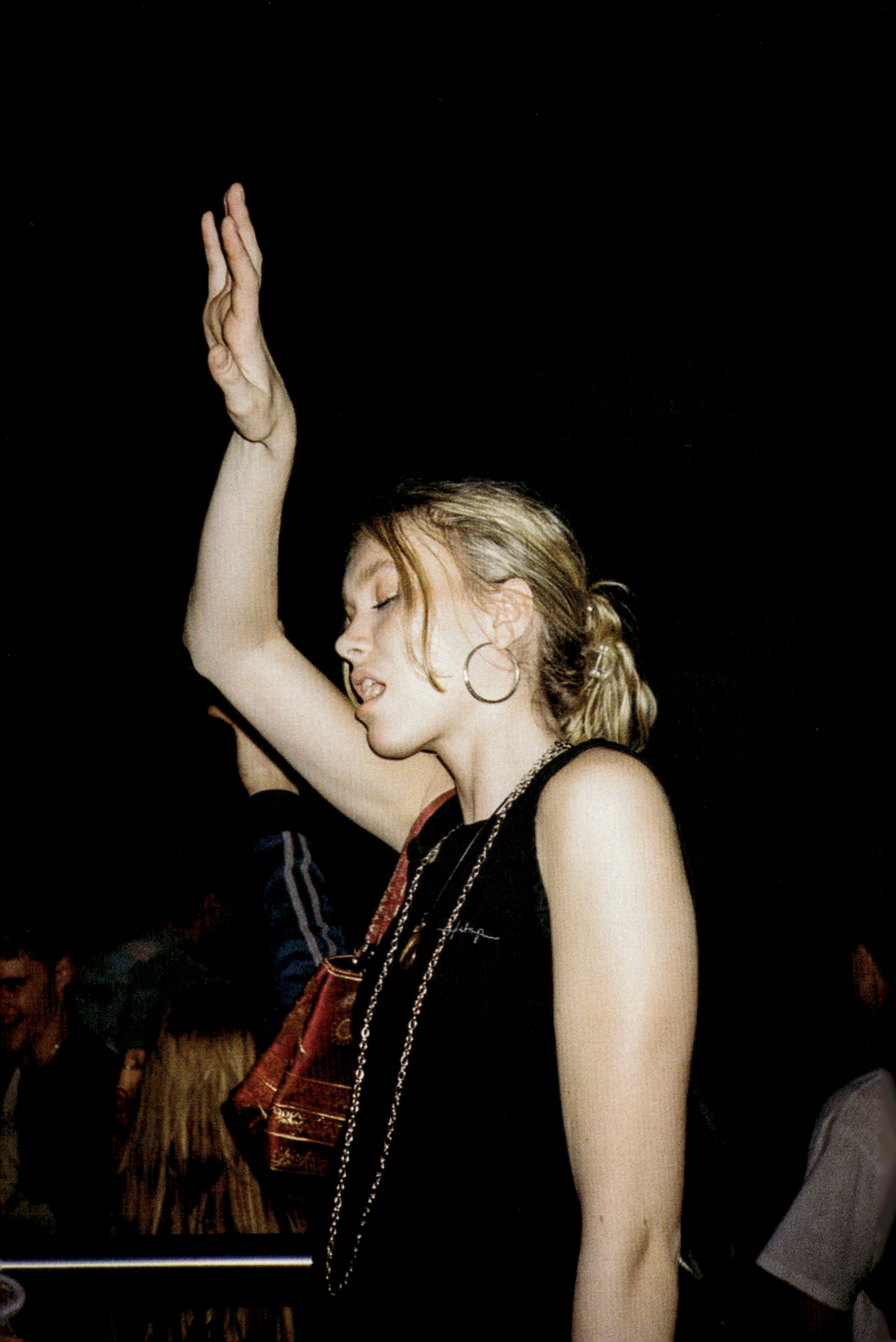

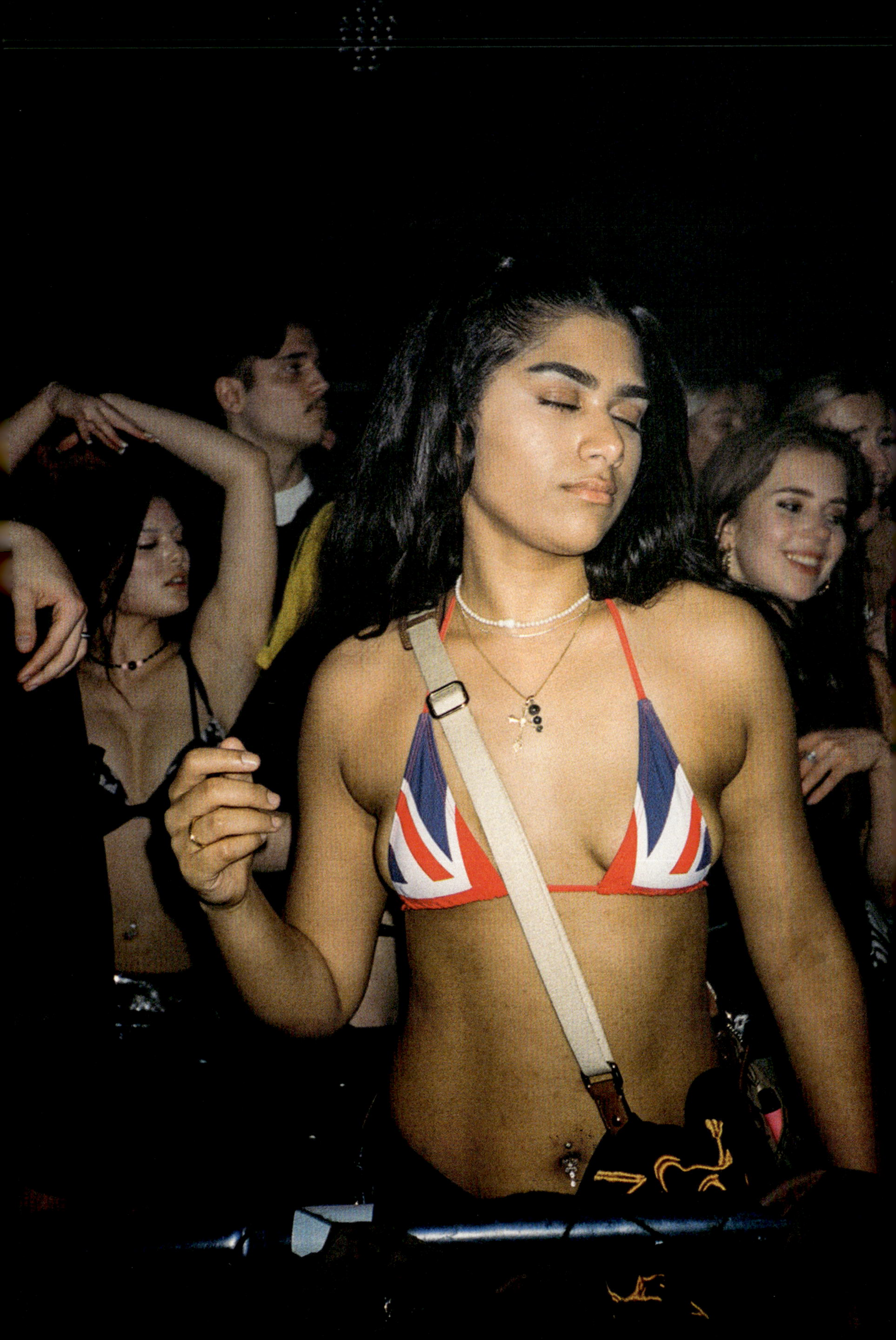

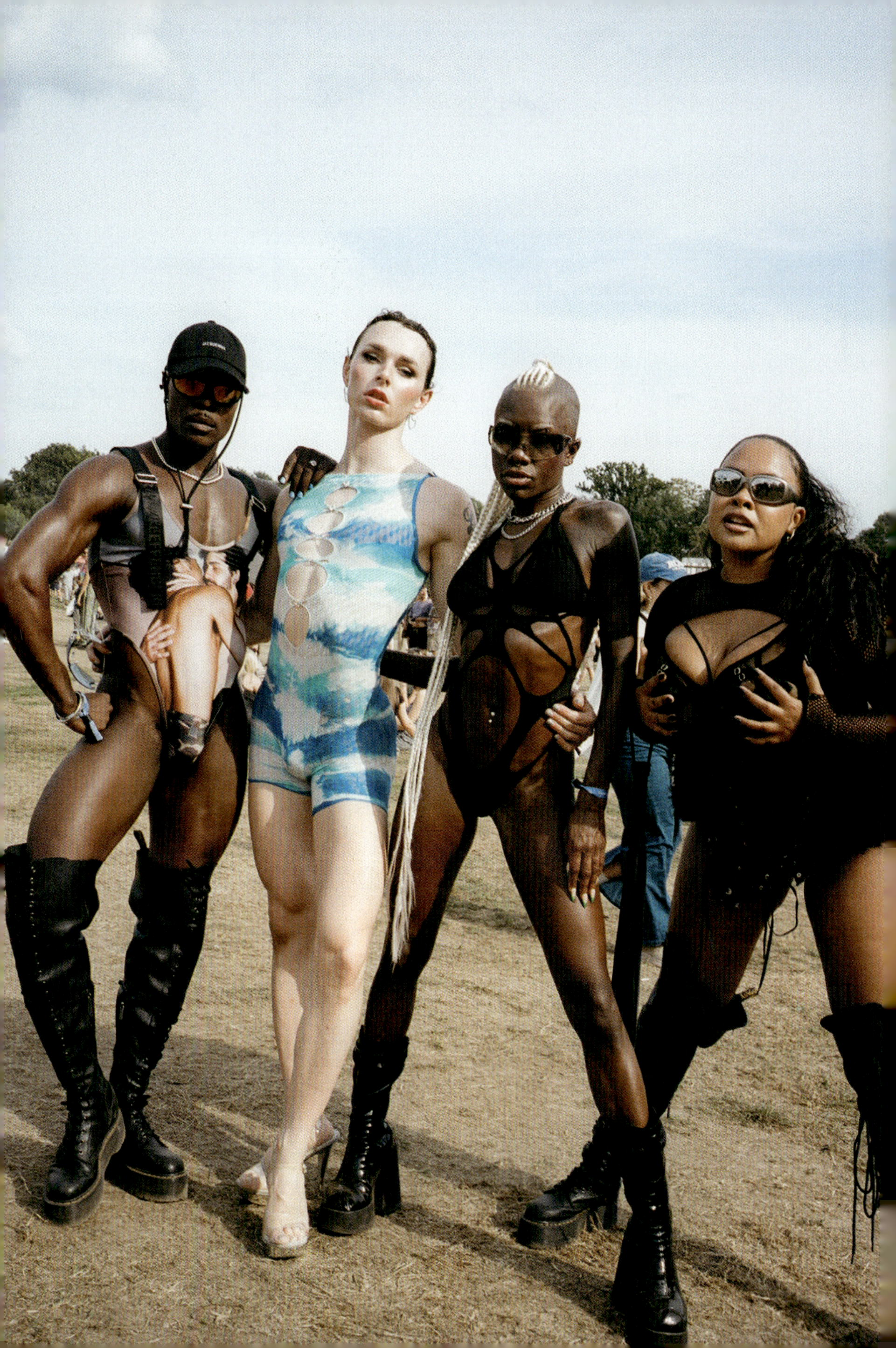

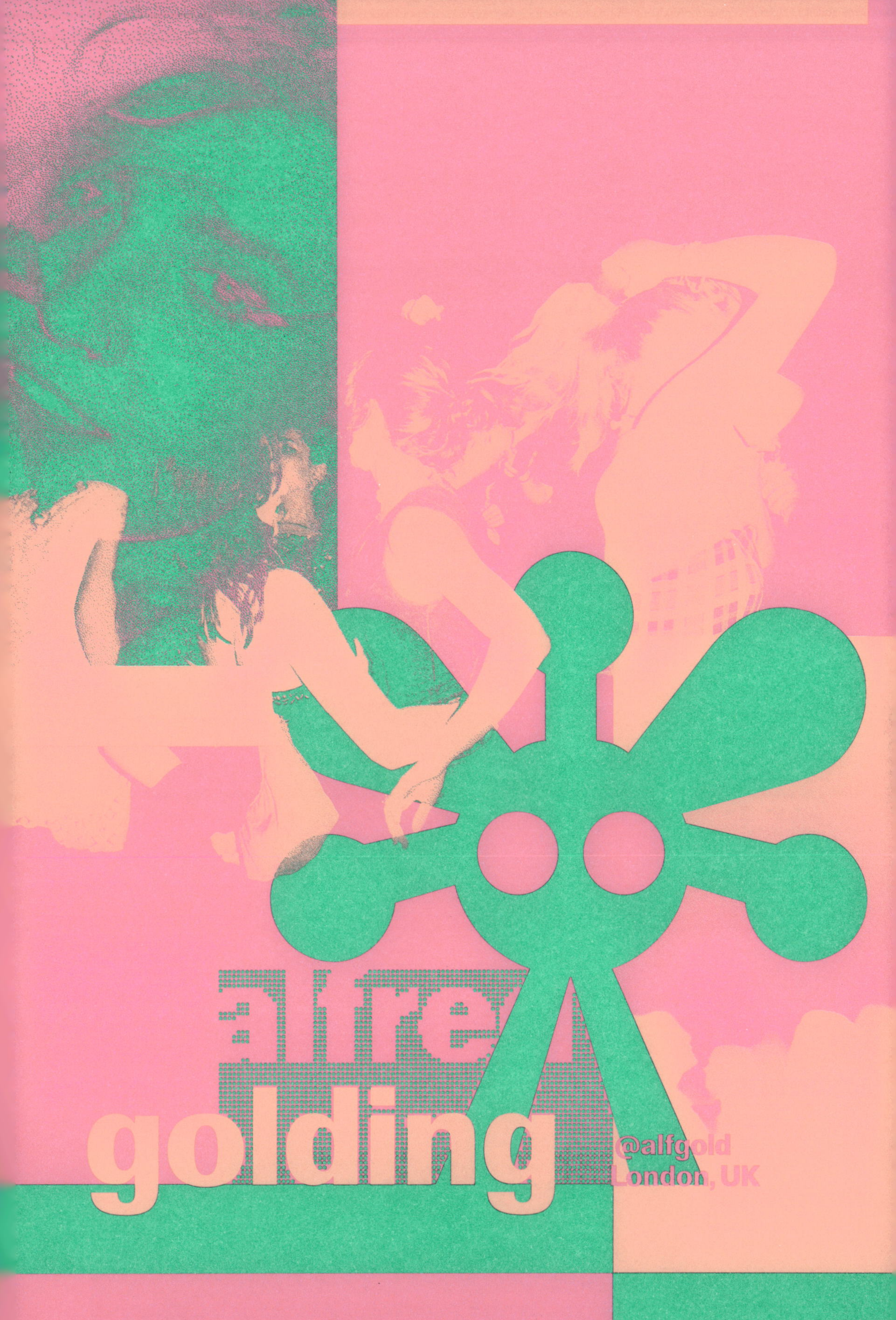

alfred
golding
@alfgold
London, UK

I started documenting my corner of London's nightlife in 2021 as the city started to properly make its way out of Covid, shooting a couple of rolls a night at the Bunker Club in Deptford. Initially just a camera test; when they came back I was surprised with the results and started looking at them a little more seriously.

Until that point I hadn't taken much interest in documenting the scene, but it soon became an obsession. I started to build relationships with venues and friendships with DJs like Deptford Northern Soul Club — who played that fateful Bunker gig that started it all — to get out as often as I could. What I aim to capture is that vibrant, electric current that takes hold of you when you step into something good, gives you that feeling of 'Yes, this is exactly what I need', and immerses you completely into a fresh community, if only for a couple of hours. And I try to cover the whole pitch: a moment of intimacy in the chaos of the dancefloor, an exchange without words, a passed lighter; these milliseconds I get to keep, and I love them all.

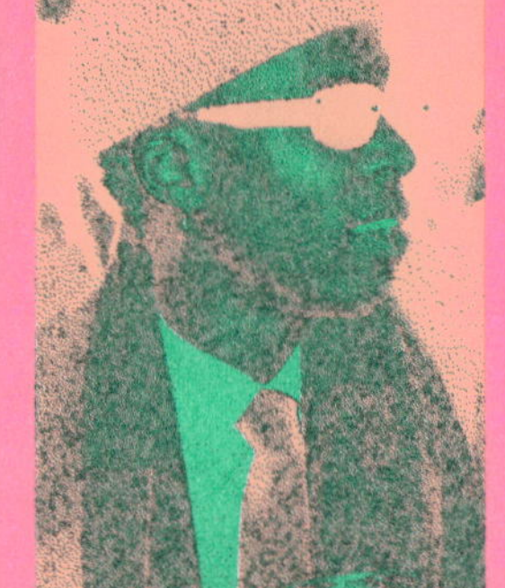

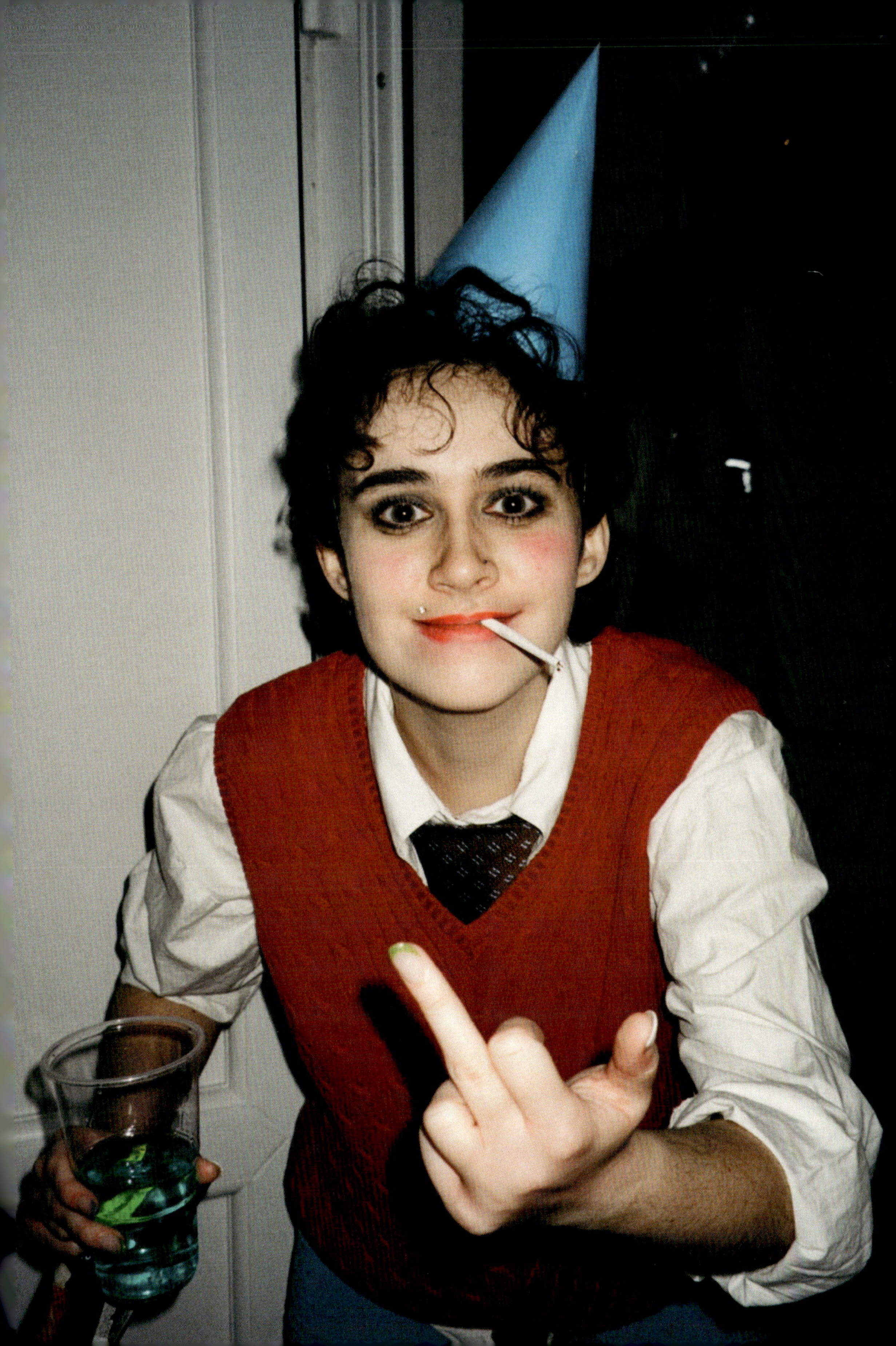

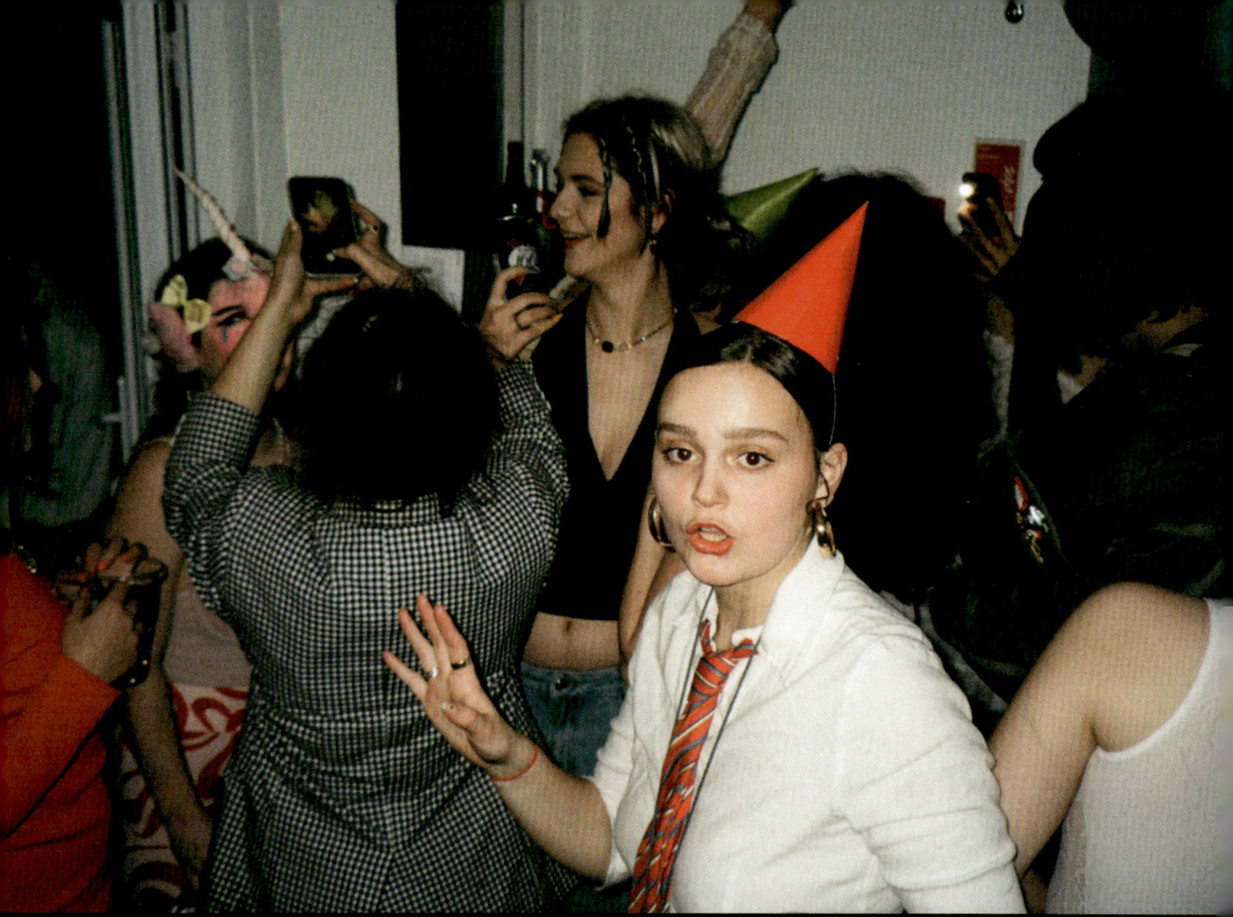

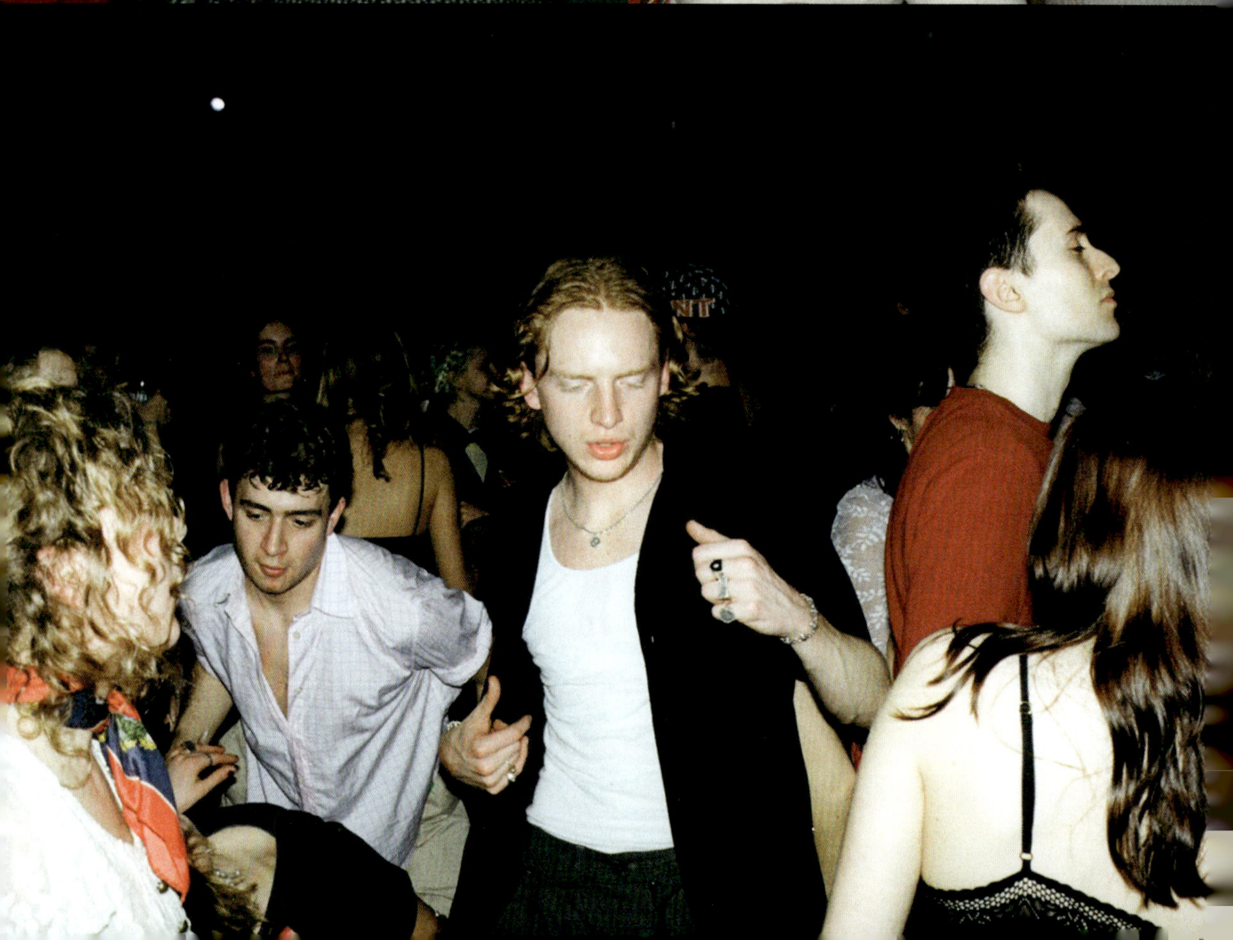

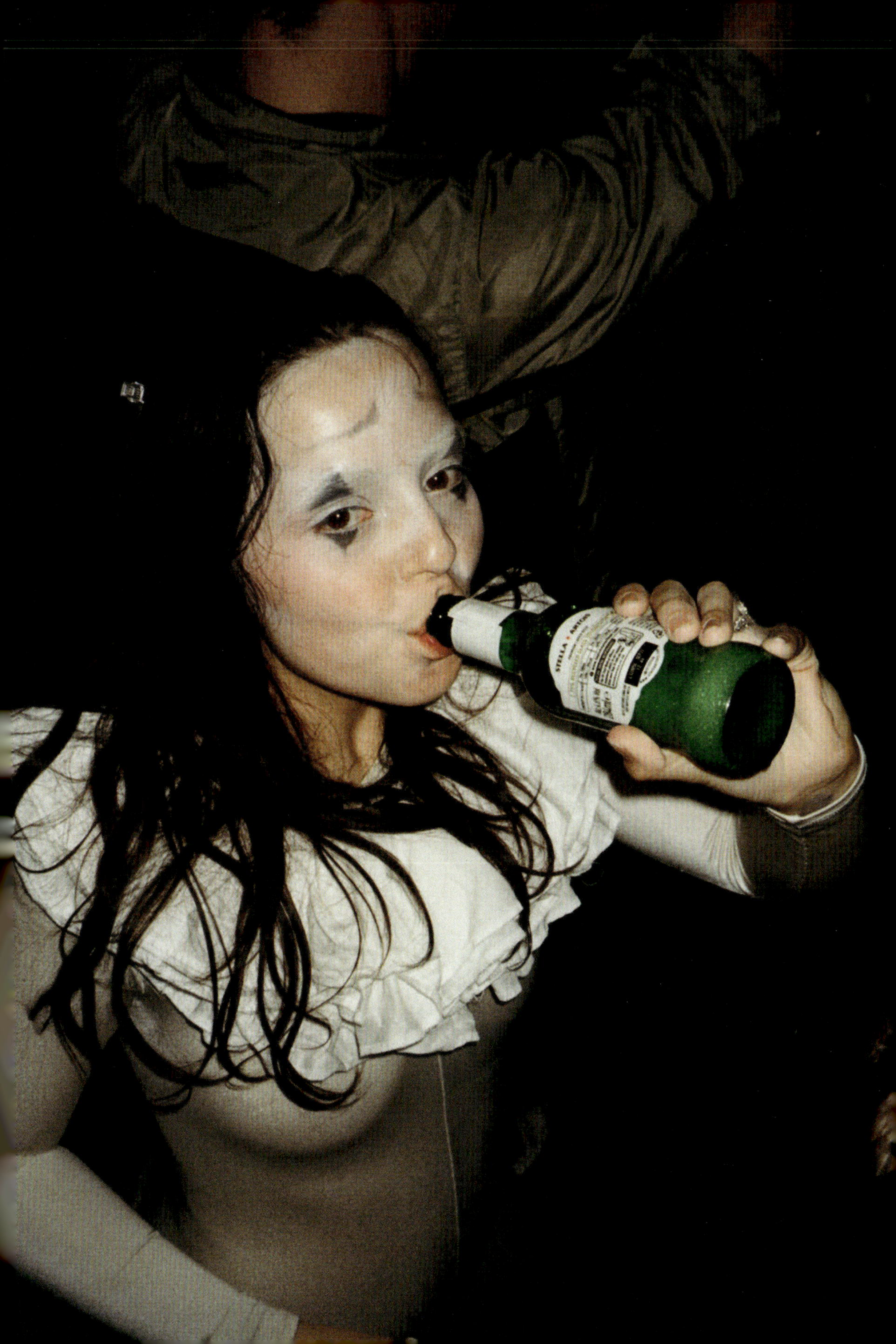

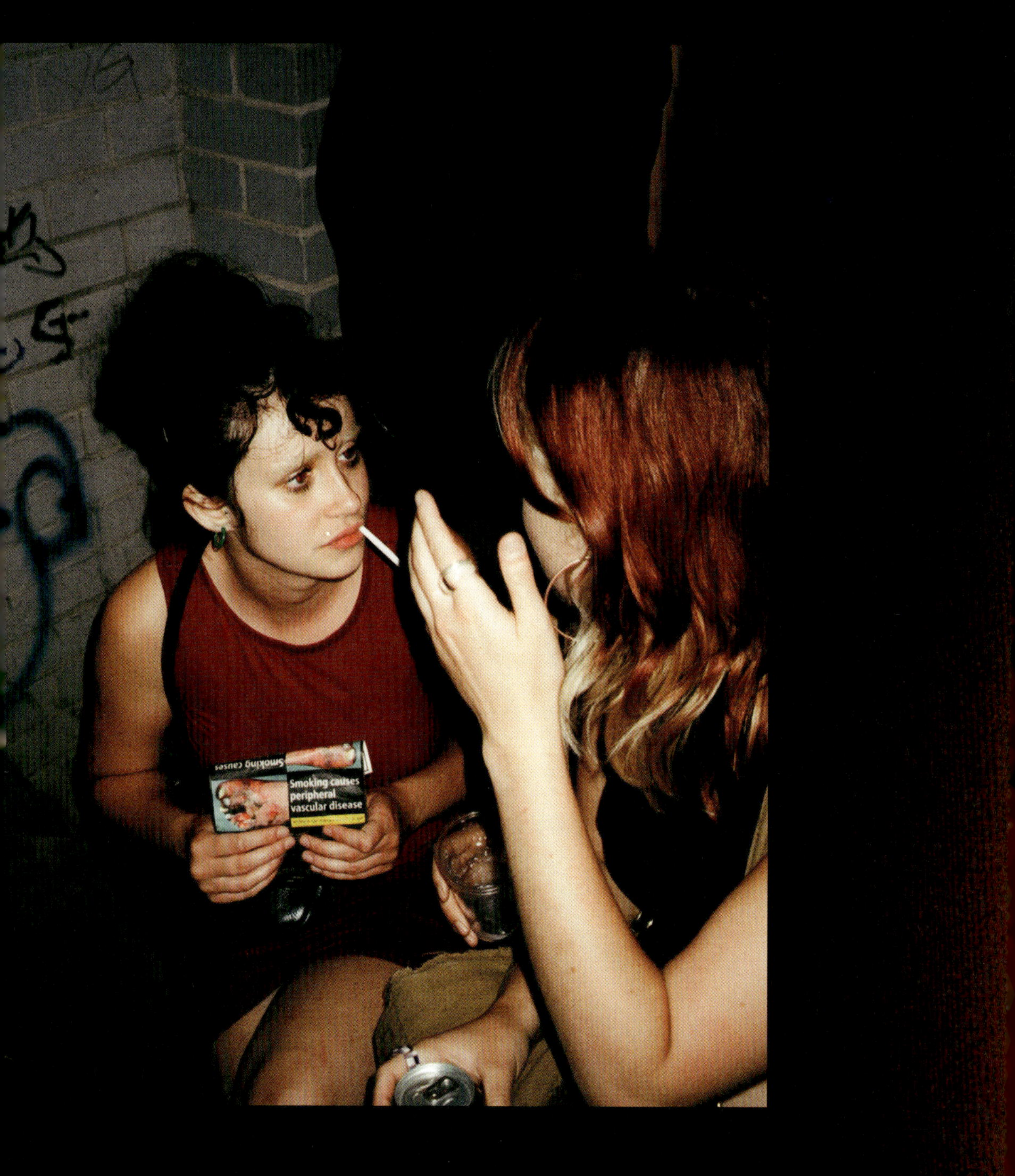
Smoking causes
Smoking causes
peripheral
vascular disease

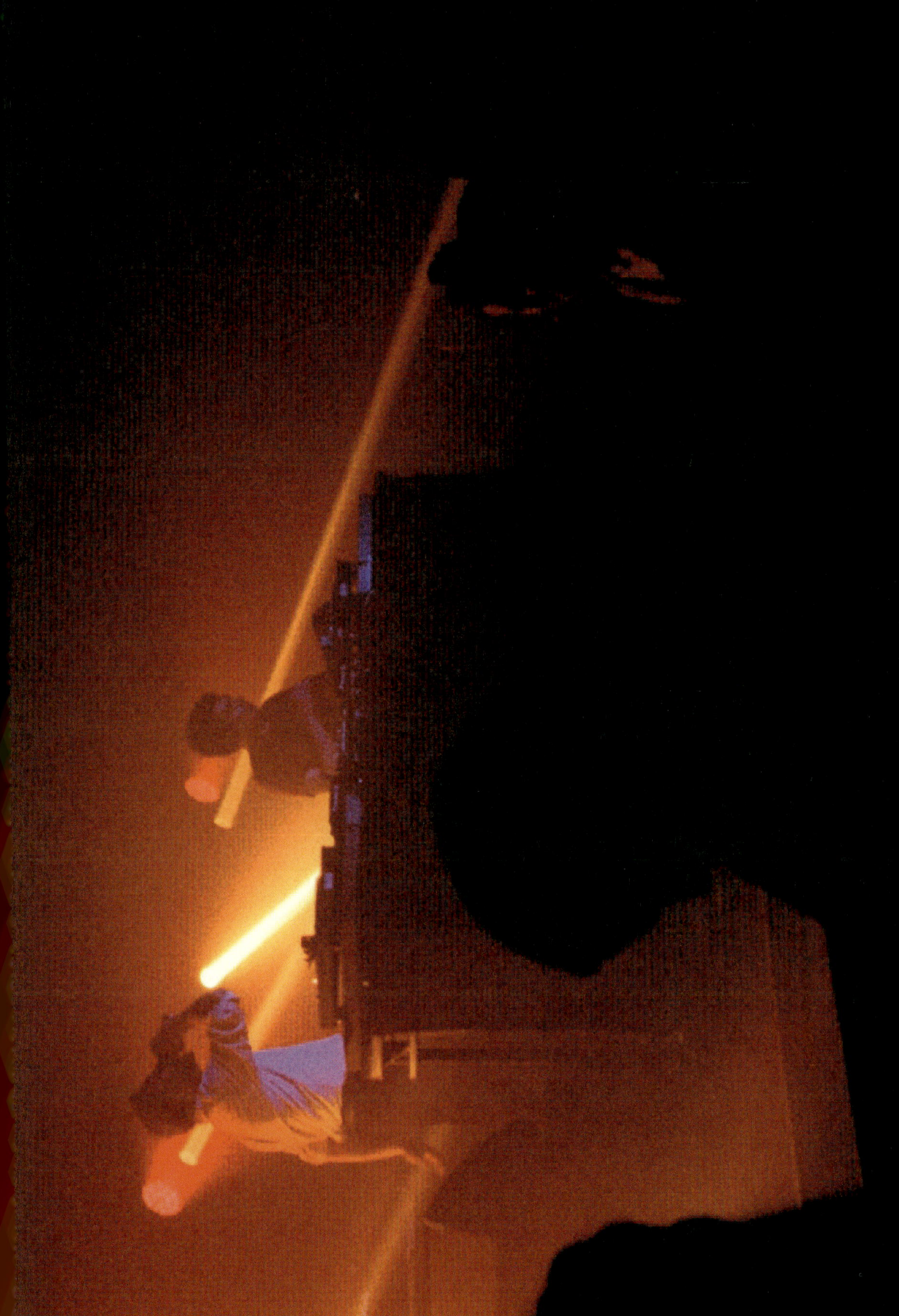

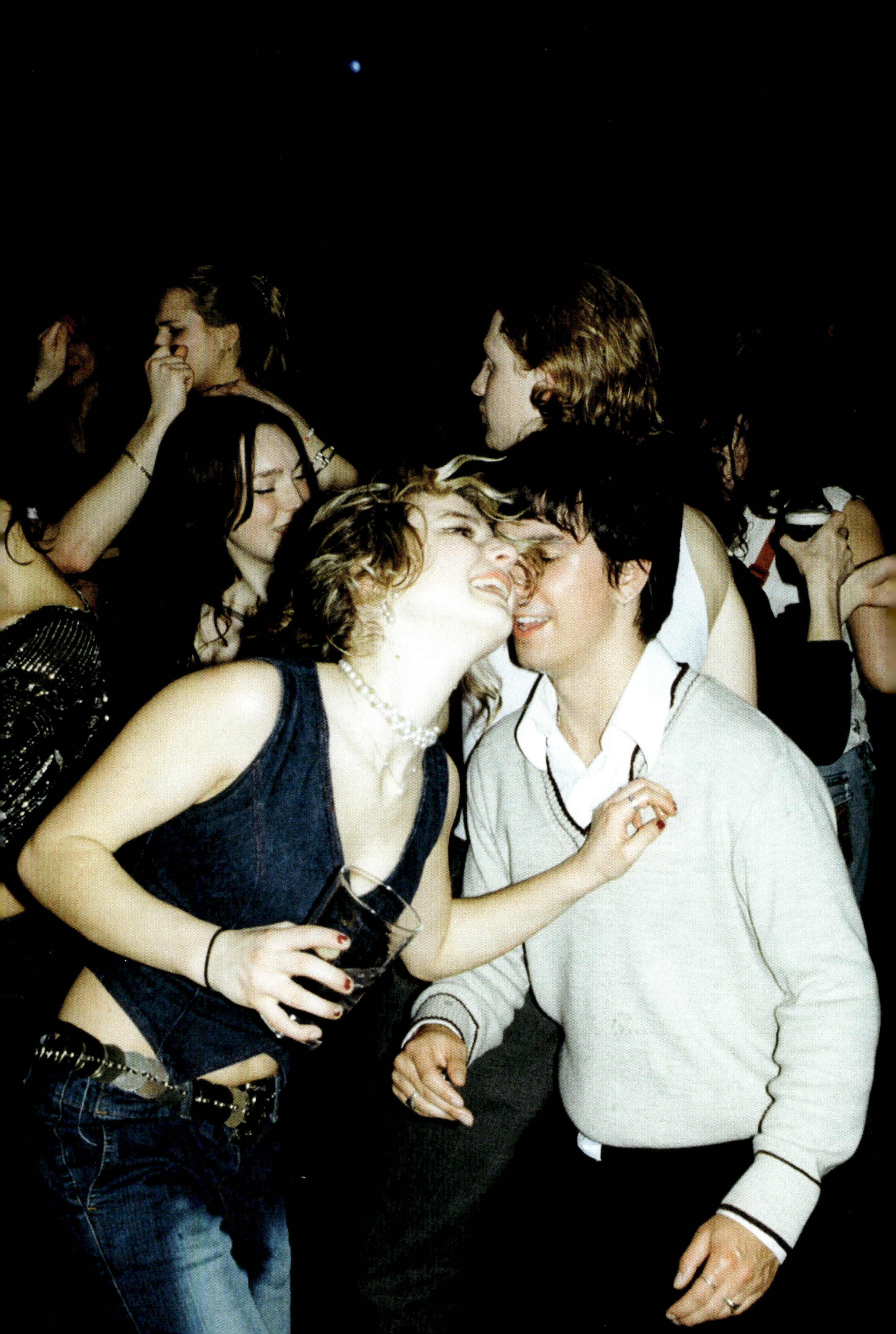

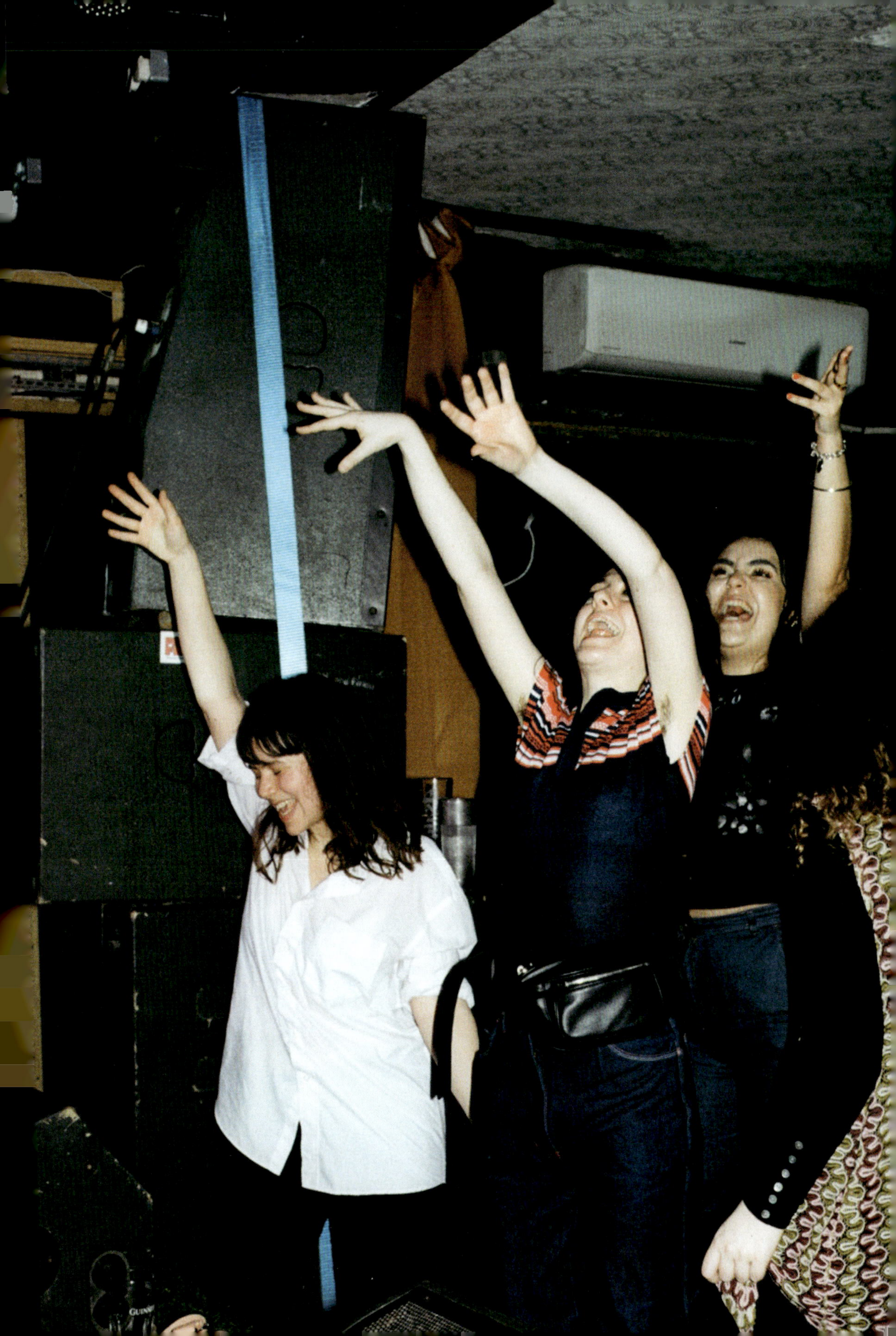

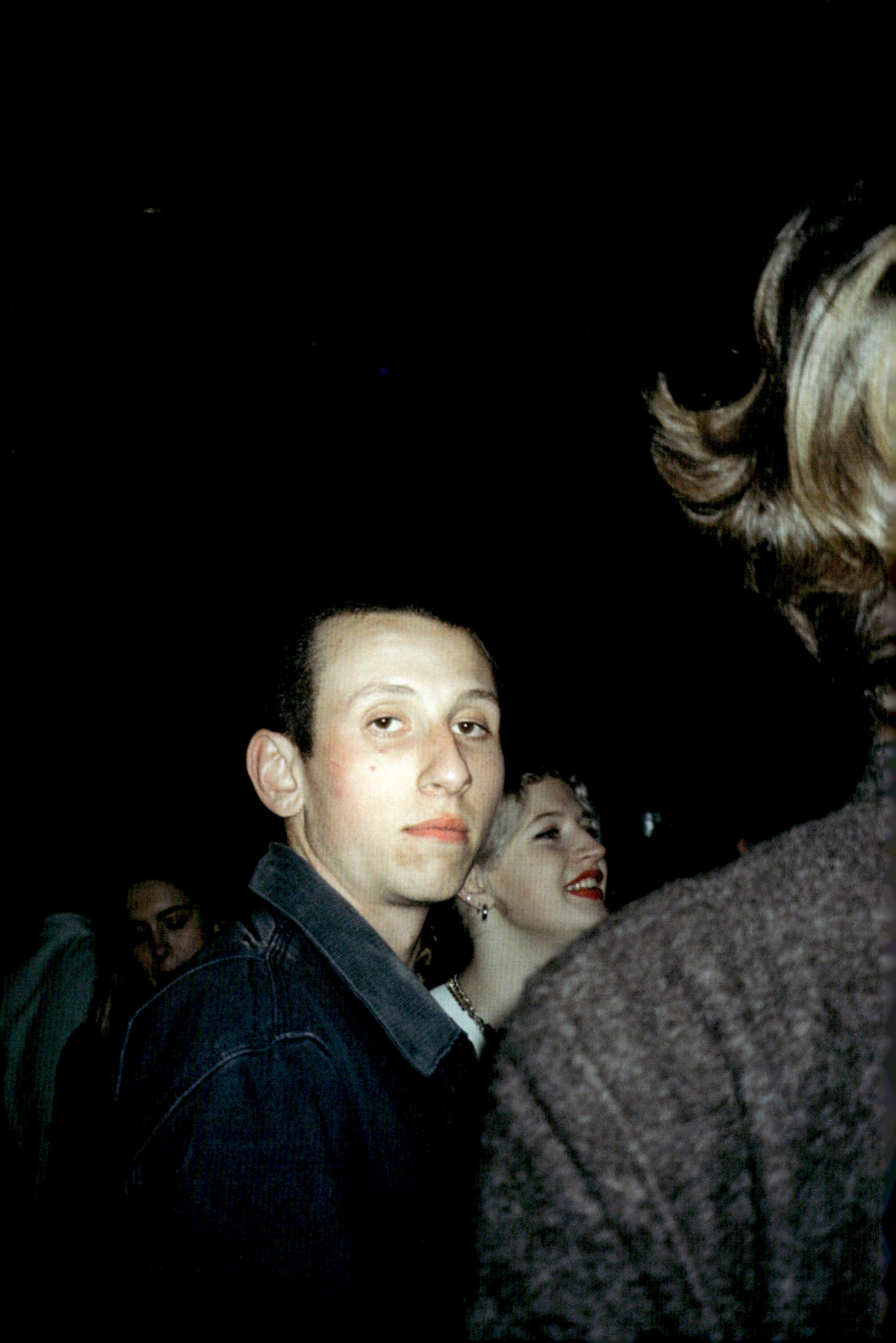

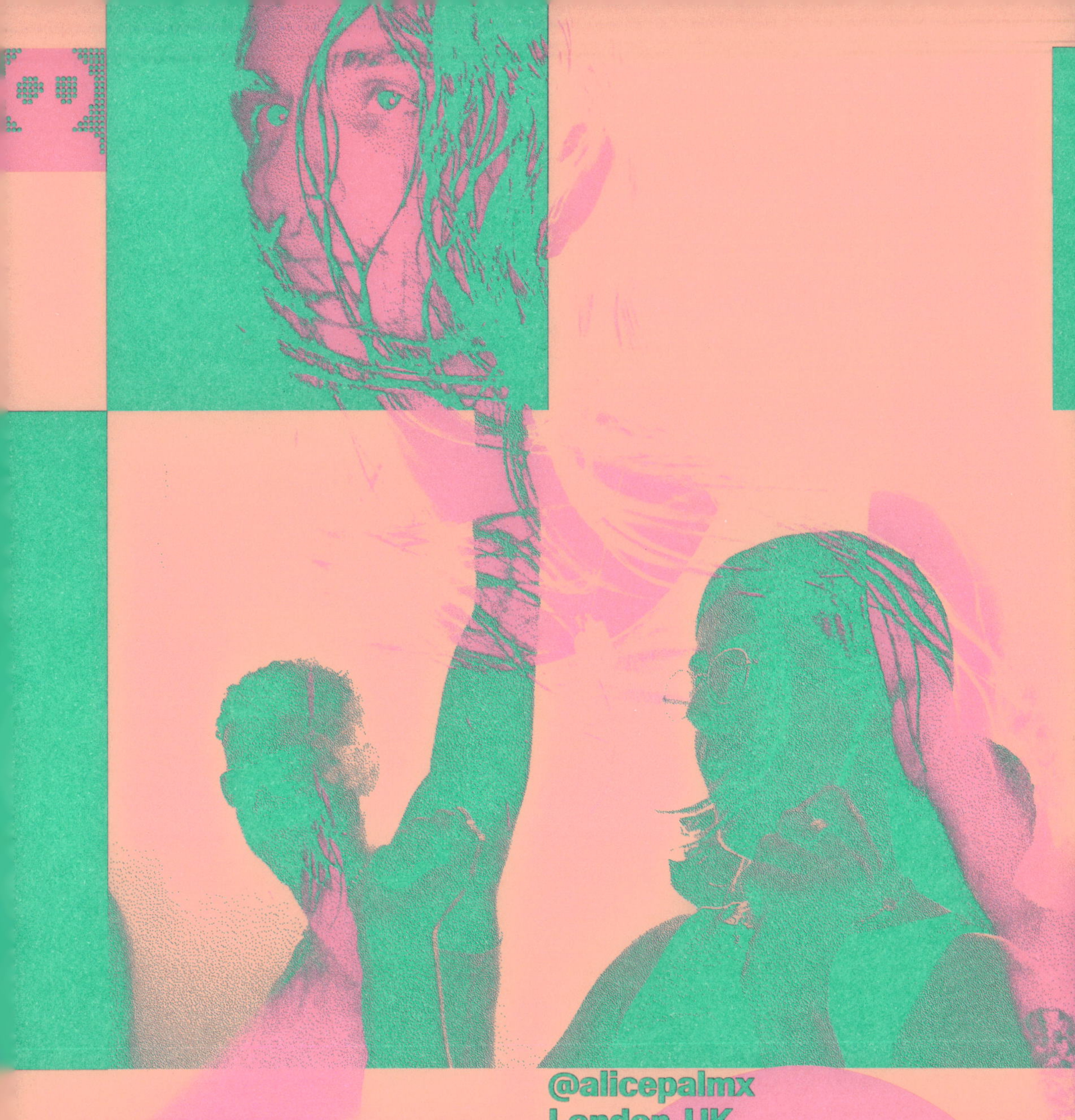
@alicepalmx
London, UK
Alice Palm

I'm a London-based photographer focusing on events and press shots. An intrigue with the human condition and connection has led me to photograph some of the best underground music events in the UK and internationally at iconic venues and events including Printworks, Maiden Voyage, Glitterbox/Defected and Fold.

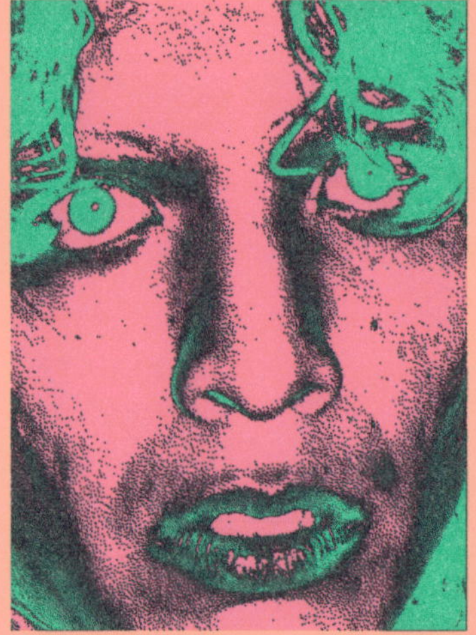

My photography is generous; it shares the beauty of human relationships that ripple through dance floors, transcending the superficial by delving into the raw, unfiltered emotions and connections that music ignites. In a world where music is the elixir of our existence, I encapsulate the visceral experience of sound and its profound impact on our souls. My photographs are not static images but testaments to the electric connection between rhythm and feeling. Each photograph is a reminder of the intoxicating fusion of sound and emotion, a sonic journey that tugs at the heartstrings and awakens the senses.

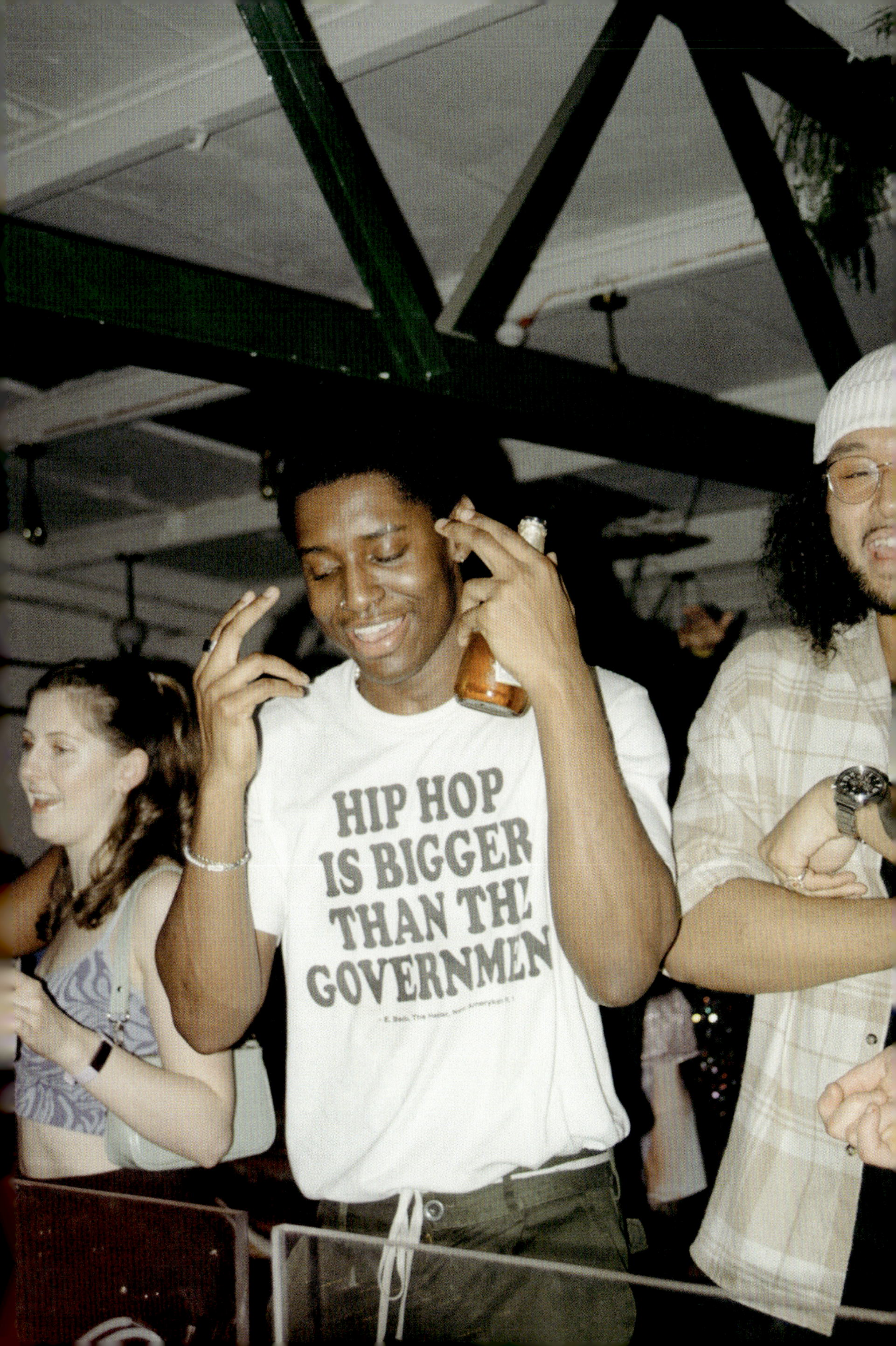
HIP HOP
IS BIGGER
THAN THE
GOVERNMEN

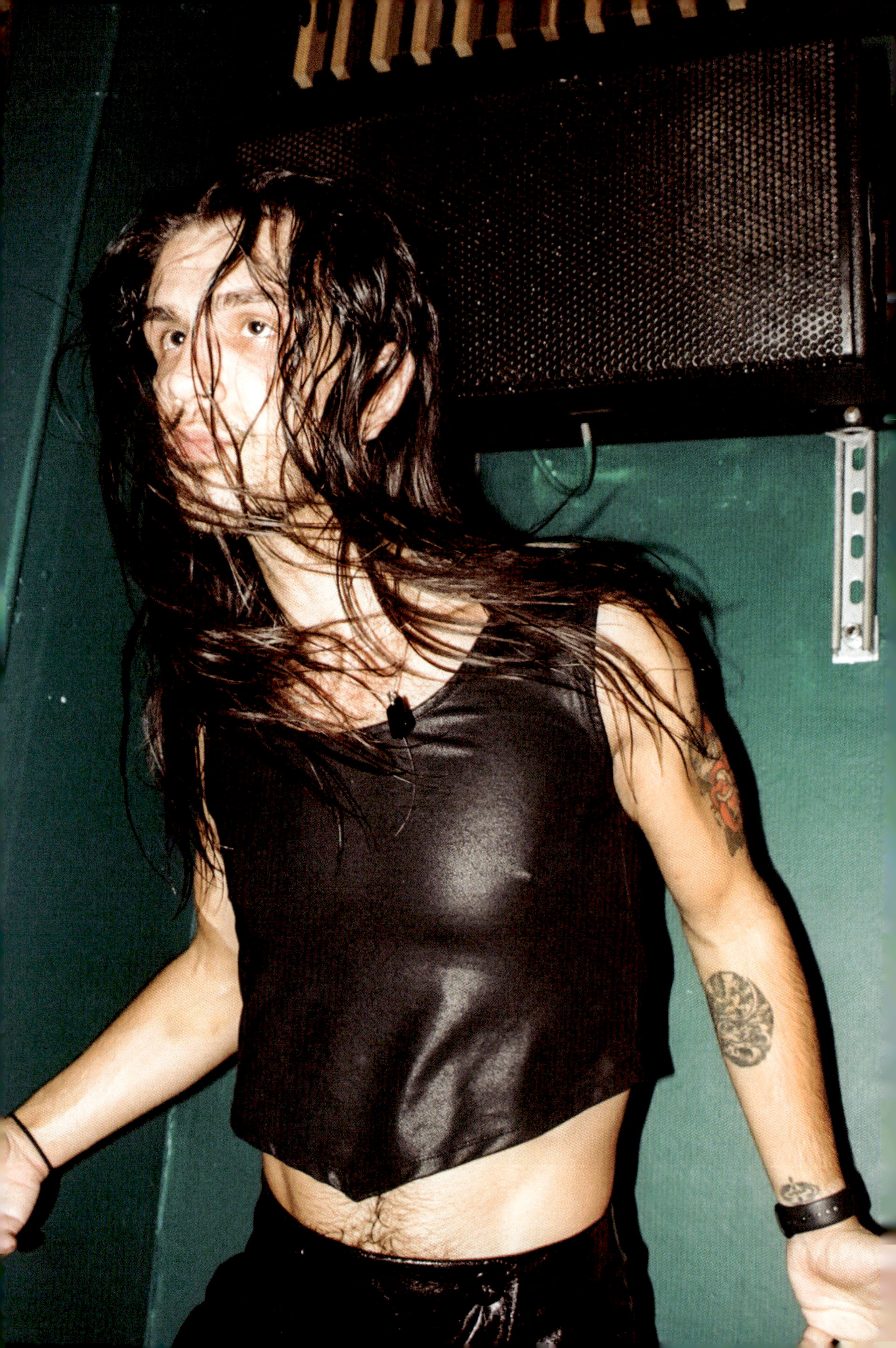

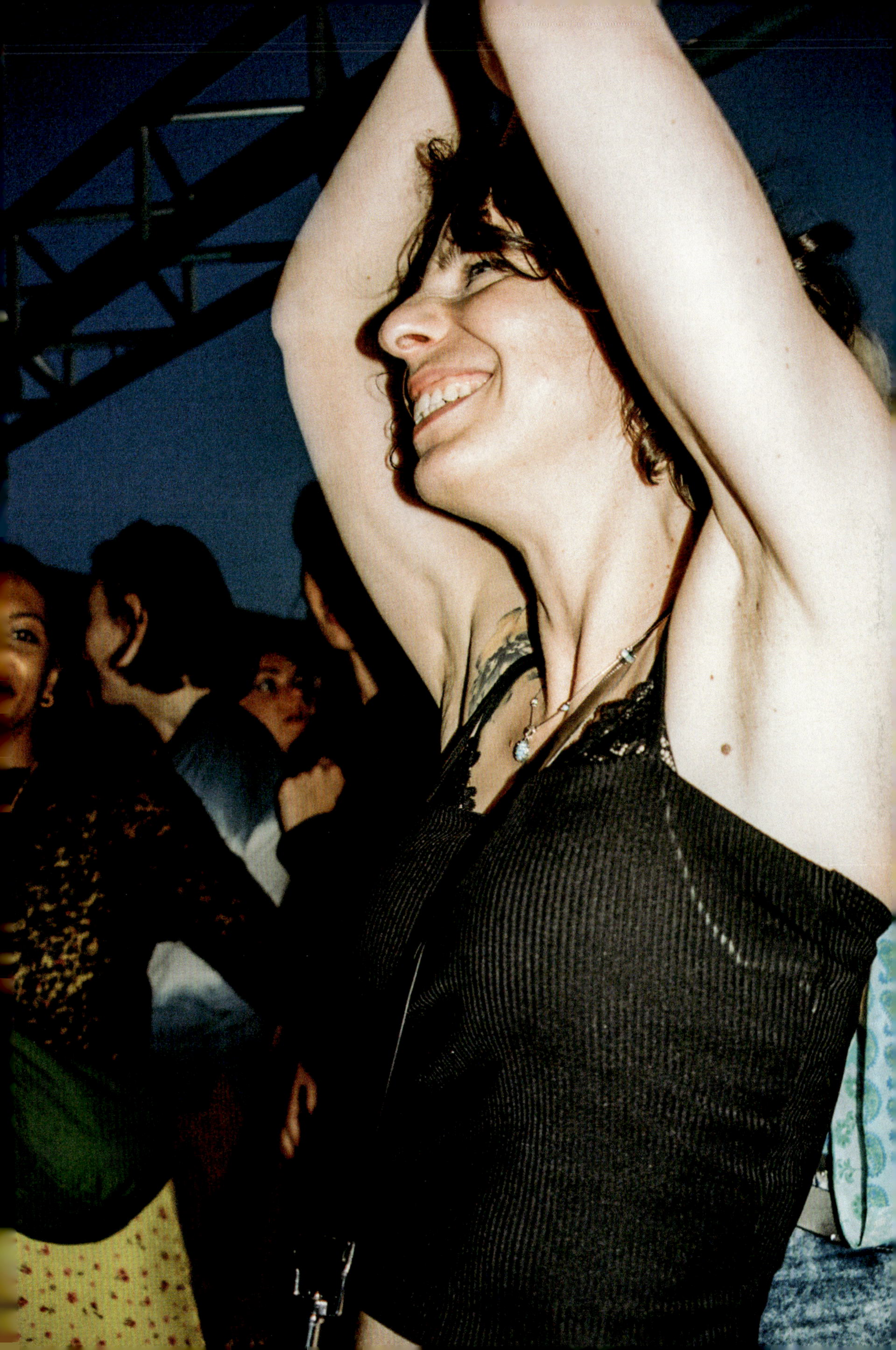

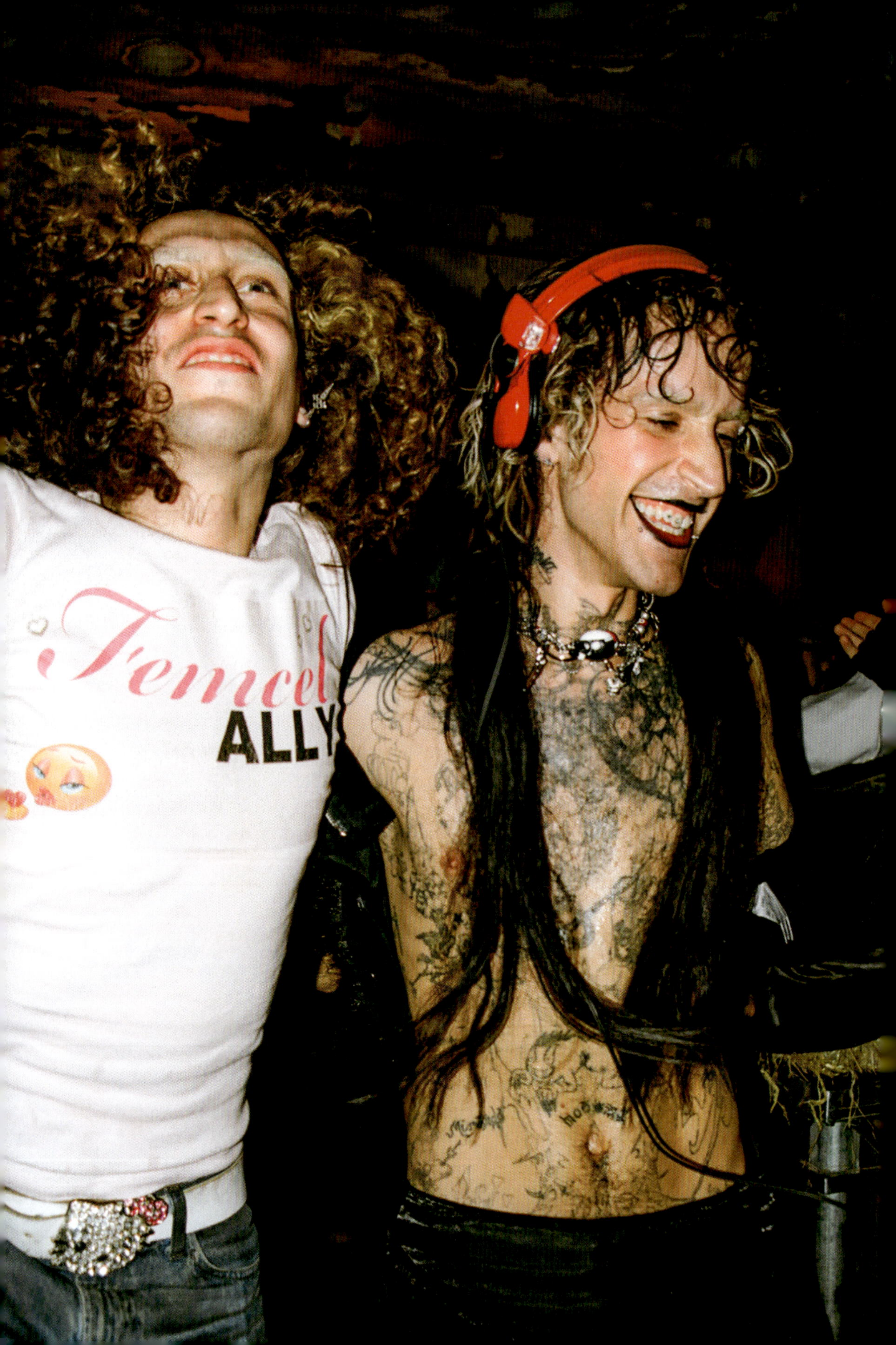

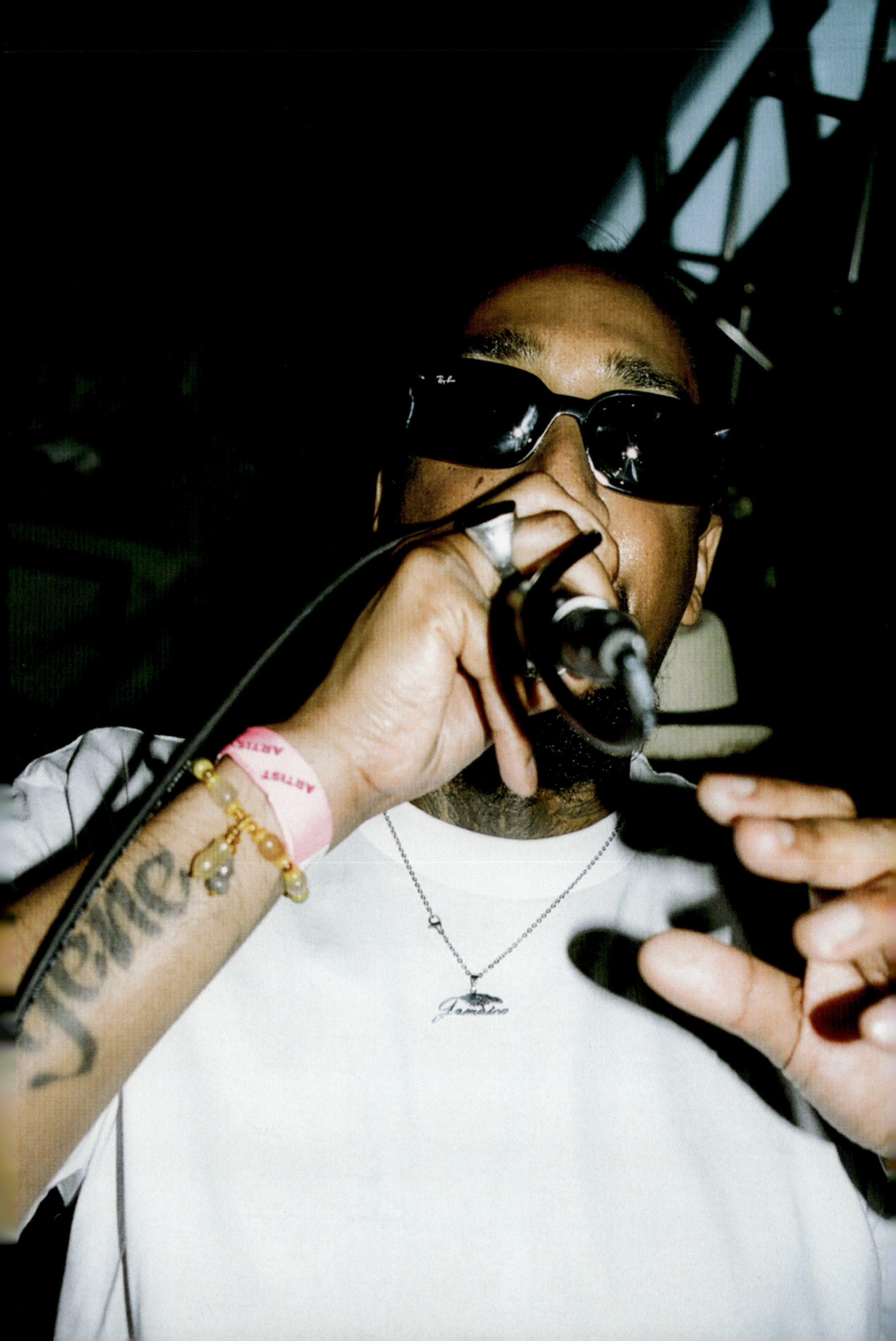

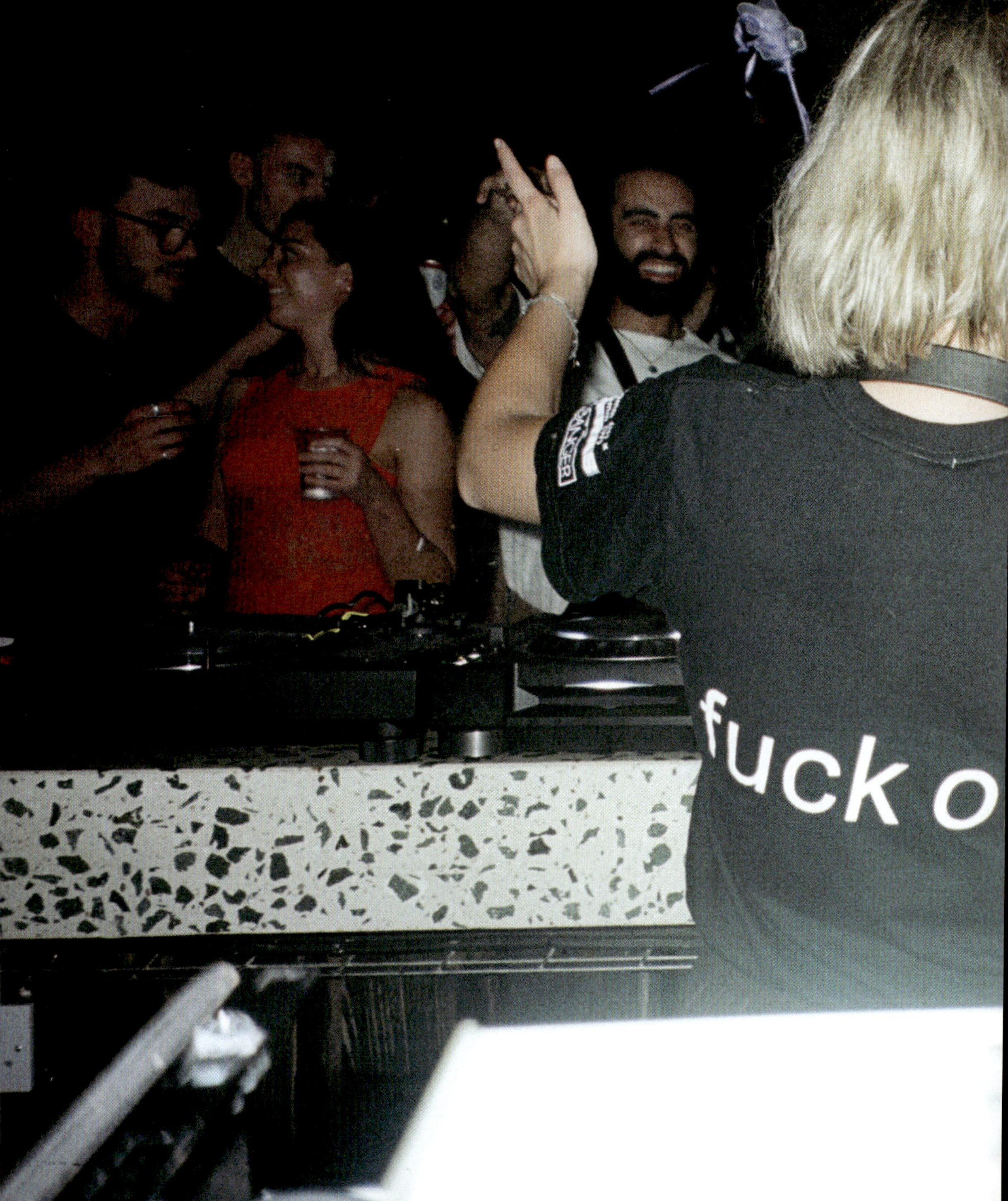

fuck o

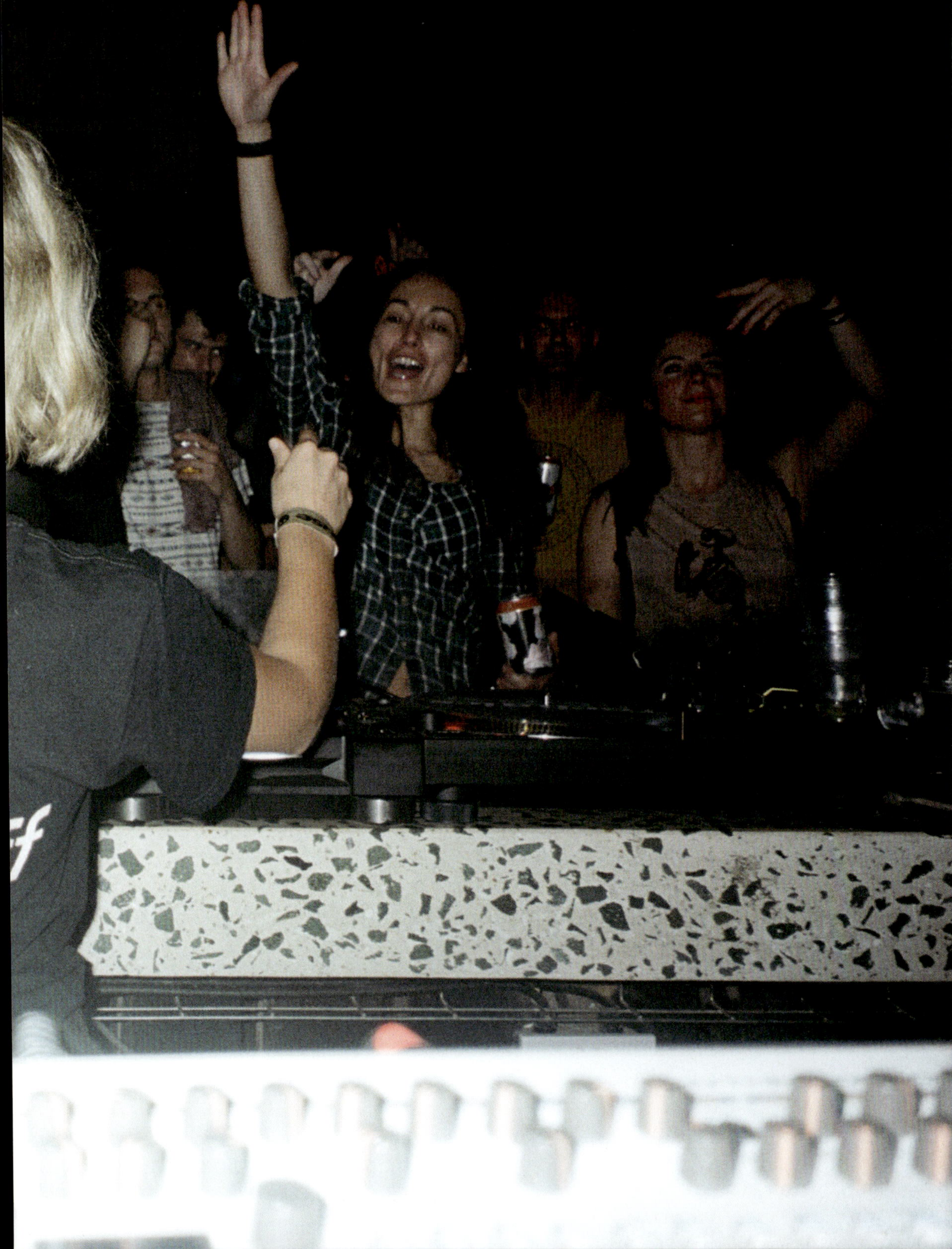

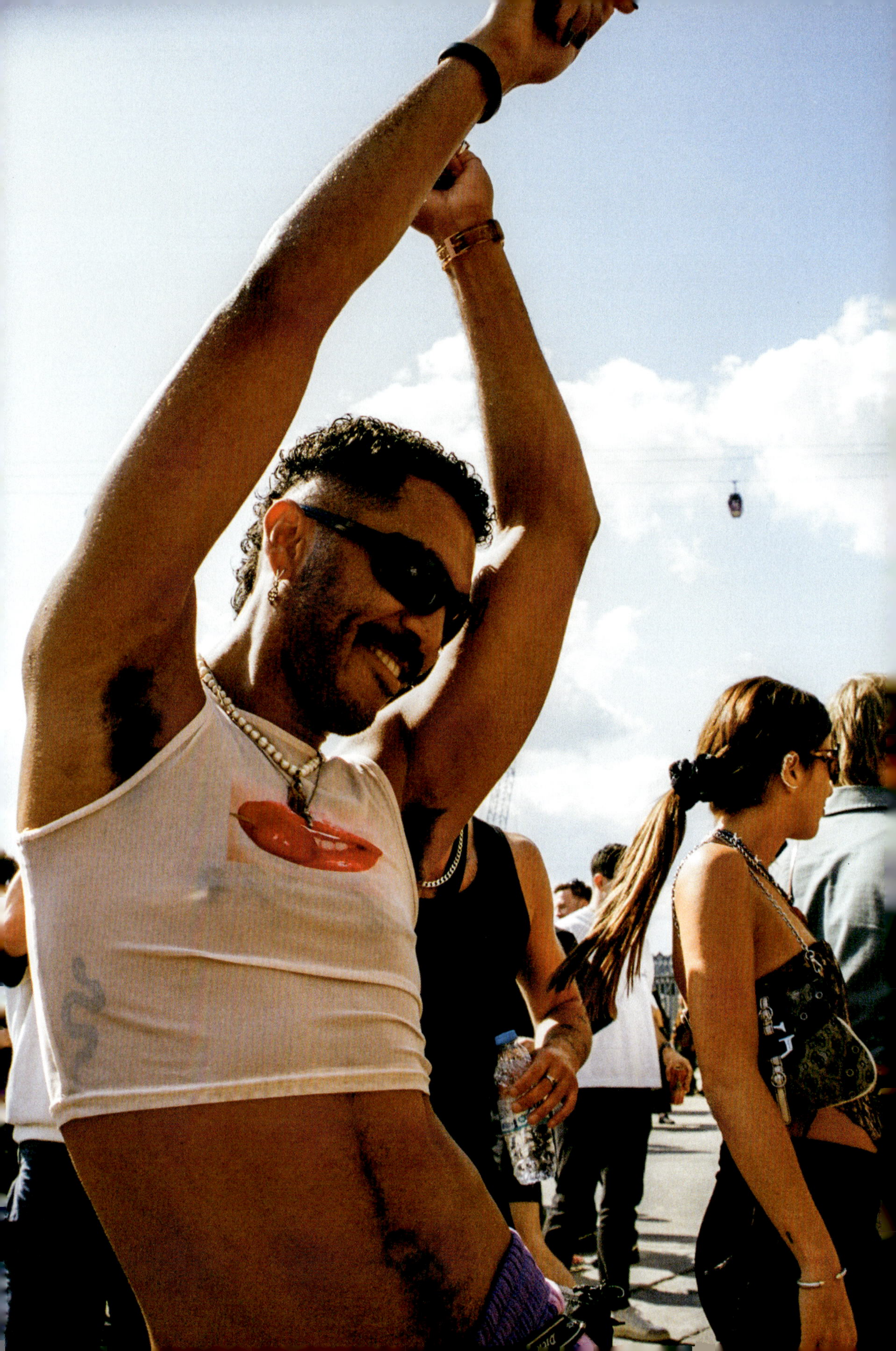

@ameliavalentiner
London, UK

Amelia
Valentiner

Music, with its profound ability to connect people, has been the guiding force behind my venture into photography.
I am particularly drawn to the hedonistic atmosphere of free parties, raves and the expansive tapestry of the UK's dynamic nightlife, as I align with the shared values of unity and expression.

In a society where government representation feels distant and legislation oppressive, these events become more than just celebrations but statements of resilience. For decades, collectives have defied legality, undertaking immense risks to create spaces free from commercial interests and I hope to preserve the spirit of these gatherings where judgment and discrimination dissipate. My work, at its core, is a celebration of the music that unifies us. I aim to reflect the story of the sound, the artists, and the deep connection binding them to the listeners and I strive to embrace the alternative and capture the authenticity that defines these subcultures.

As a photographer navigating the UK's diverse nightlife, I am not just documenting moments; I am shaping a narrative that echoes the beats of resistance, community, and the honouring of freedom. It's about respecting the roots of the scene and the underground culture from which these events were born.

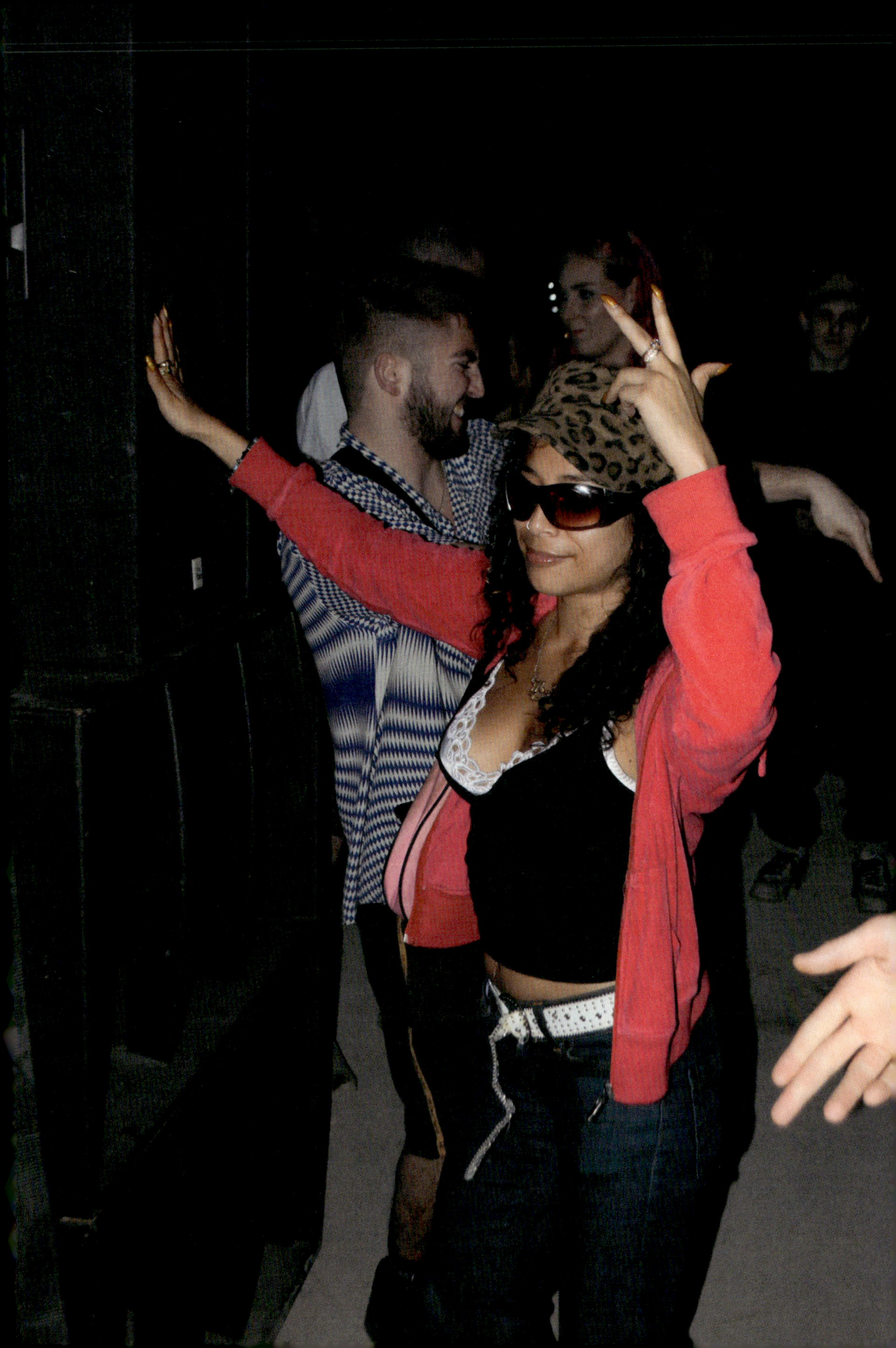

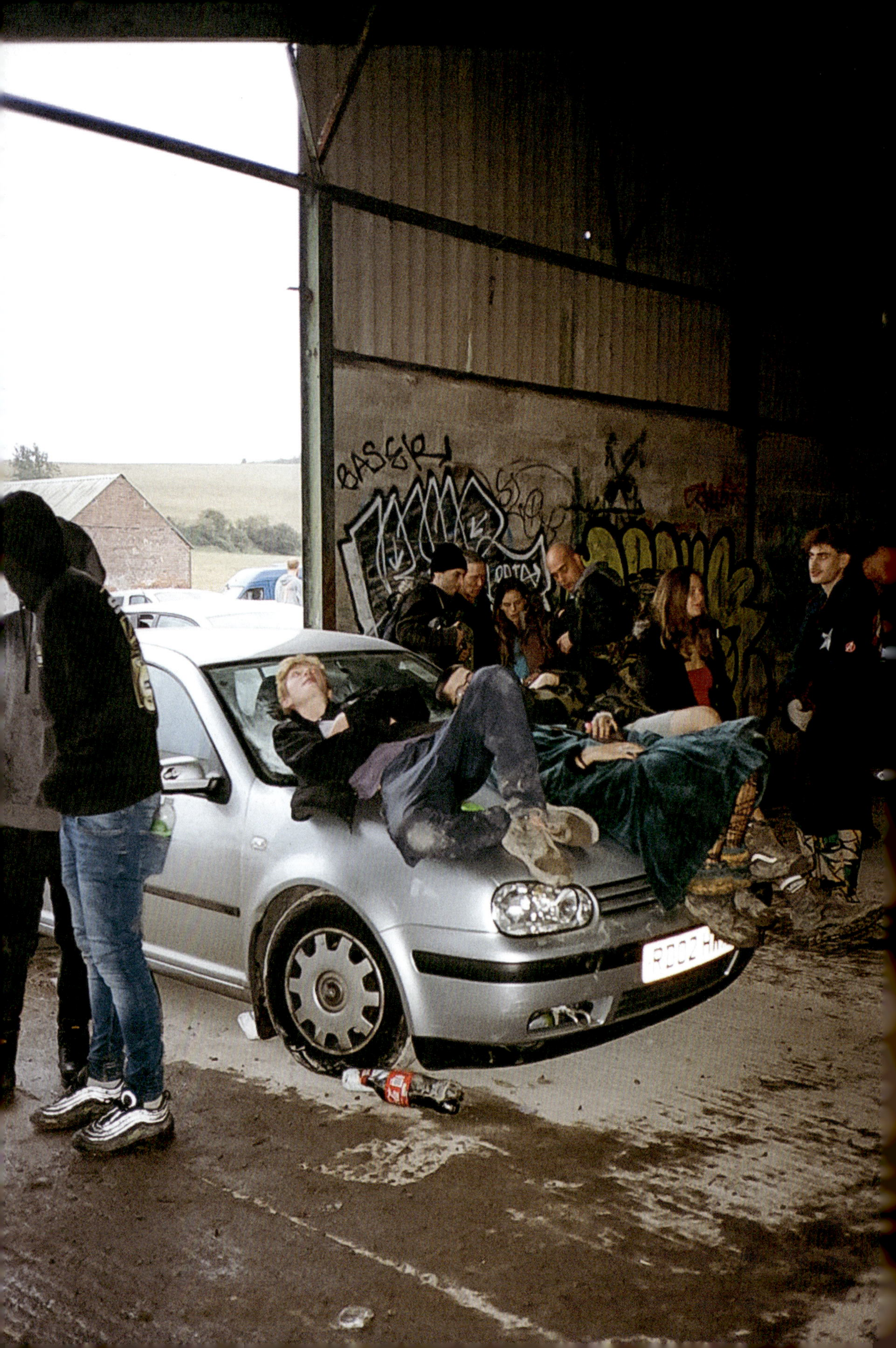

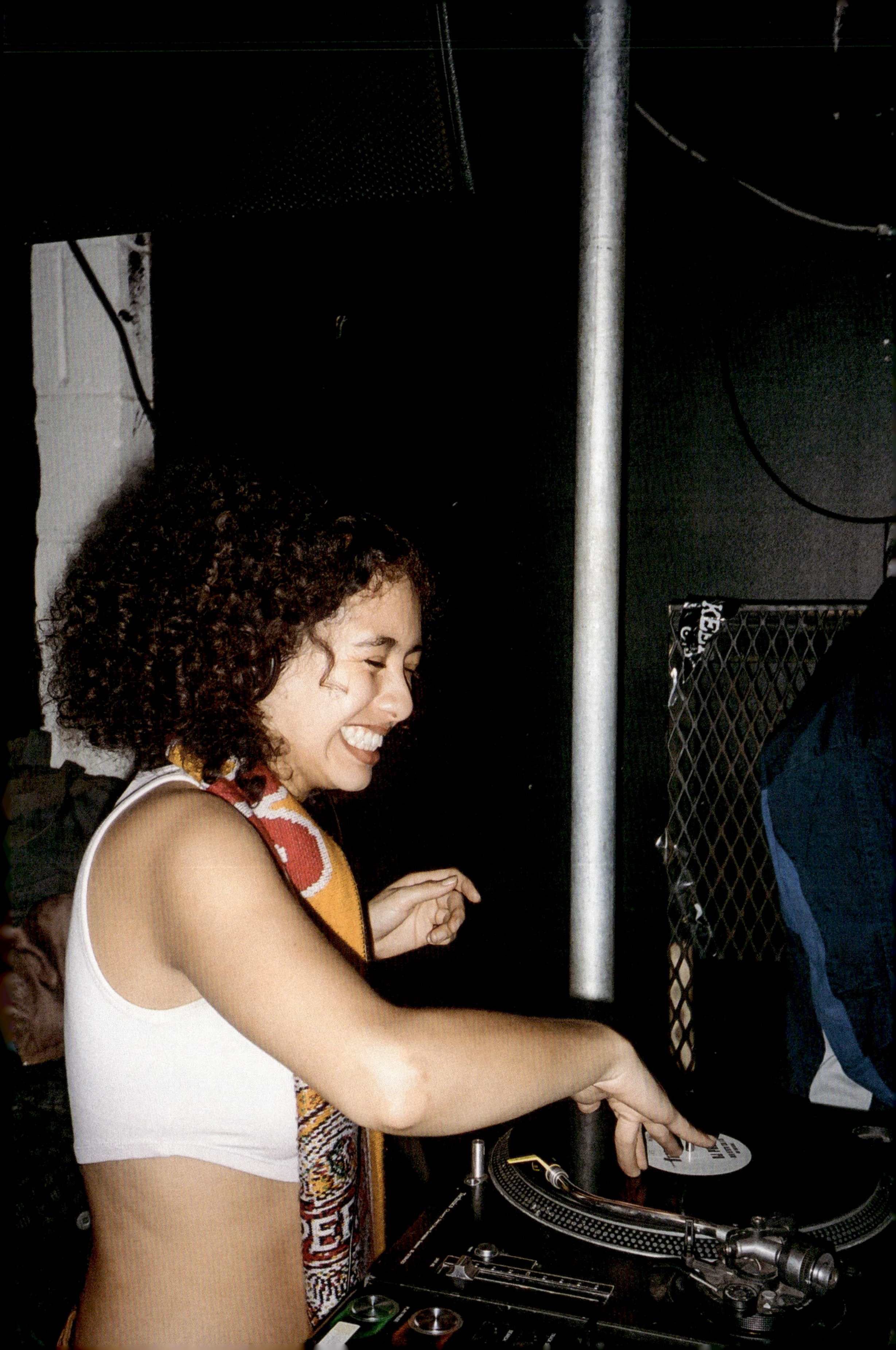

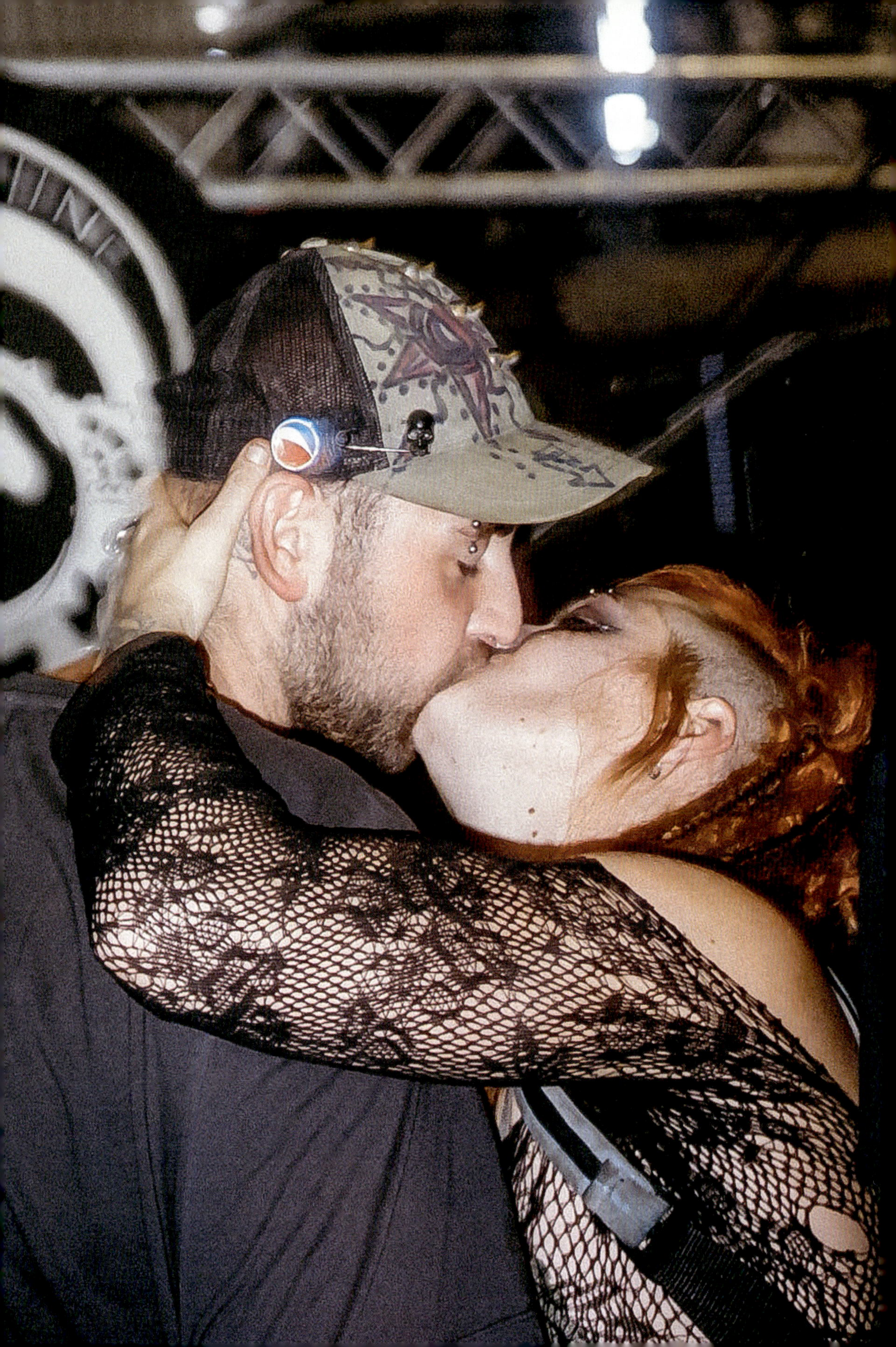

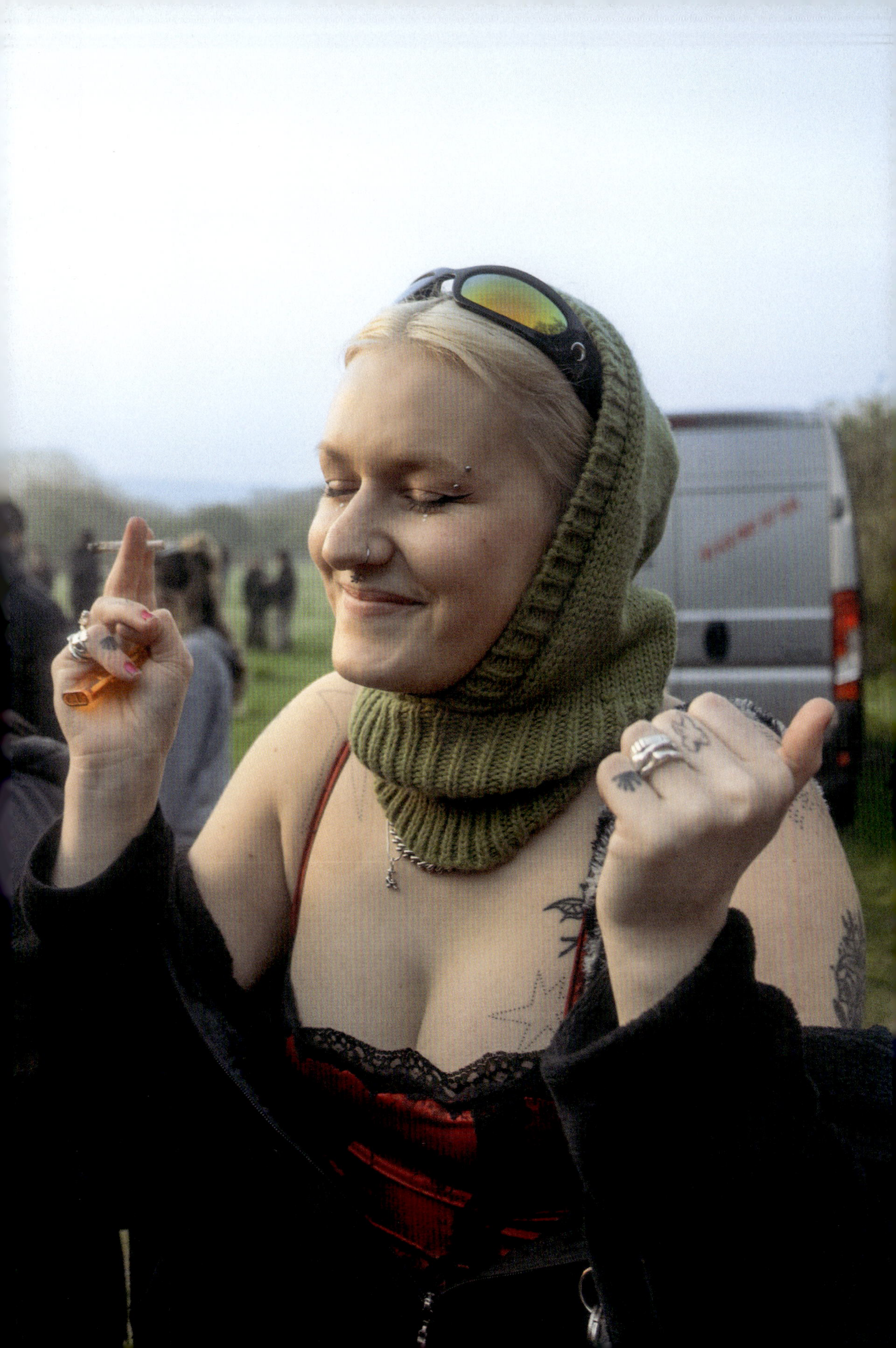

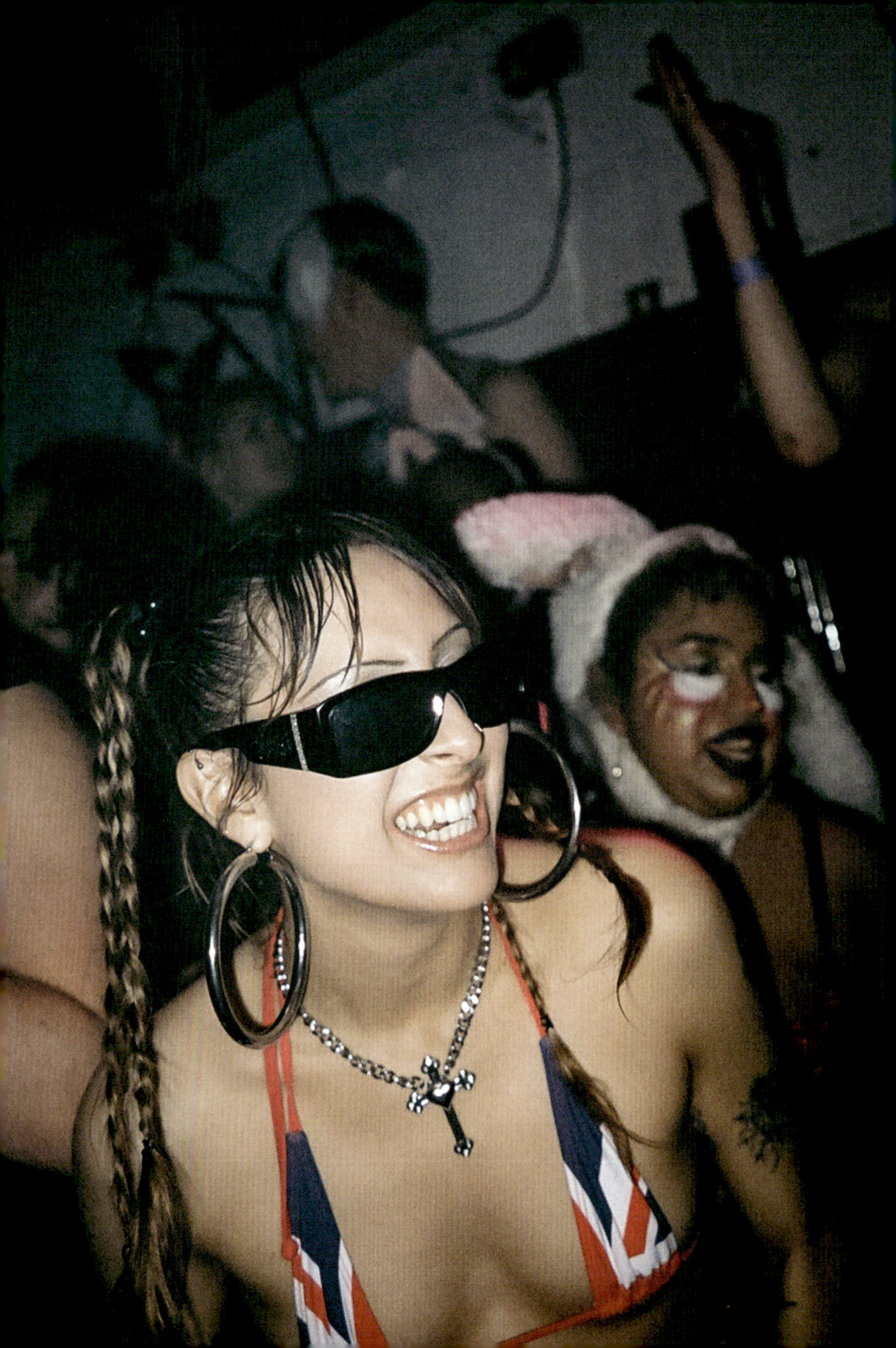

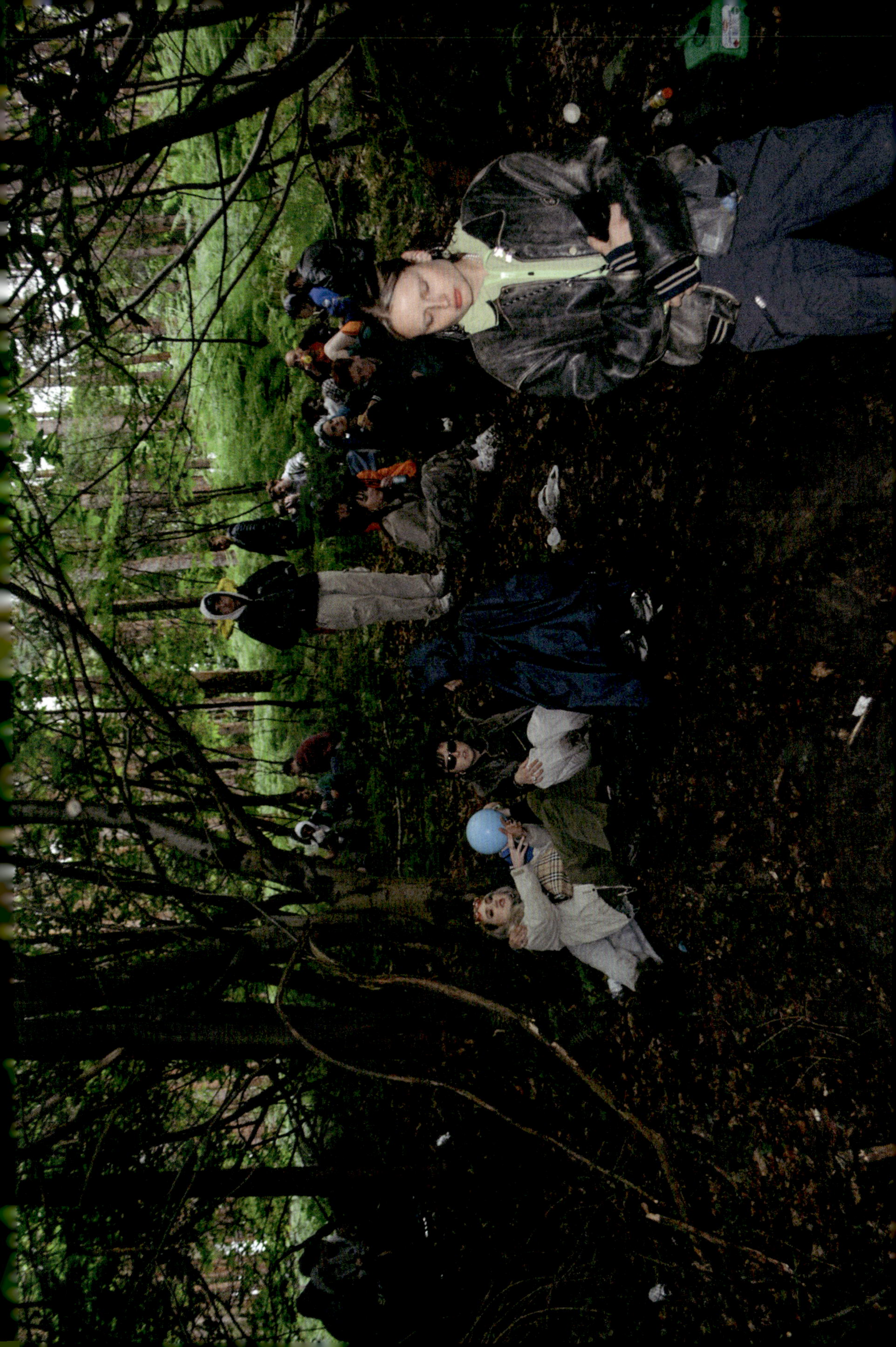

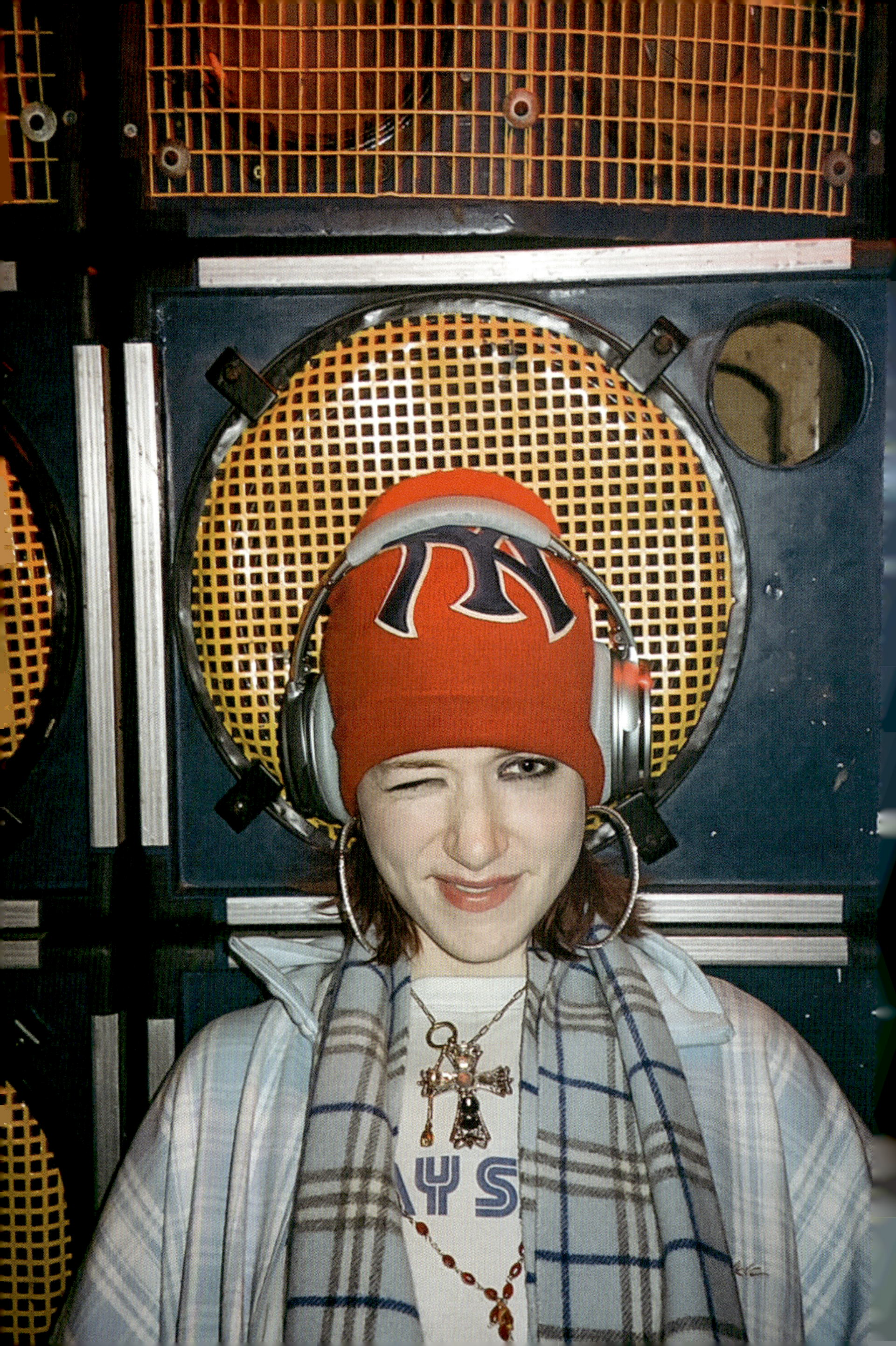

Bruna Blumenberg

@blumenbergph
São Paulo, BR

Born and raised in the southern region of Brazil, I currently reside in Santa Catarina and work in São Paulo. Through art and photography, I have not only showcased a form of expression but also presented a vivid narrative of reality. Photography has taken me to places where I could carry along my art and my perspective, aiming to transform and offer new insights into the artistic world. Celebrating a lifestyle that involves music, fashion, and art.

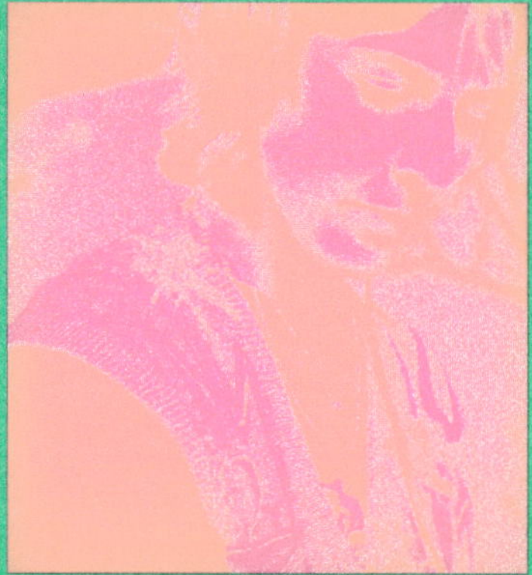

Immersing myself in the contrasts that inspire my vision, I assert the photographic journey is more than a visual record; it's an optical testimony of my experiences.

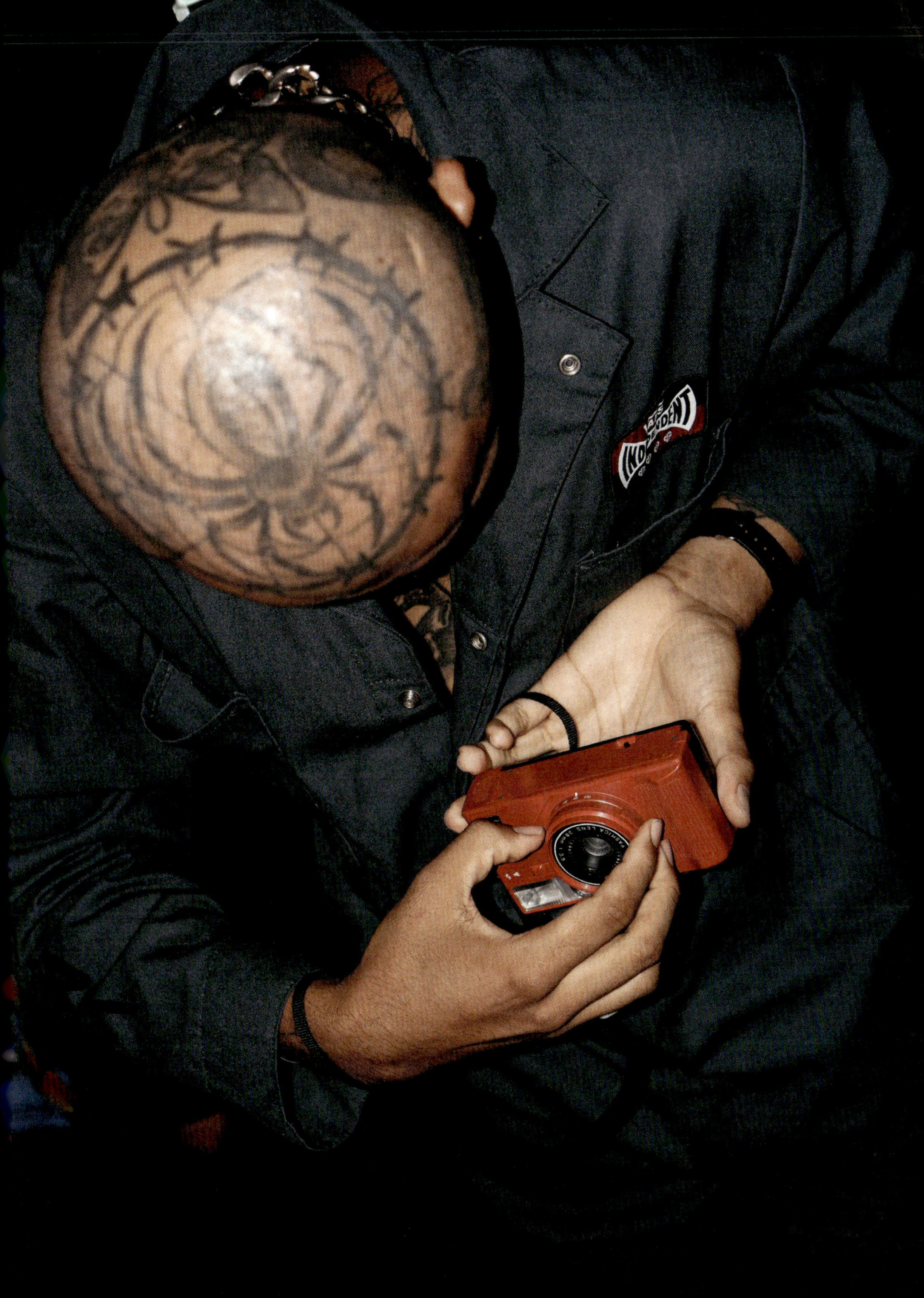

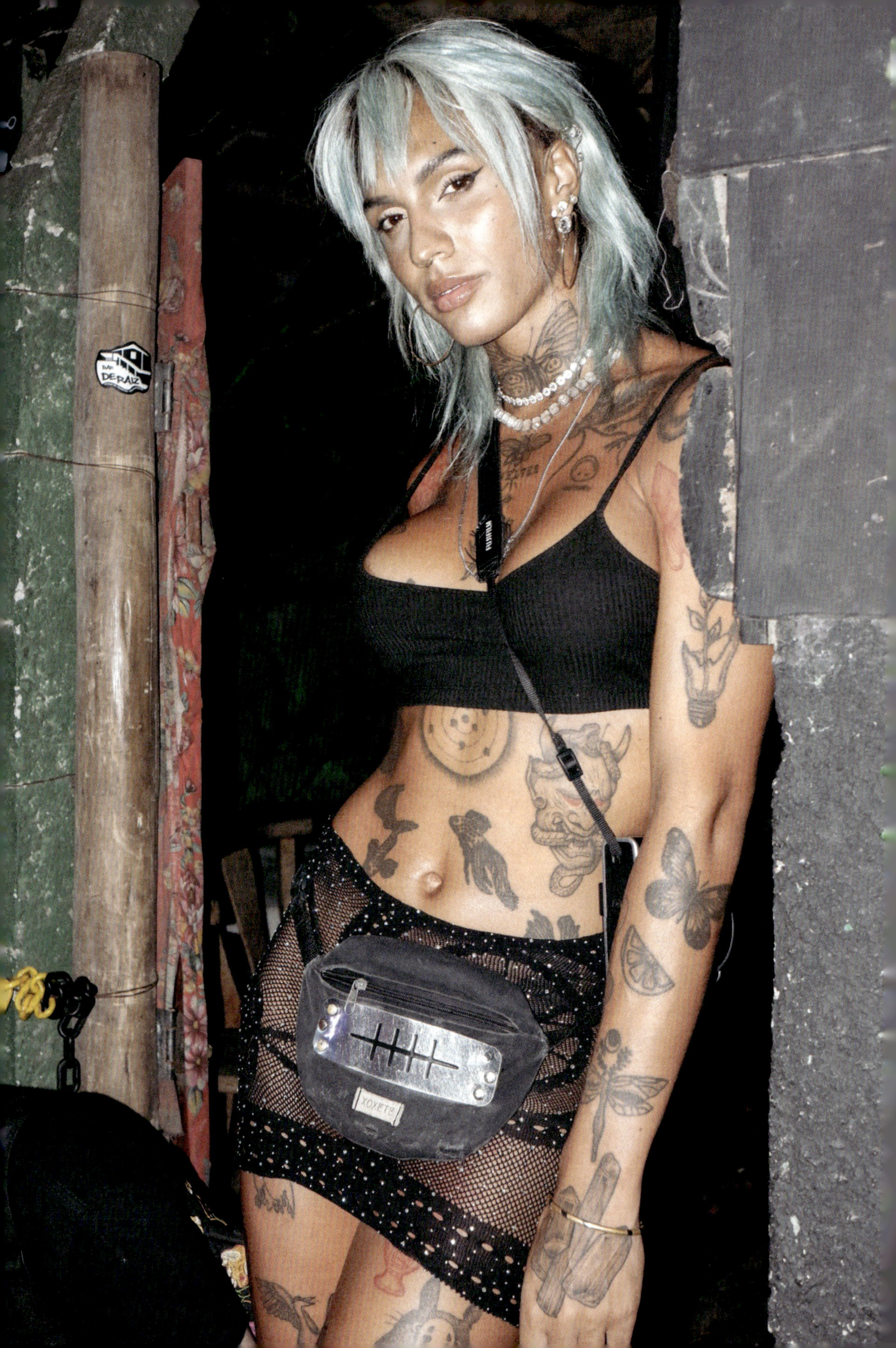

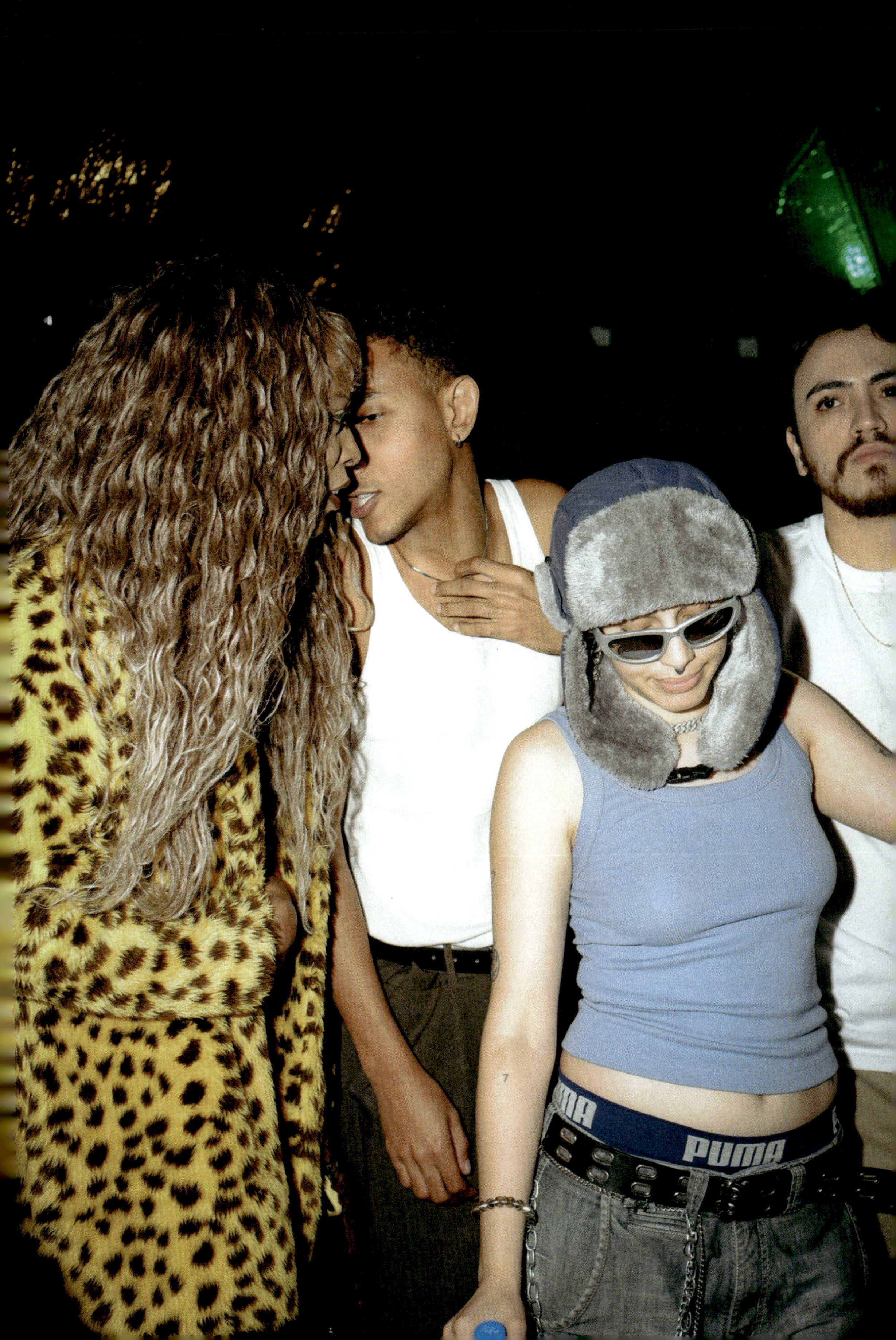

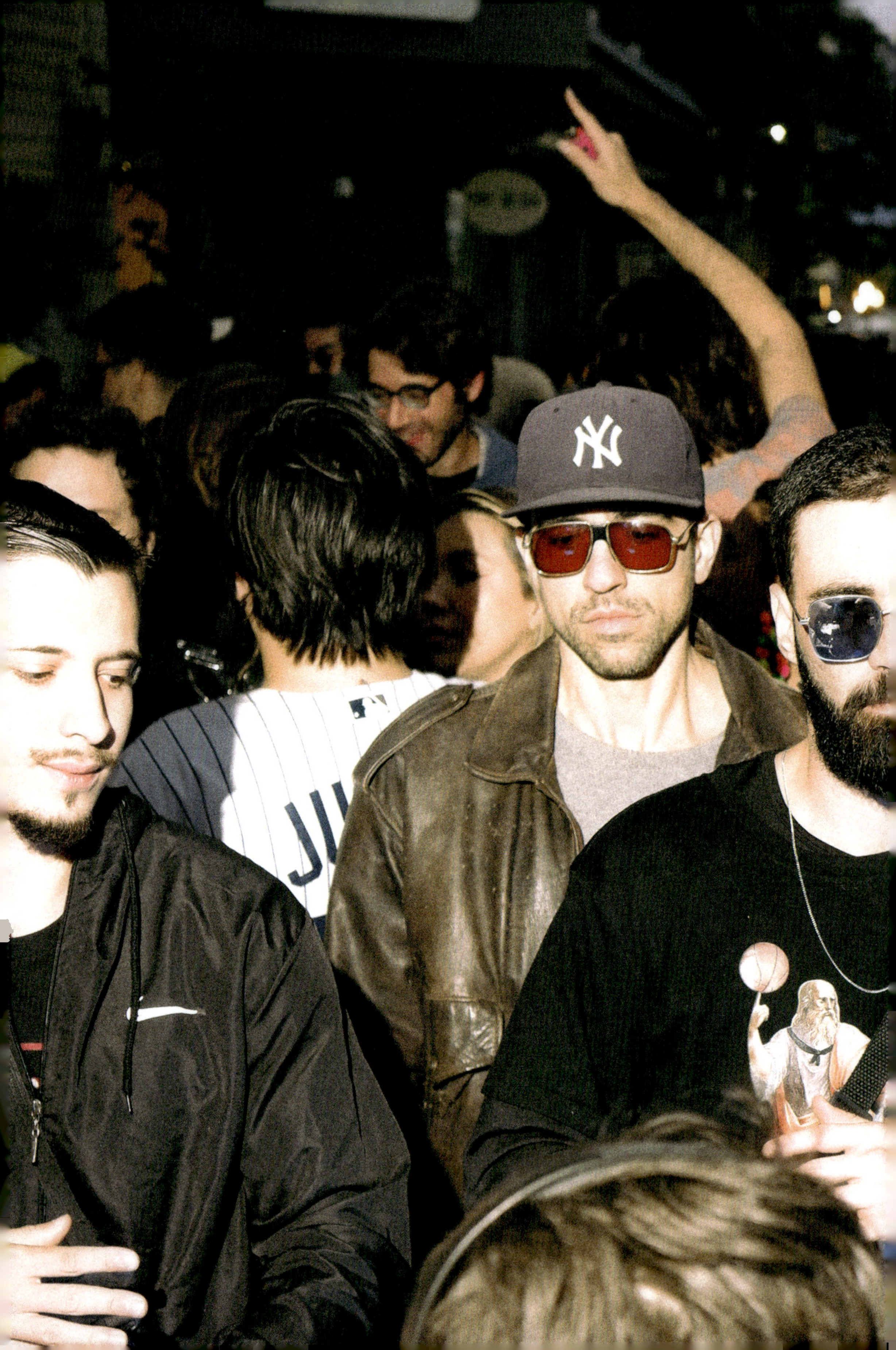

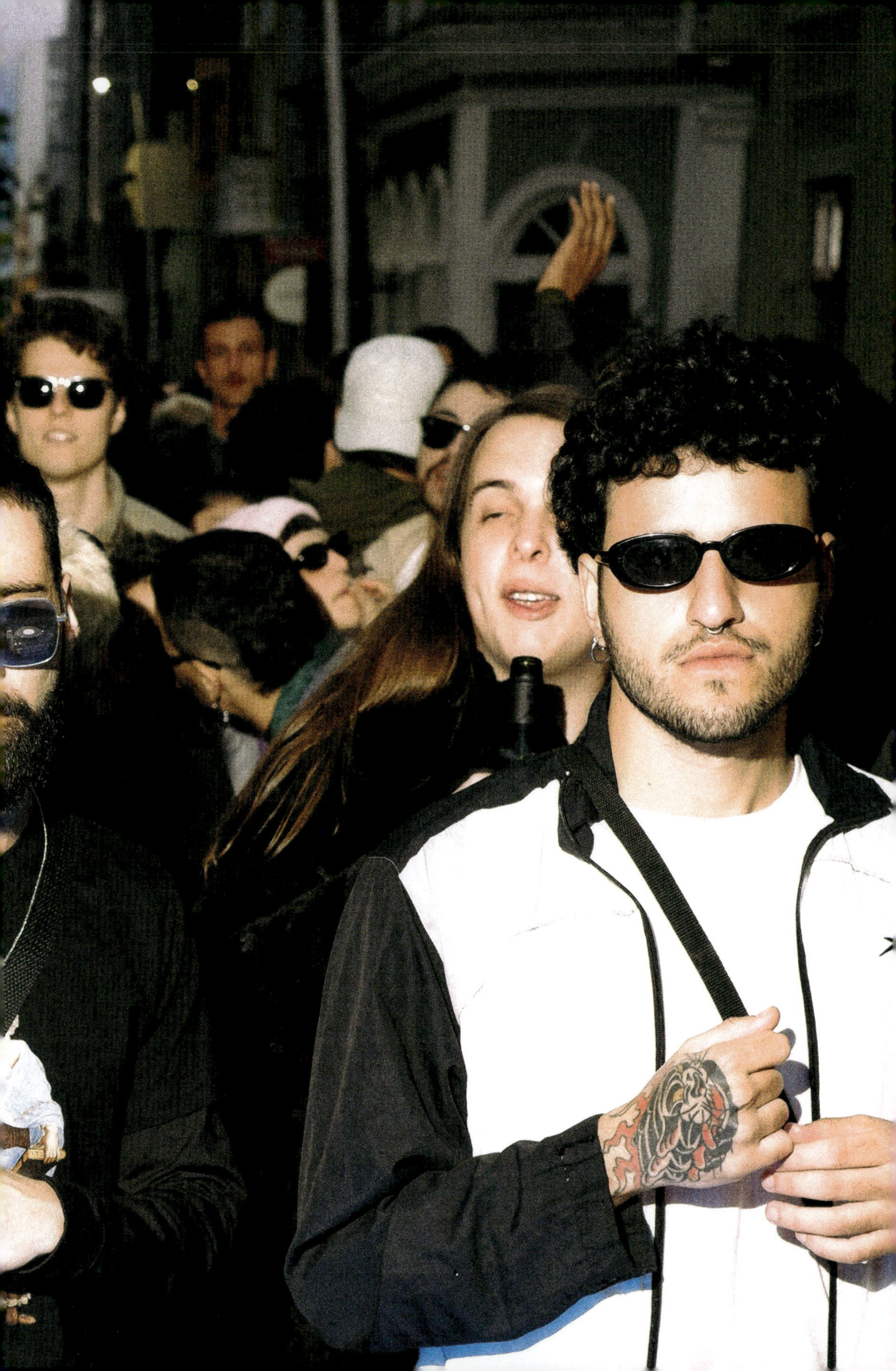

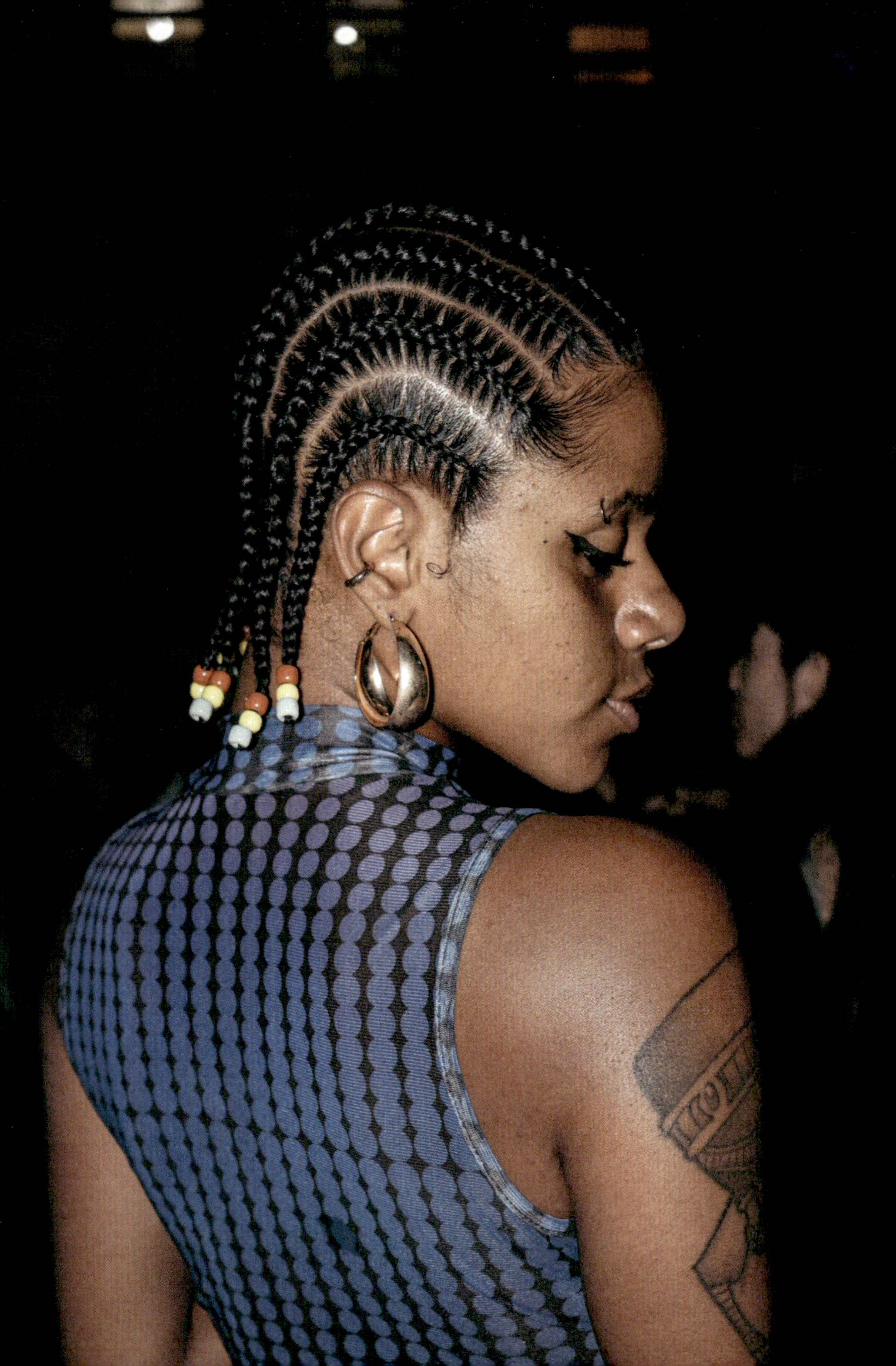

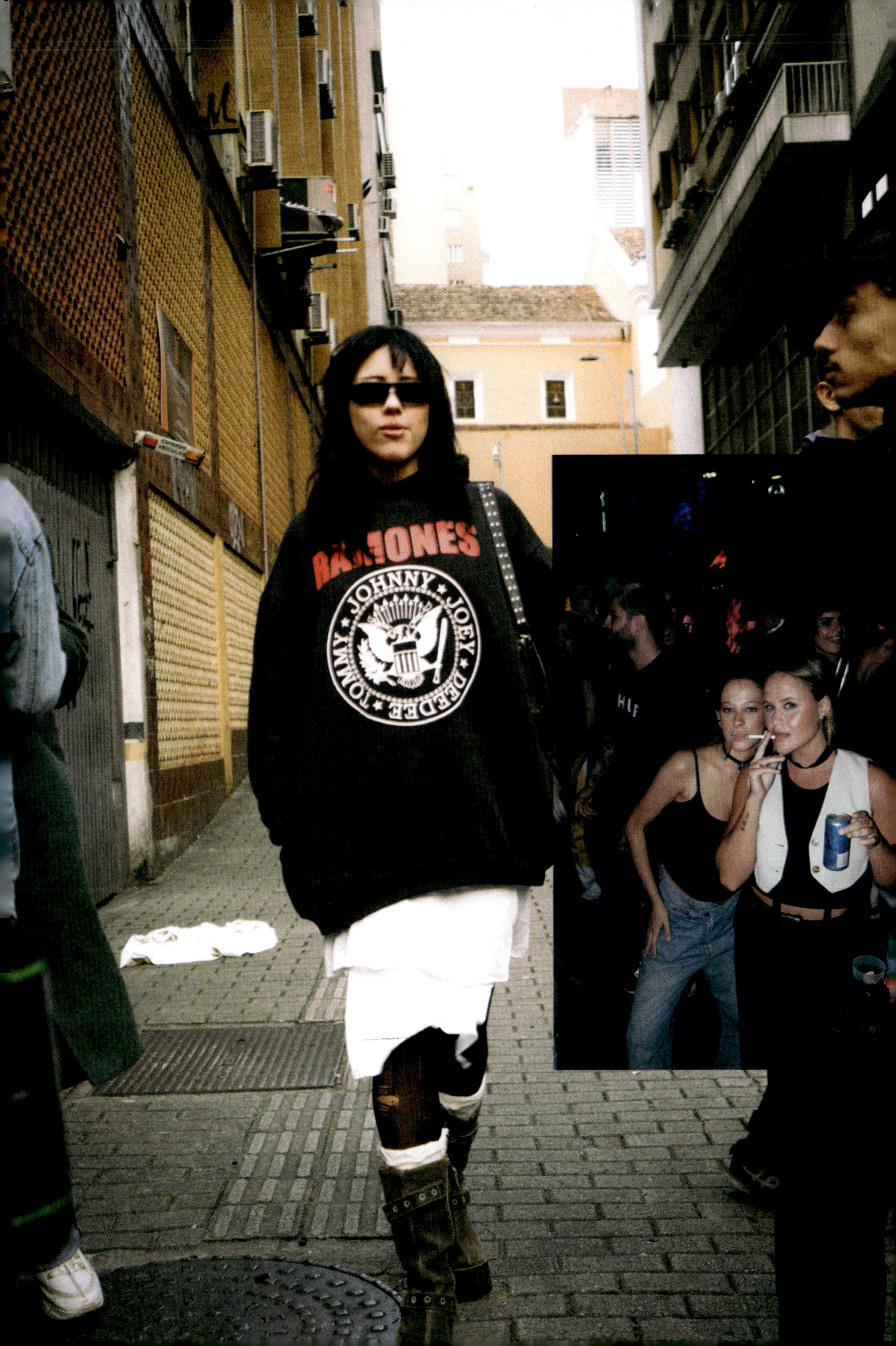

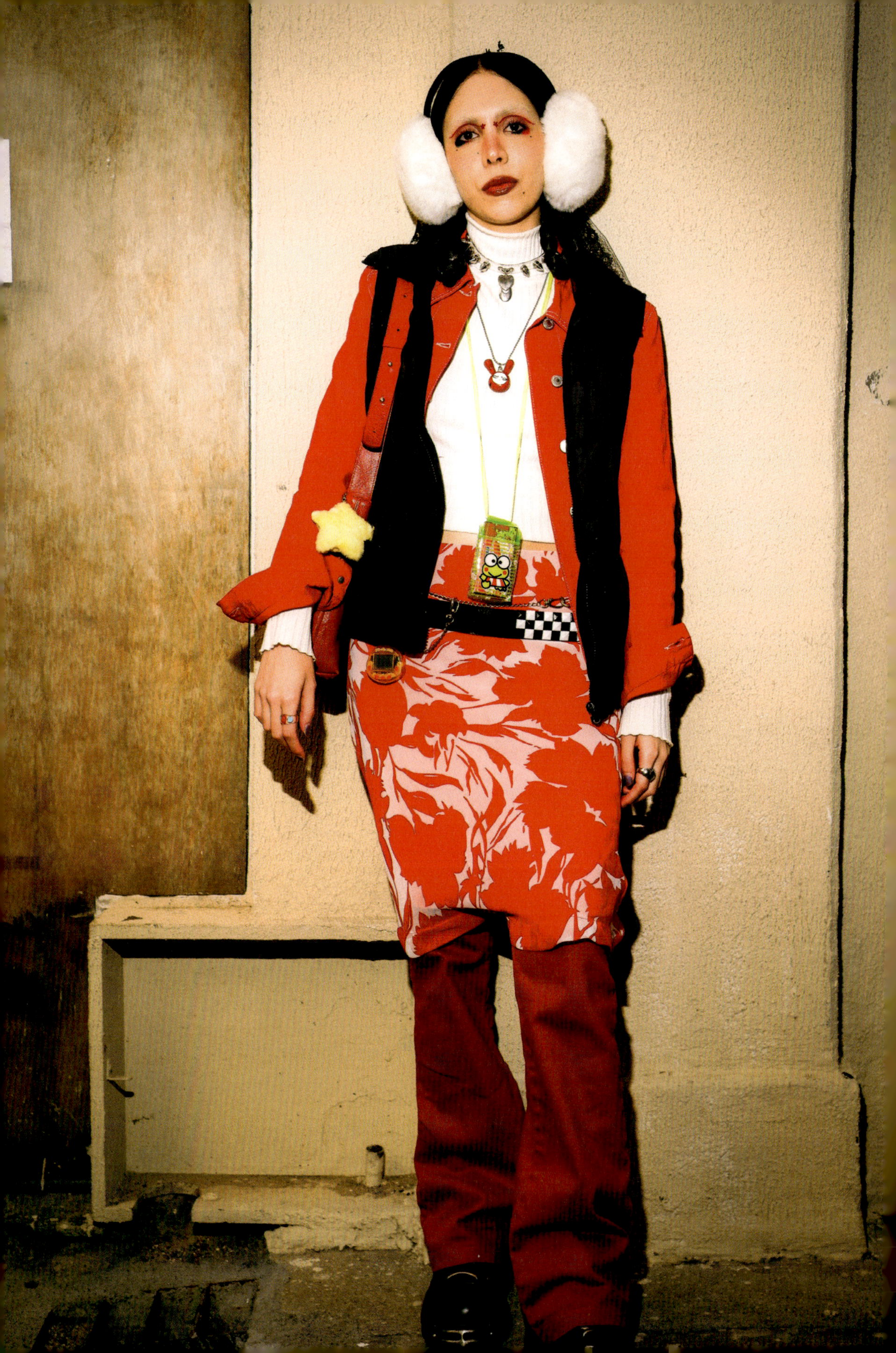

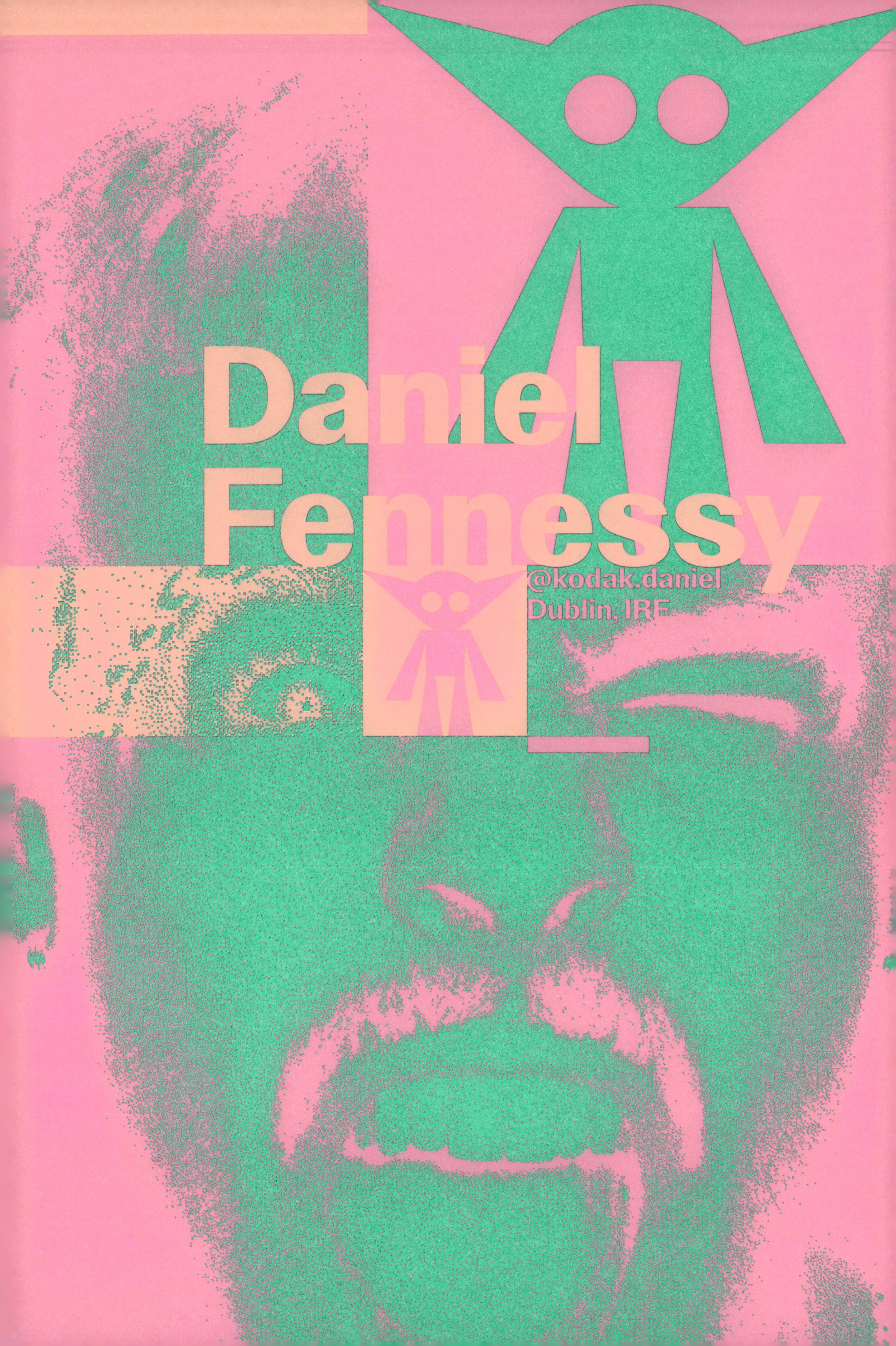

Daniel Fennessy

@kodak.daniel
Dublin, IRE

I'm Daniel, Irish Photographer and Videographer under the alias Kodak Dan. First starting my journey back in December 2022 living in Dublin, I was drawn to shooting discrete candids of ravers at several techno nights in the city. Since then I've made a career out of my love for the scene, having a worldwide photo deal with DICE and having my photos on posters in New York, Barcelona and London, Shooting multiple festivals across Europe and touring with many different artists.

The simplicity of capturing a moment where the dancer is lost in the music makes the photo more natural and real as if you were seeing it with your own eyes. That really makes a photo euphoric.

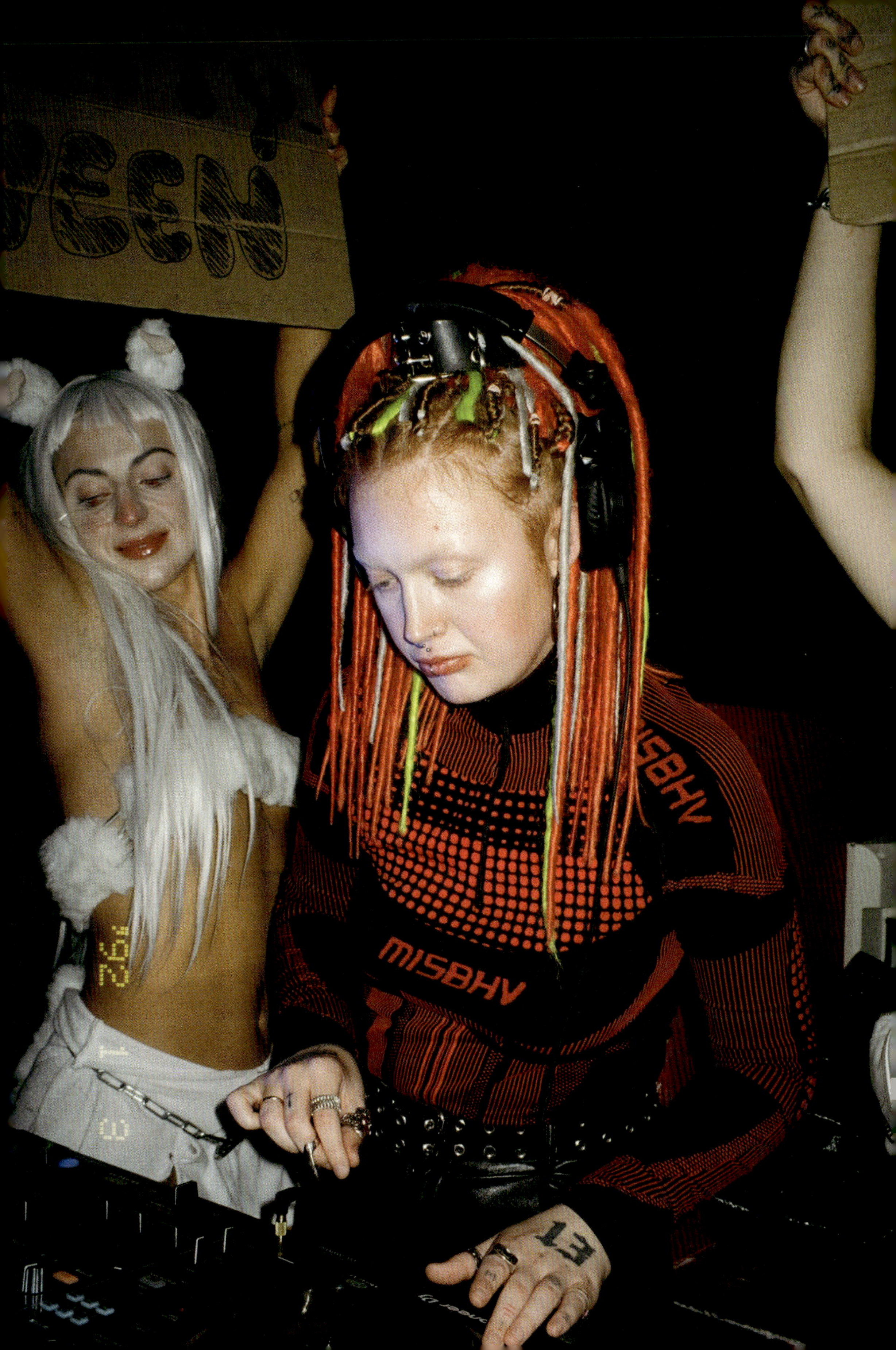

MISBHV
MISBHV
13

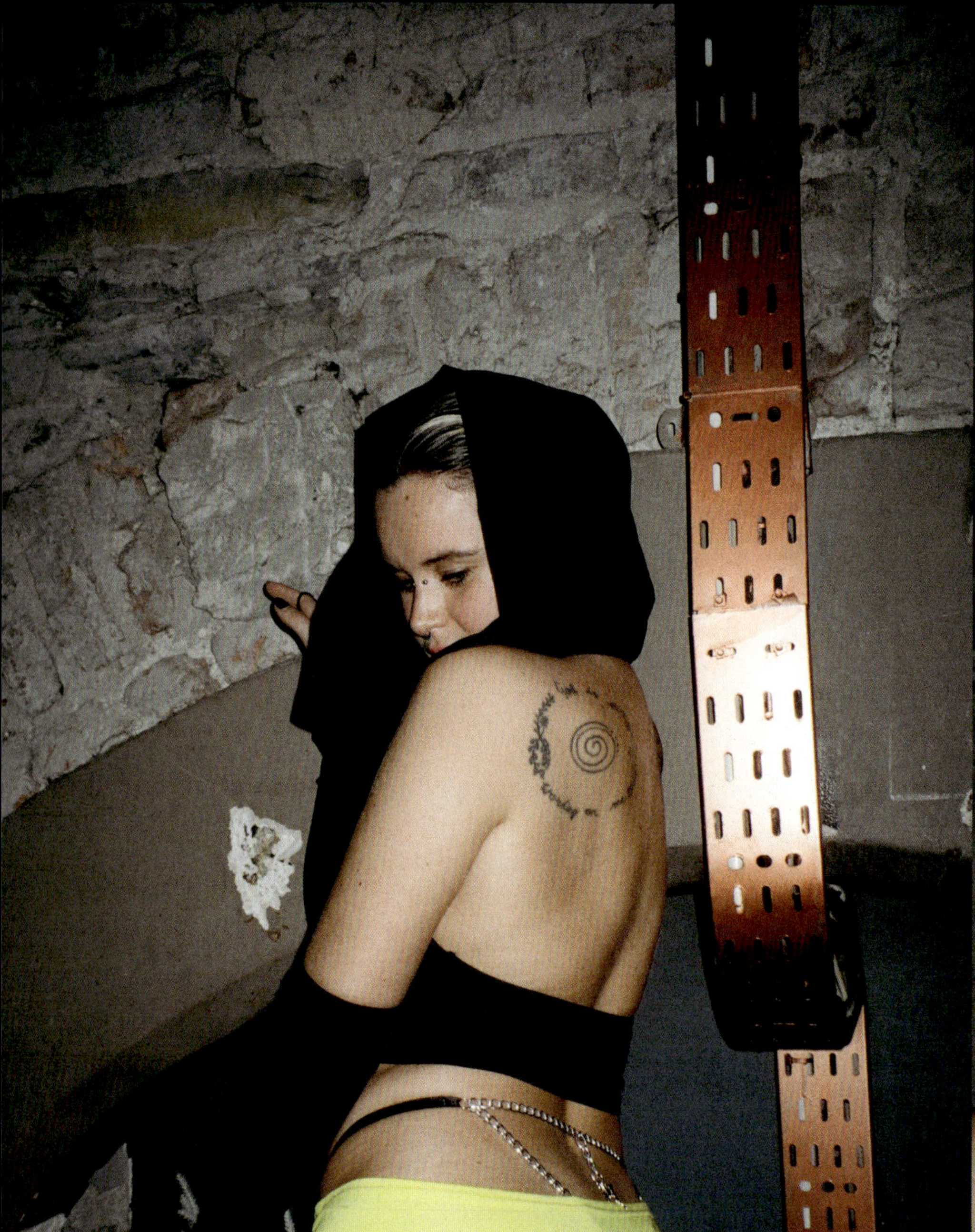

WRITTEN AND DIRECTED
BY
QUENTIN

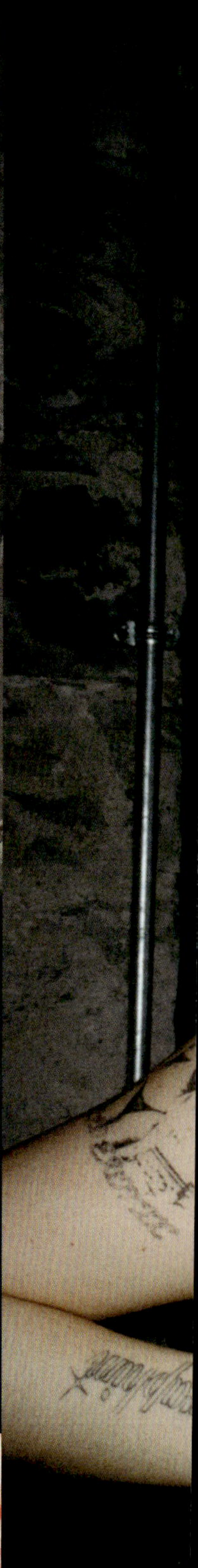

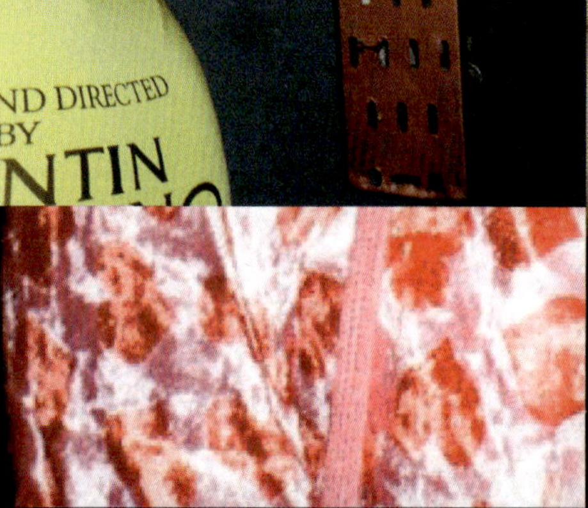

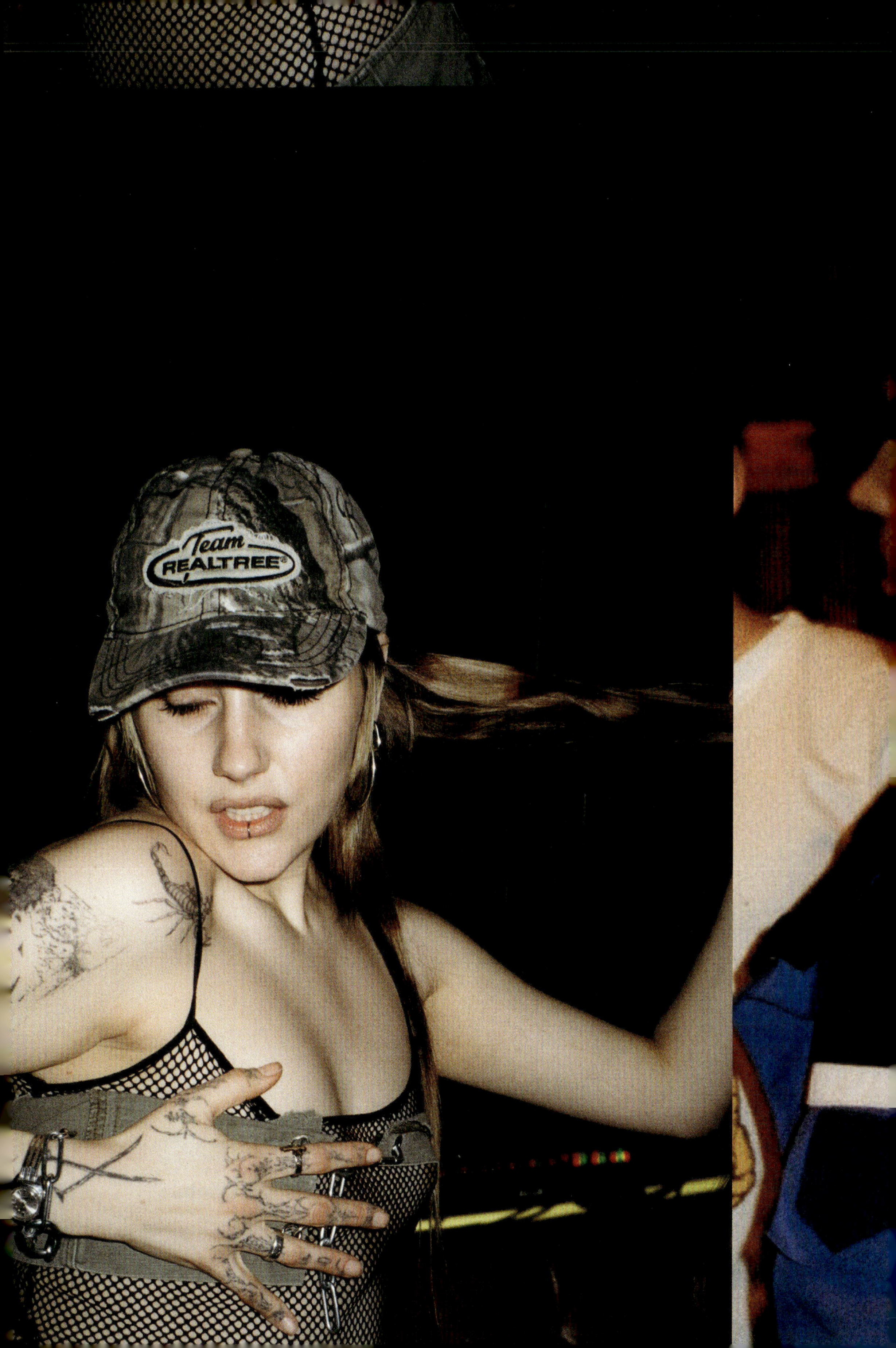
Team
REALTREE

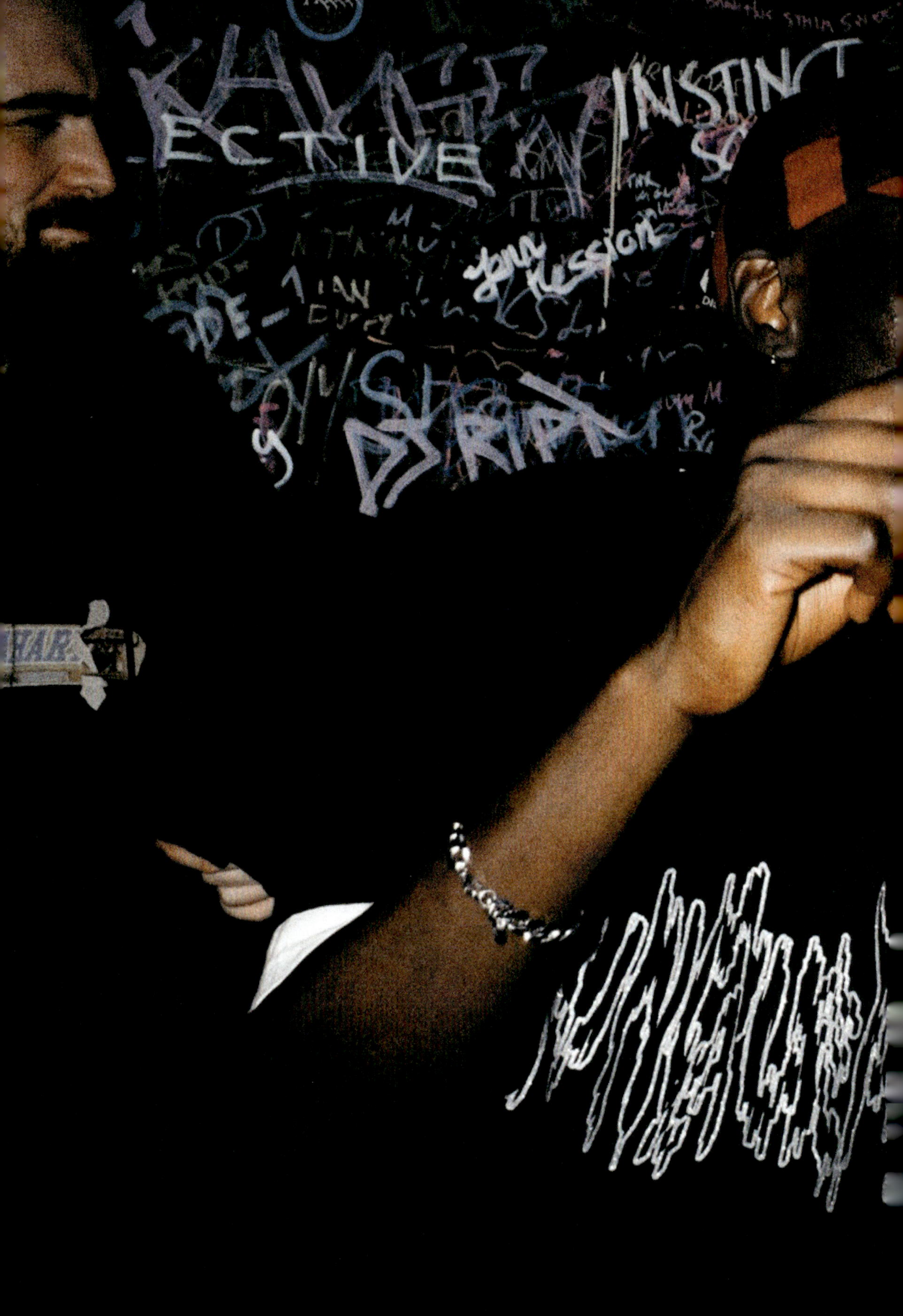

ECTIVE INSTINCT
DJ
session
DISTURBA
INSTINCT

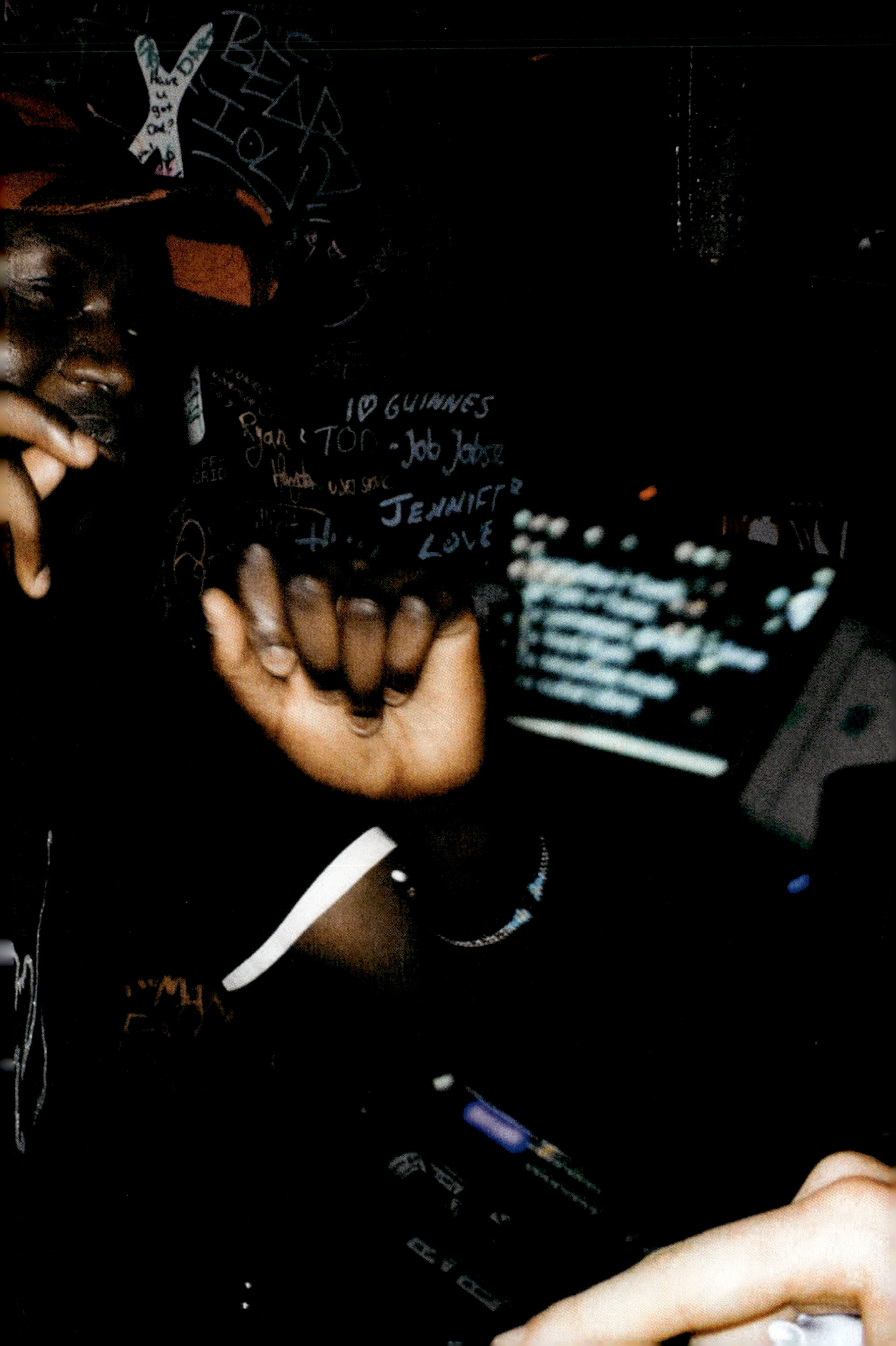

I ♥ GUINNES
Job Jobse
JENNIFER LOVE

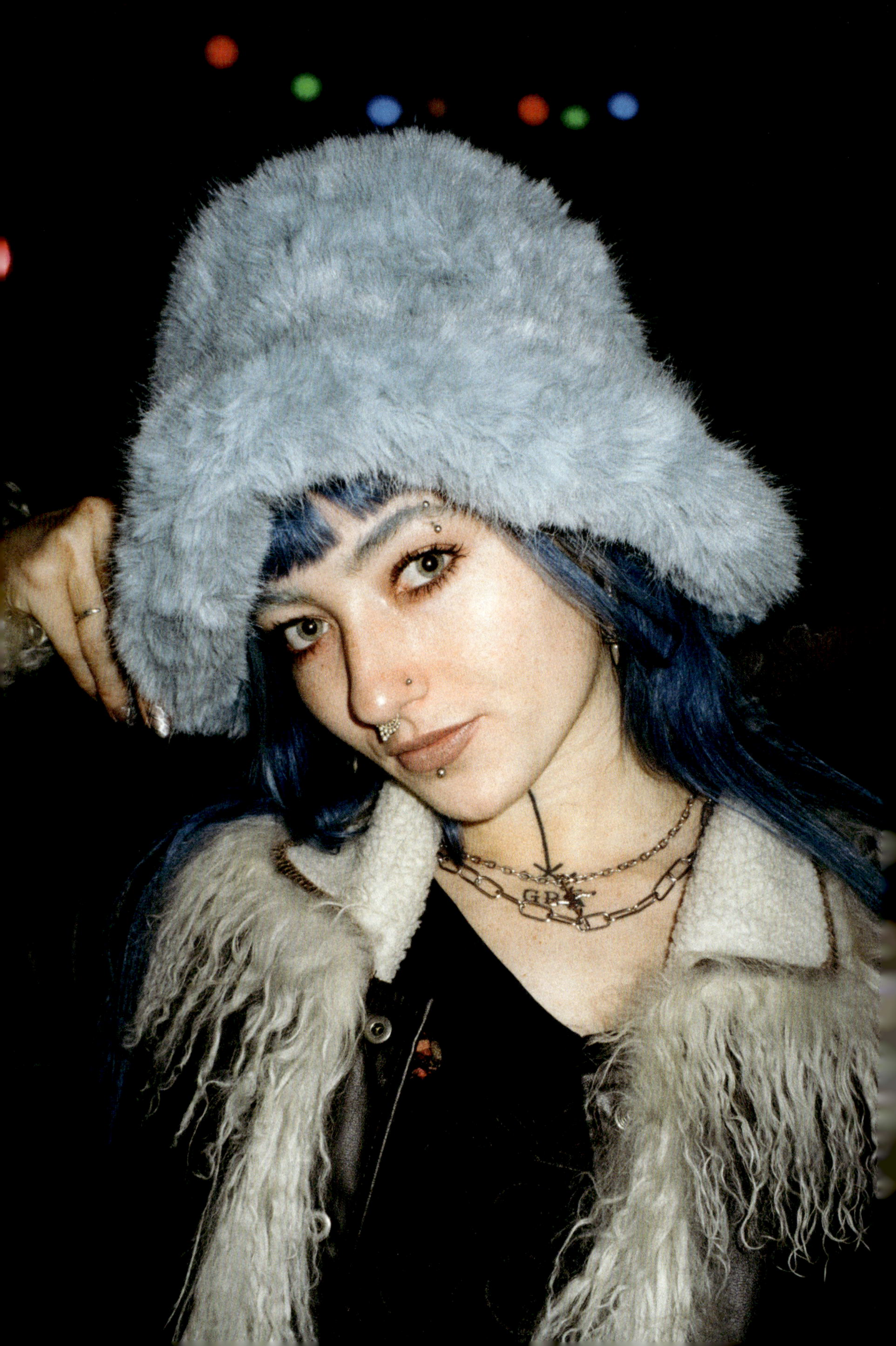

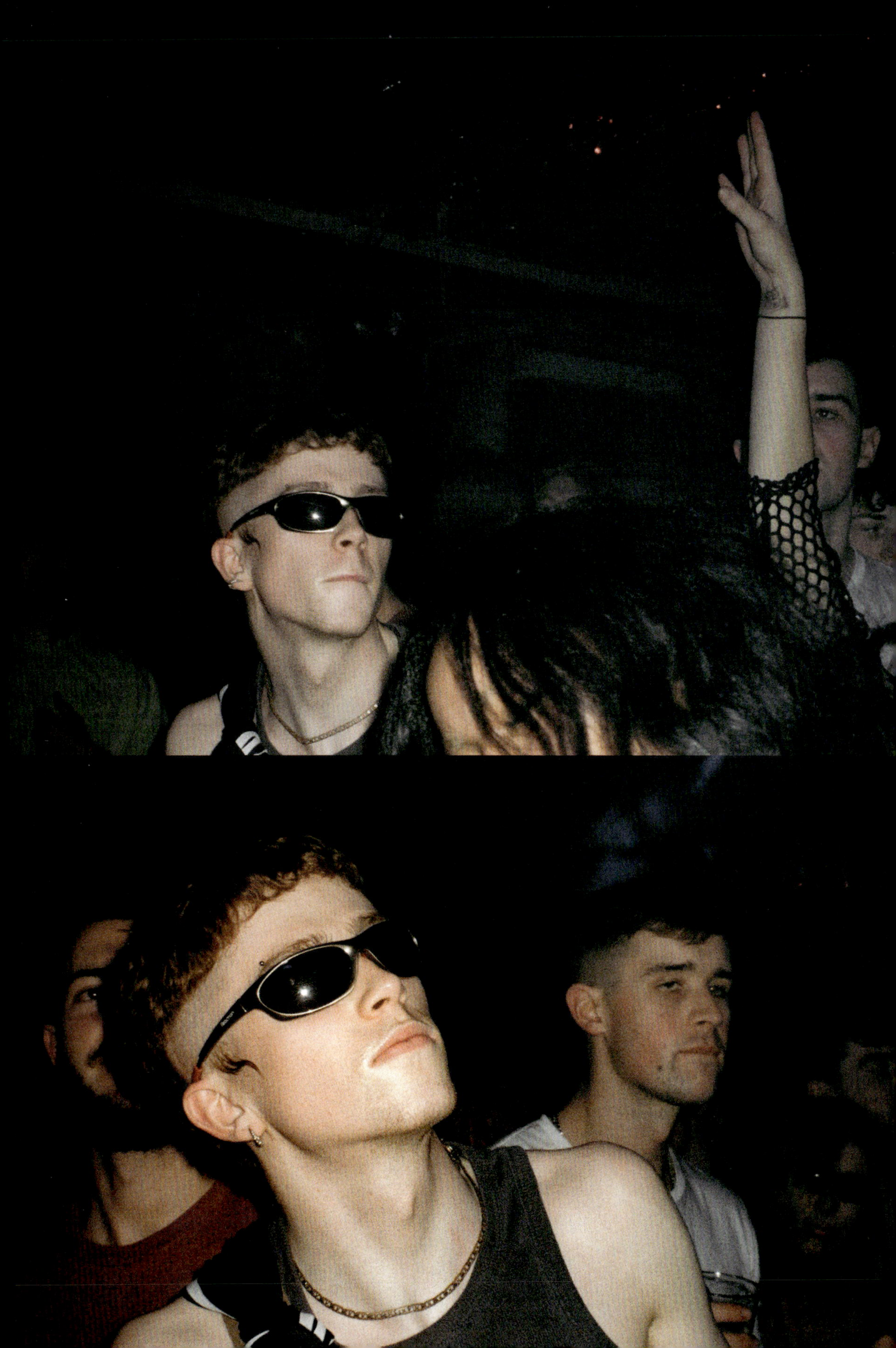

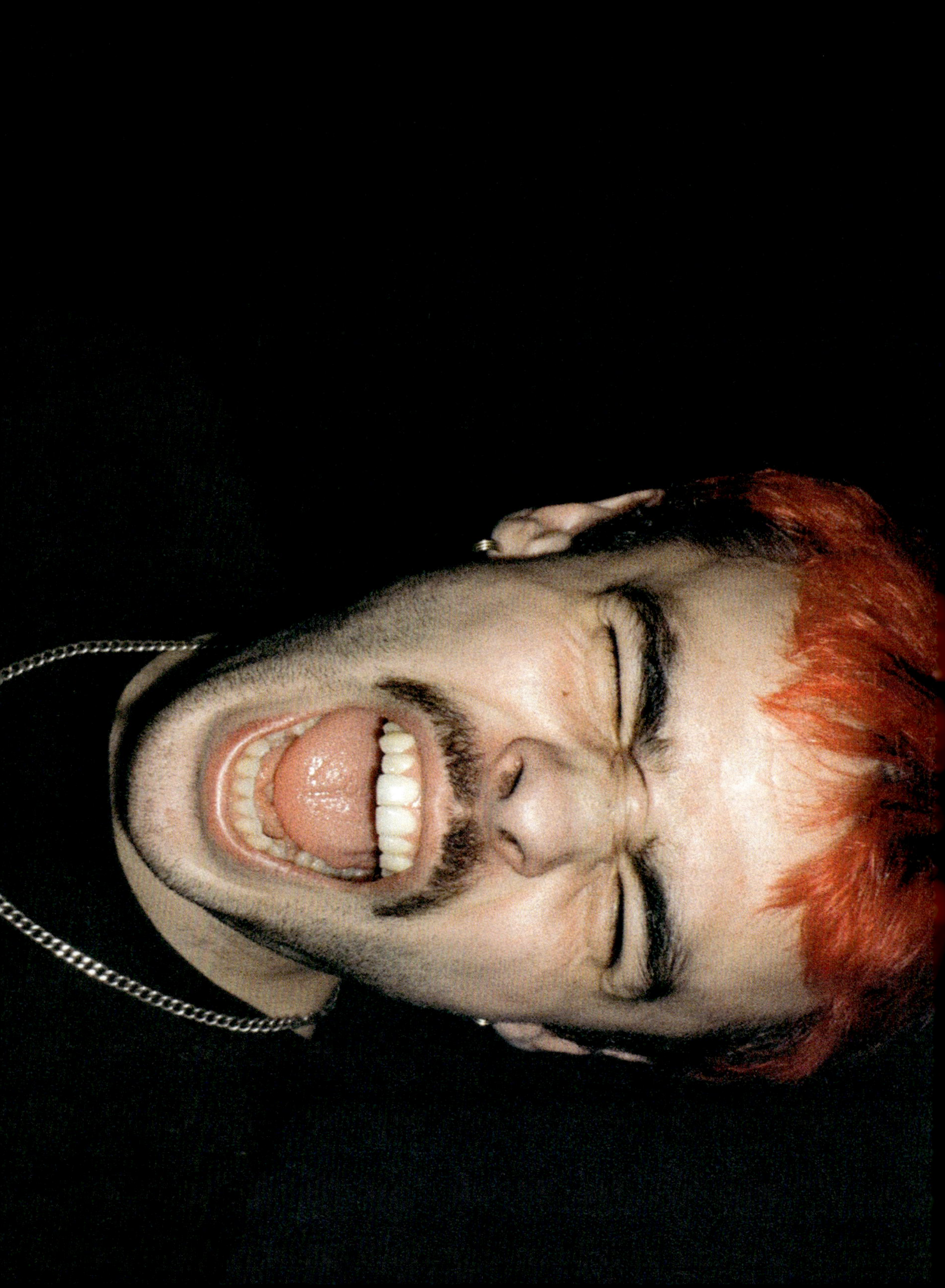

Distorted
@distorted.__
Newcastle / Sydney AUS

Raw, authentic, capturing the real, gritty, and distorted side of the Australian electronic music scene. Distorted is a dynamic photography duo between Azel and Tom natives of the land down under. With our shared passions for music and the dance scene, we try to bridge the gap with our fresh and authentic perspective of capturing unique moments through film photography.

Tom, deeply rooted in the diverse music scene of Newcastle, brings a wealth of local knowledge and a lifetime of involvement. Stemming from a musically diverse family, Tom naturally had a strong interest in all things music. Photography became an instinctive extension of involvement in these creative scenes. Thus, allowing Tom to blend his passions and immerse himself in the art of visual storytelling. Azel carries with her a rich appreciation for the music and dance culture in her home city. Originally coming from Sydney, a place where diverse music and dance culture thrives, she recognised a need for more originality in the music photography scene in Newcastle. Partnering with Tom, Azel's love of music, the dance scene, as well as film photography sparked the idea of collaboration. The partnership was a natural progression, driven by our shared dedication to supporting and celebrating the essence of music and dance through film photography.

Together we formed DISTORTED.

Leveraging our unique backgrounds, shared passions, and artistic visions to capture distinct moments. We capture the real scene, real people, real interactions. Our efforts aim to infuse the music and dance scene with an authenticity and creativity that sets us apart from others. Photography gives us an avenue to involve all the things we love into one which makes it so enjoyable for us.

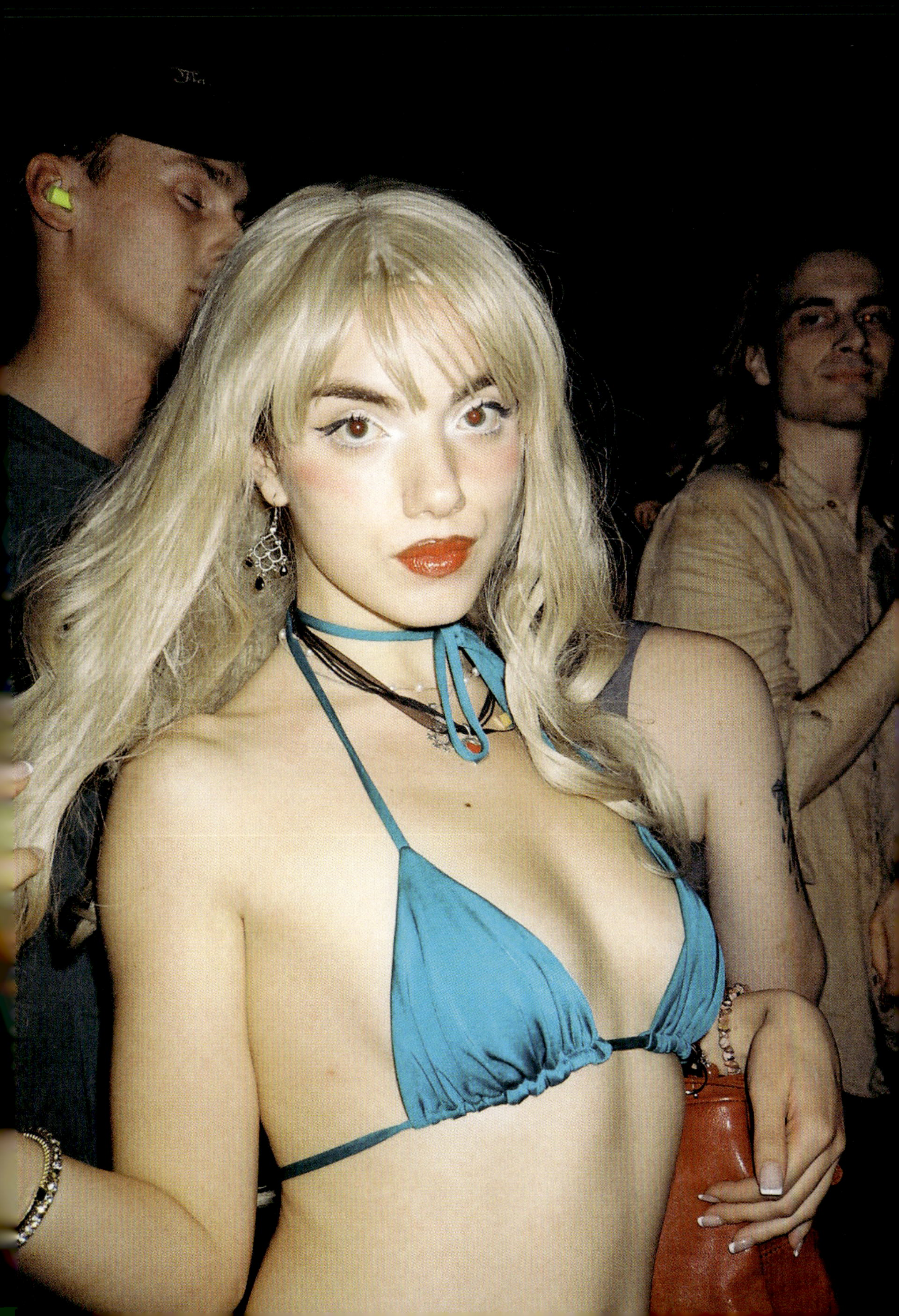

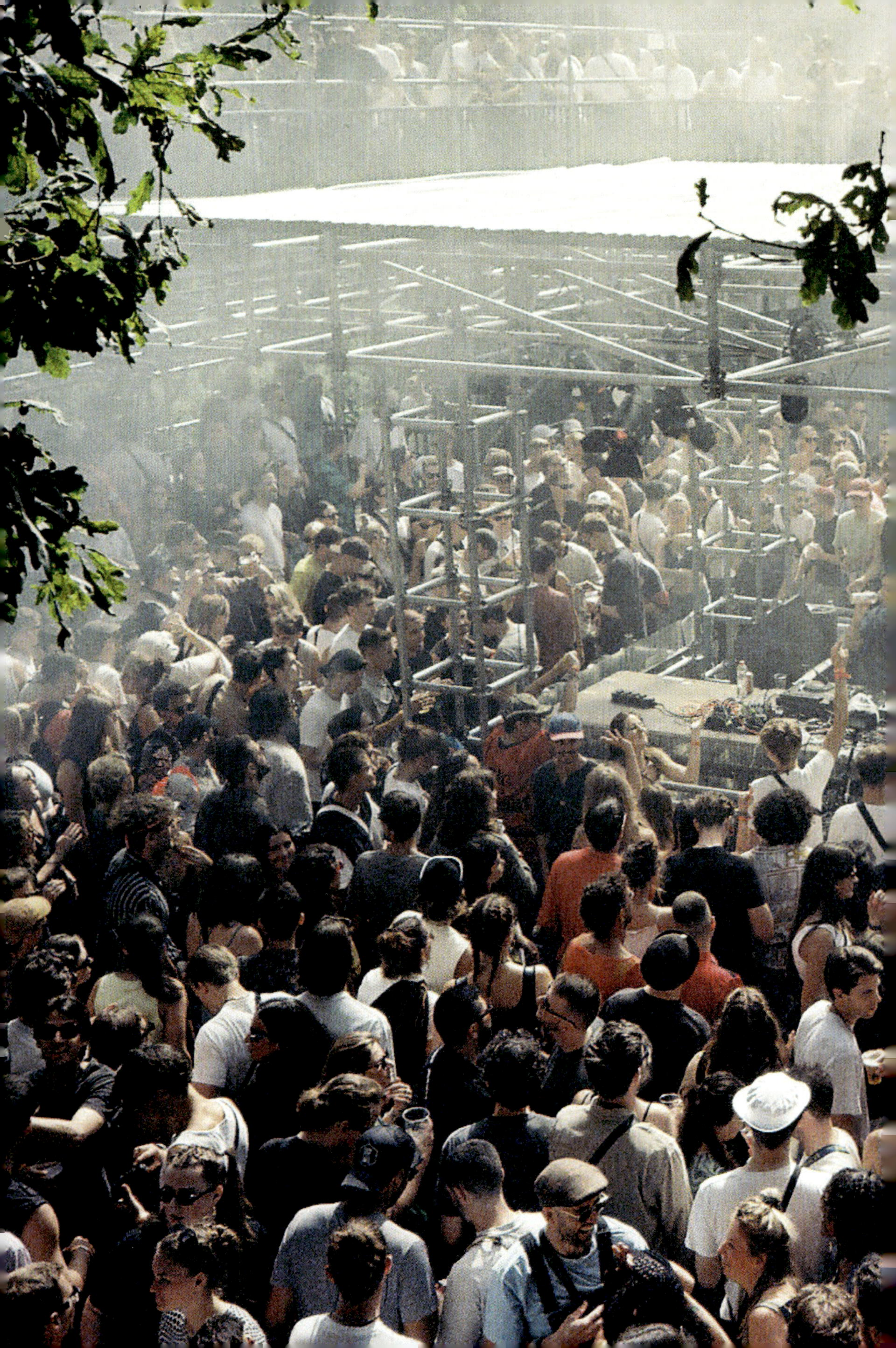

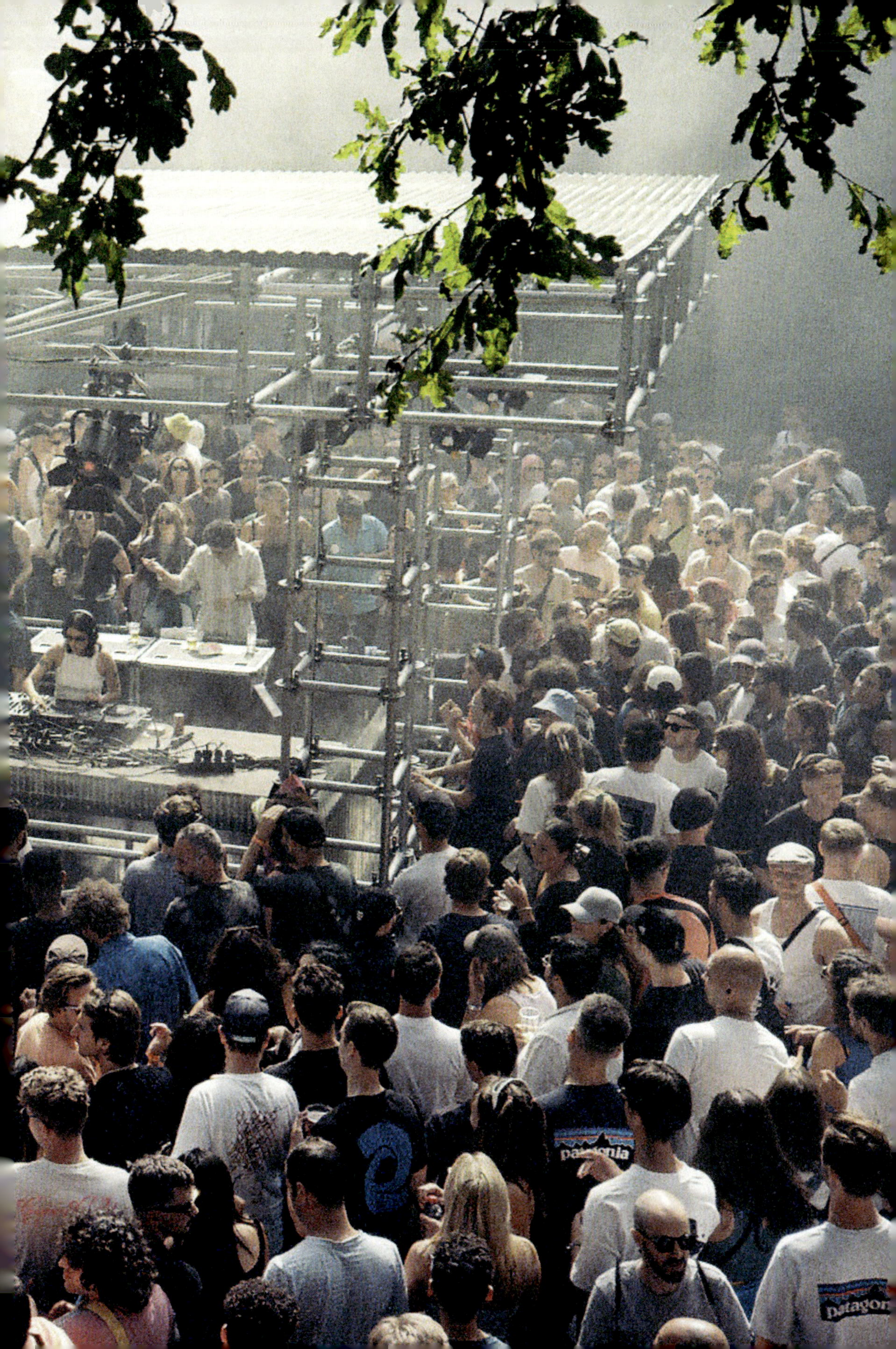

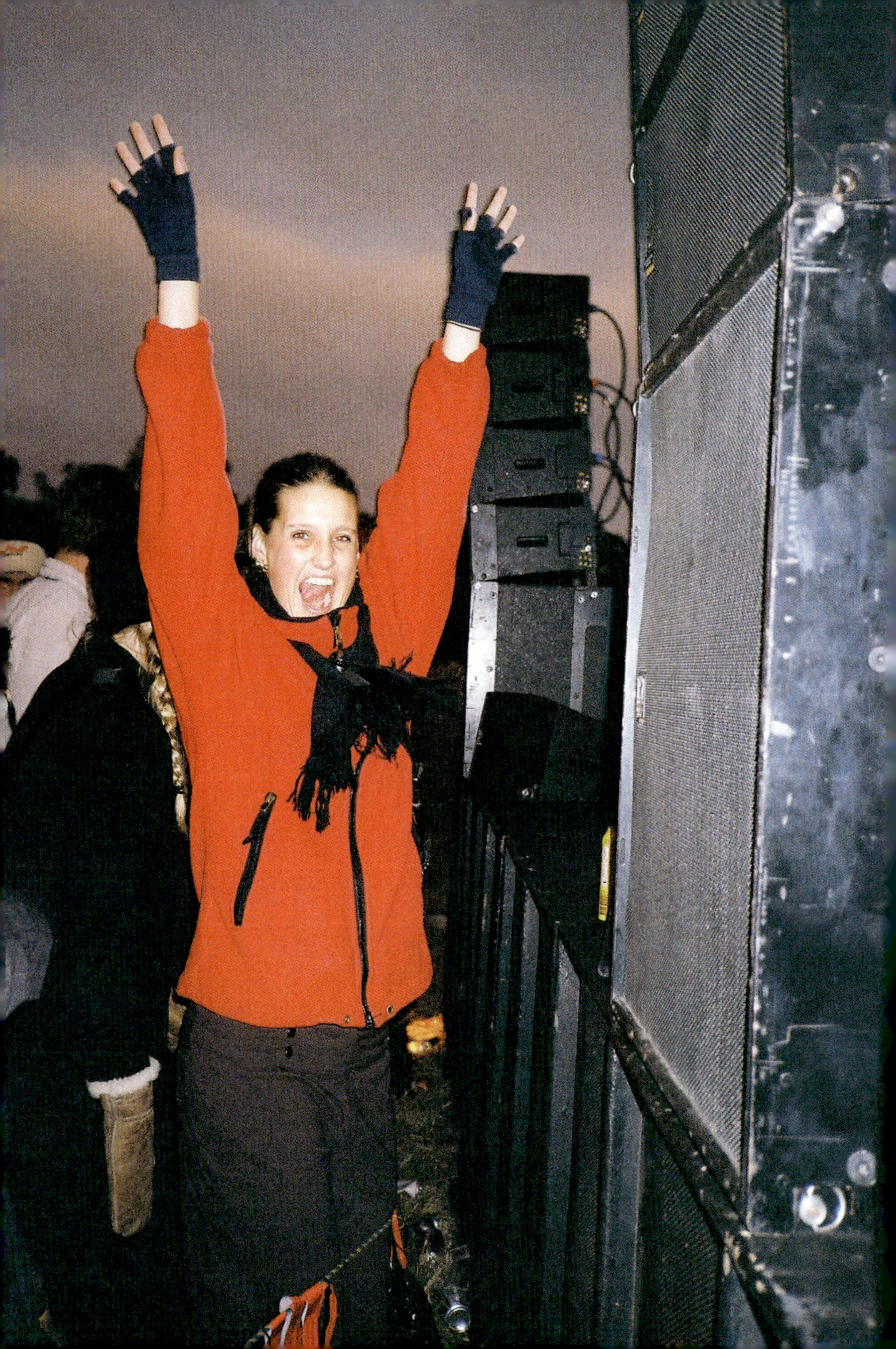

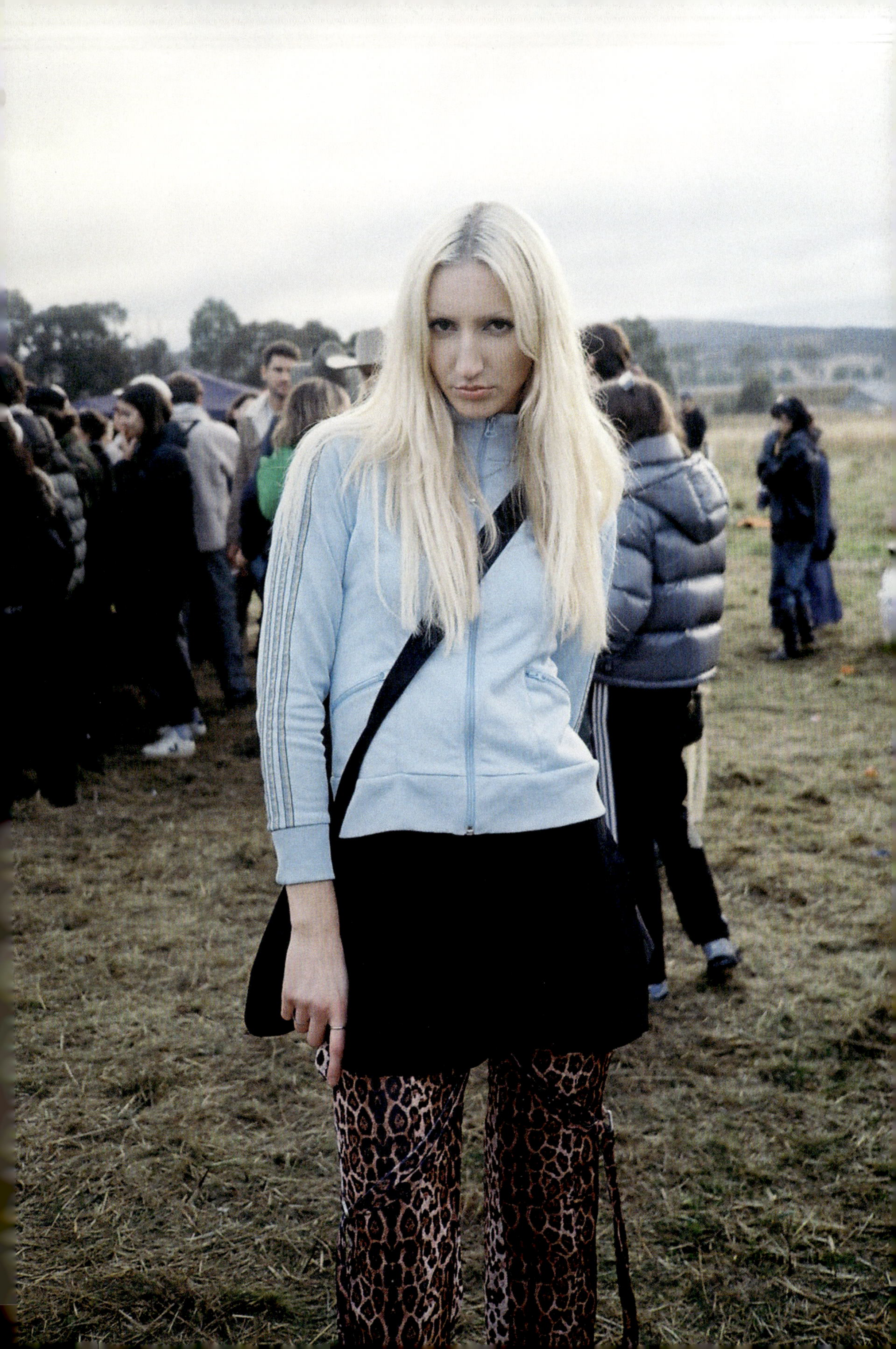

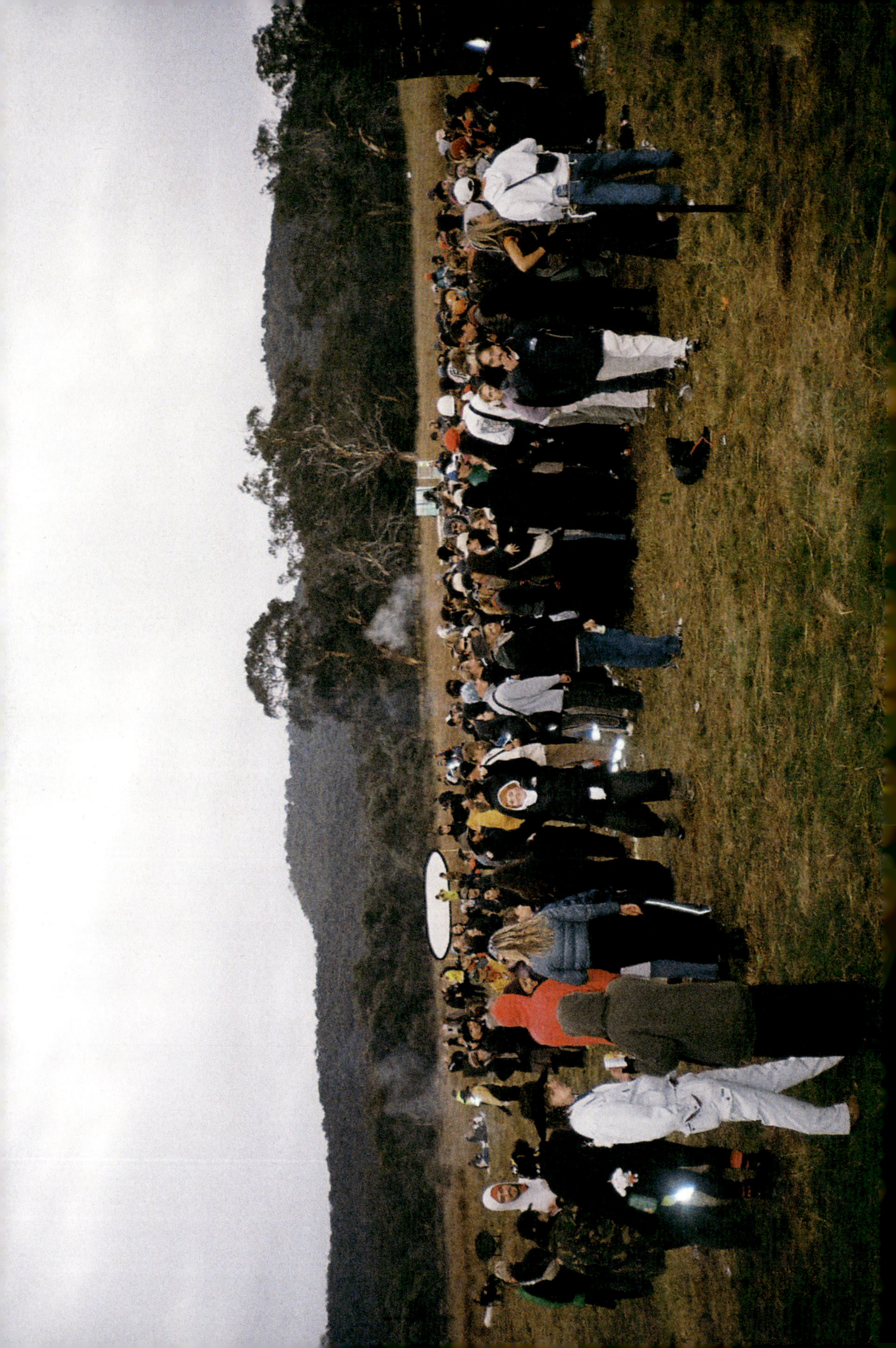

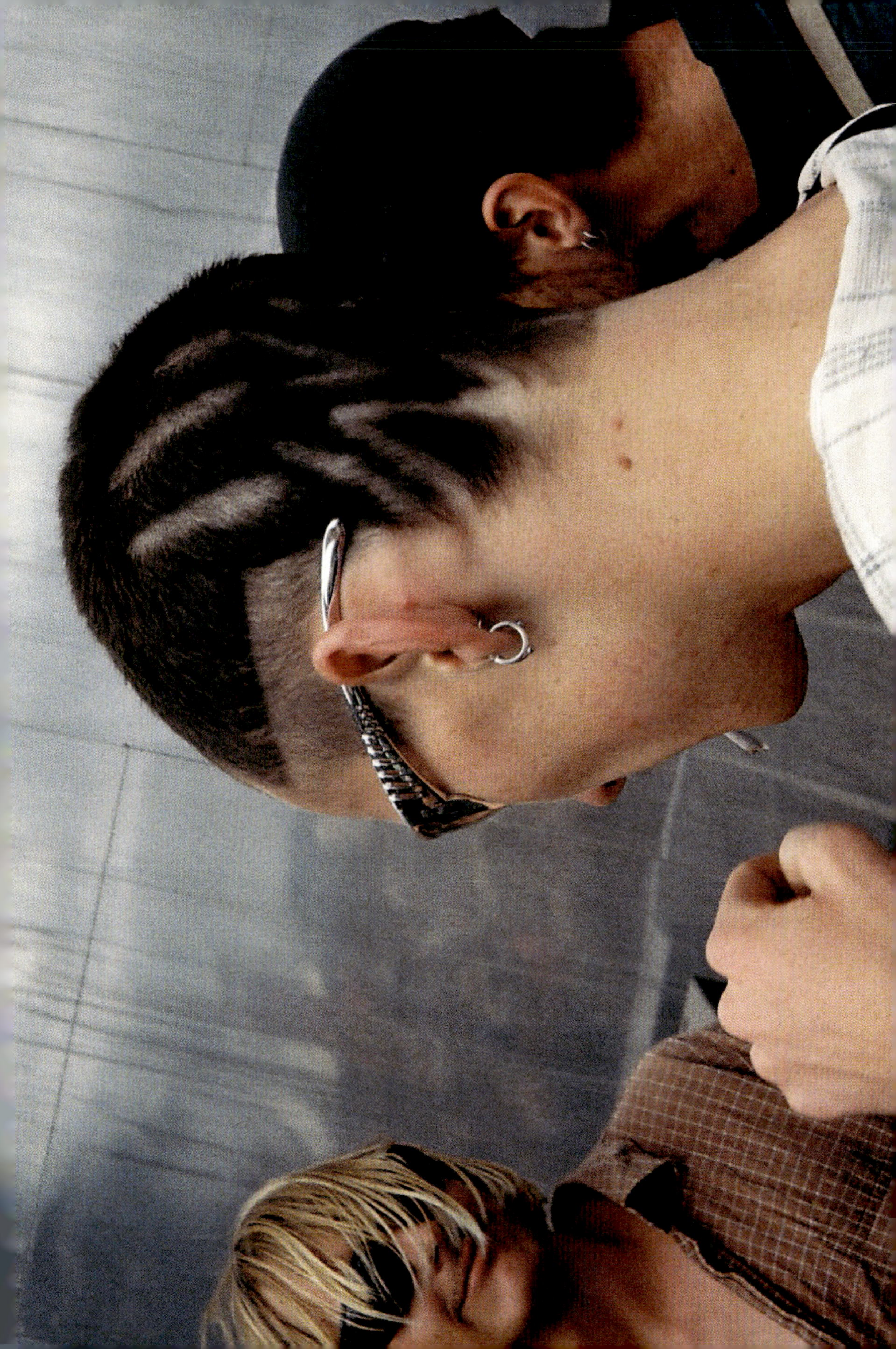

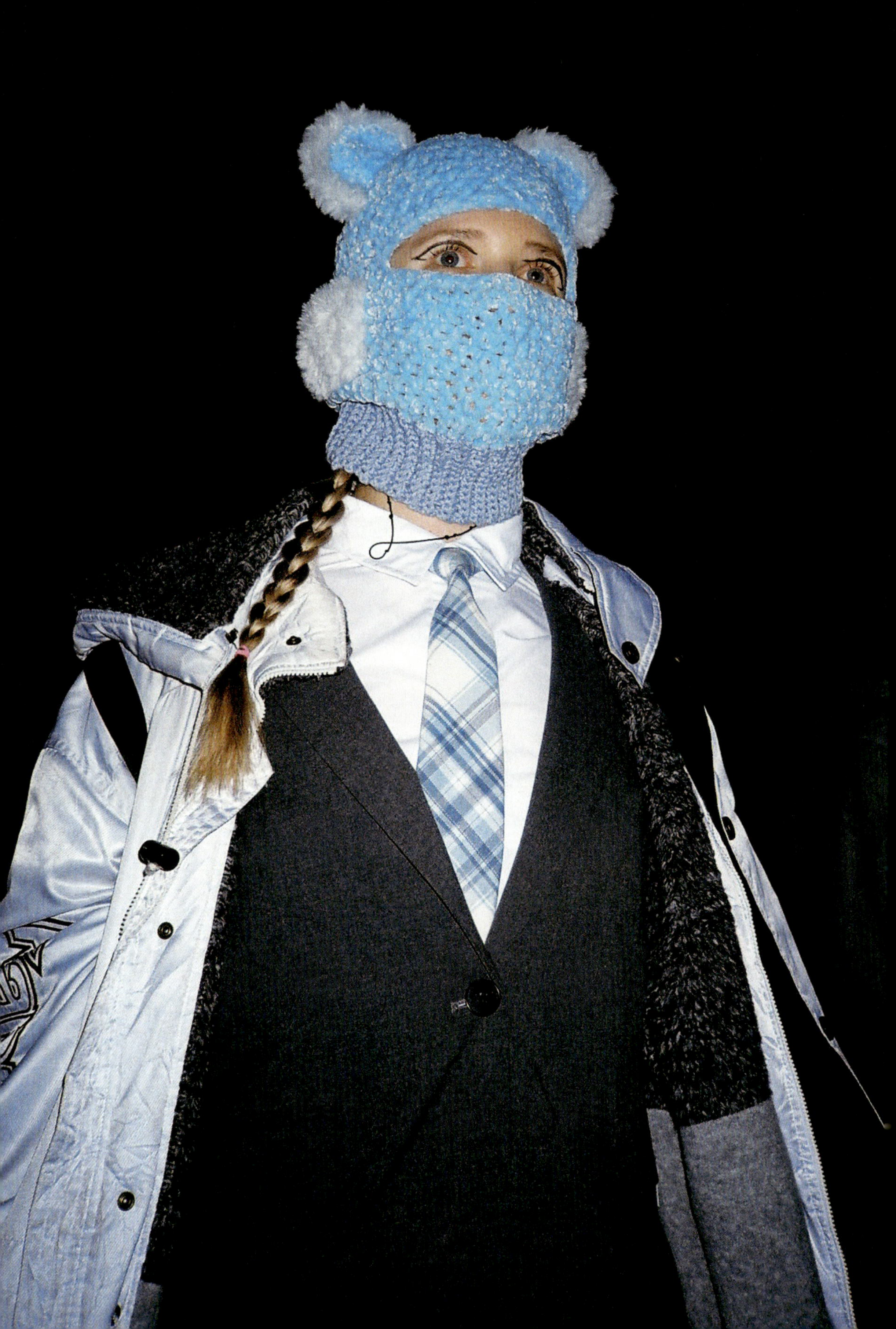

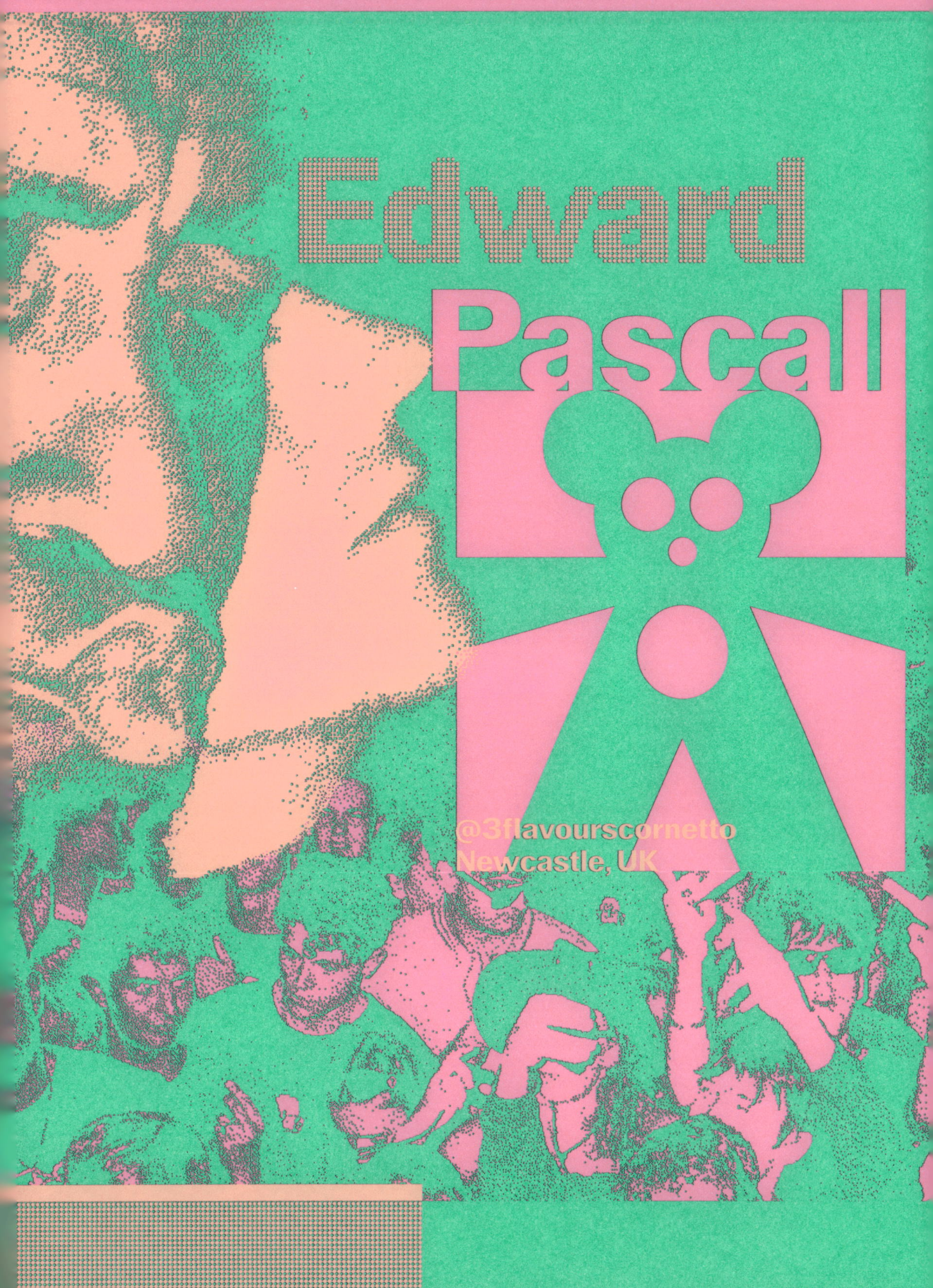

Edward
Pascall
@3flavourscornetto
Newcastle, UK

Being brought up with a love for punk music, I grew a deep passion for the DIY music scene, with pure expression and hedonism at the focal point.Before hitting my teens, I discovered dubstep on YouTube and proceeded to infiltrate my elder brother's laptop with loads of viruses as I tried ripping the sounds of Digital Mystikz onto my MP3 player. The sounds of dubstep, dub, and reggae opened my eyes to the UK's wider sound system culture.

My love and passion for this culture inspired me to pick the camera back up and document the scene I love so much. I really value the importance of documenting things. Any moment is a piece of history, so those special ones lost in the dance deserve to be captured.

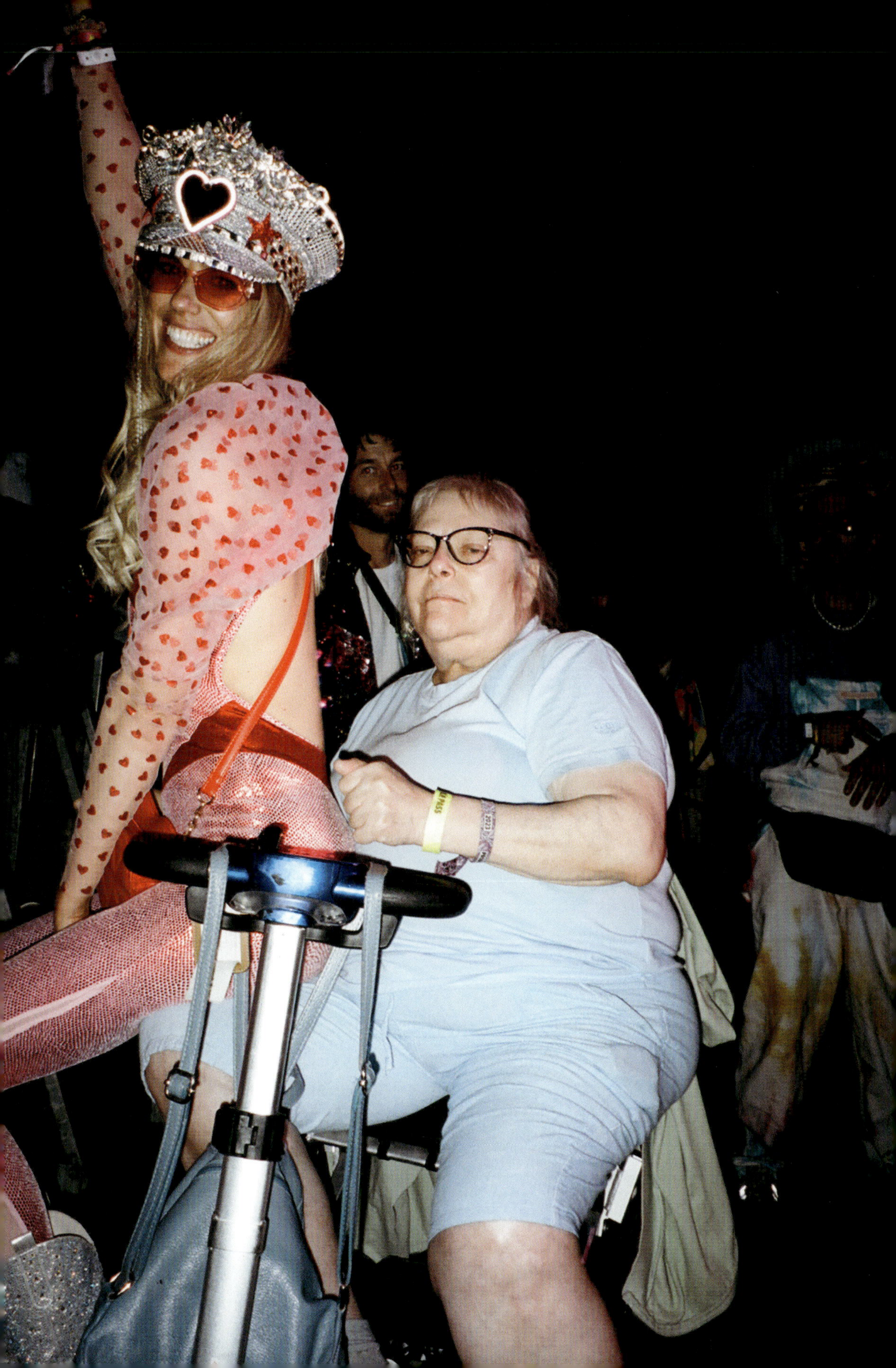

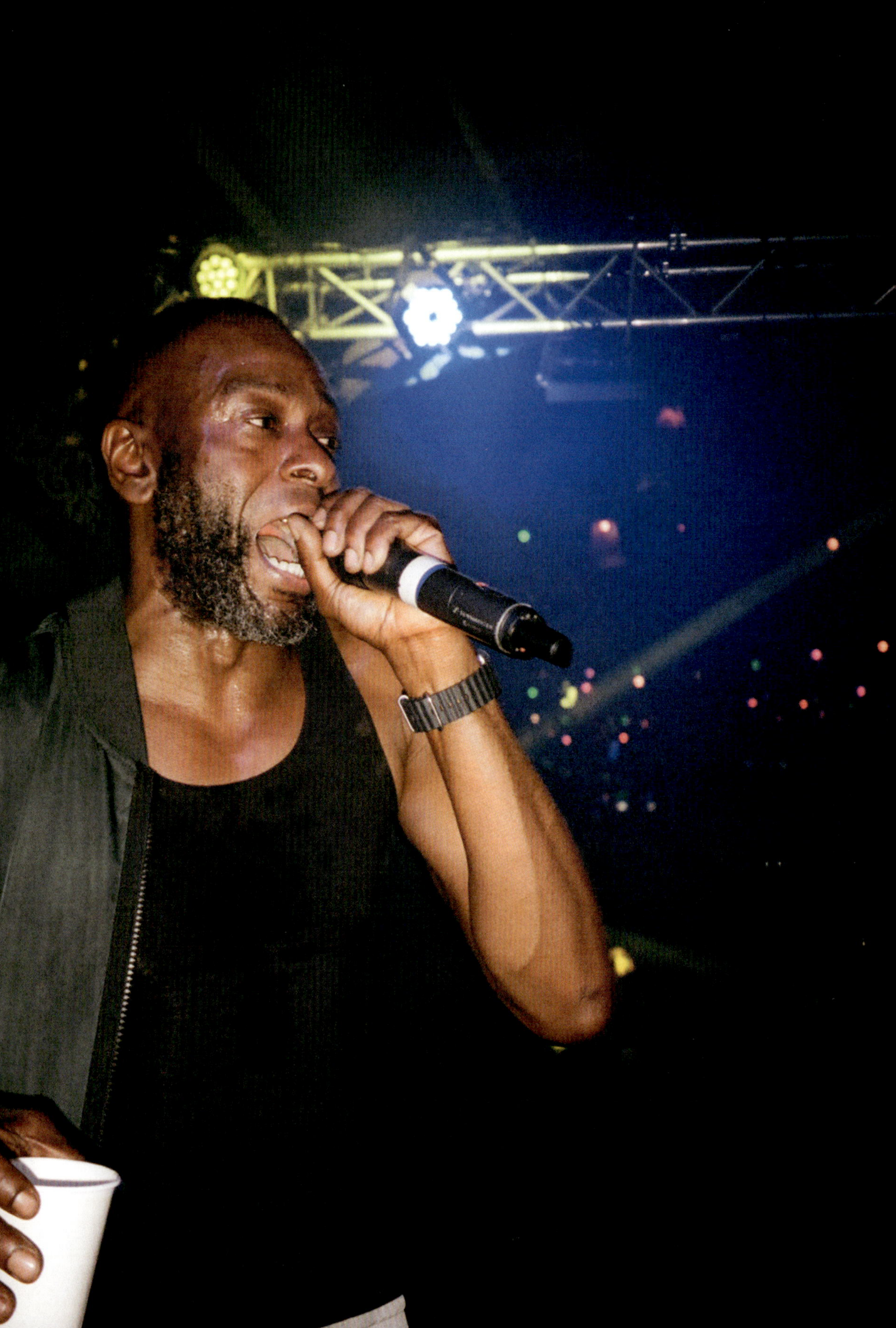

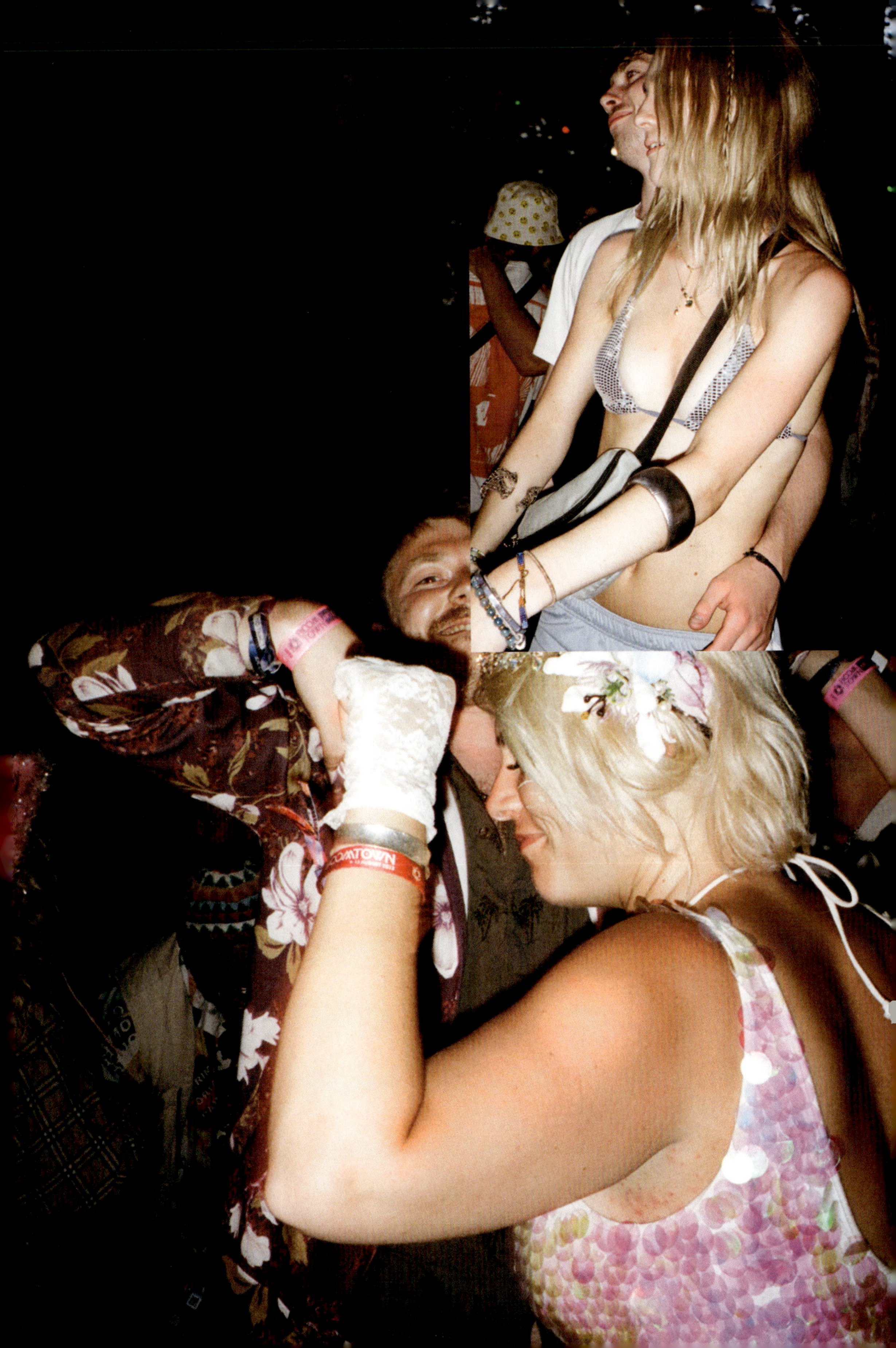

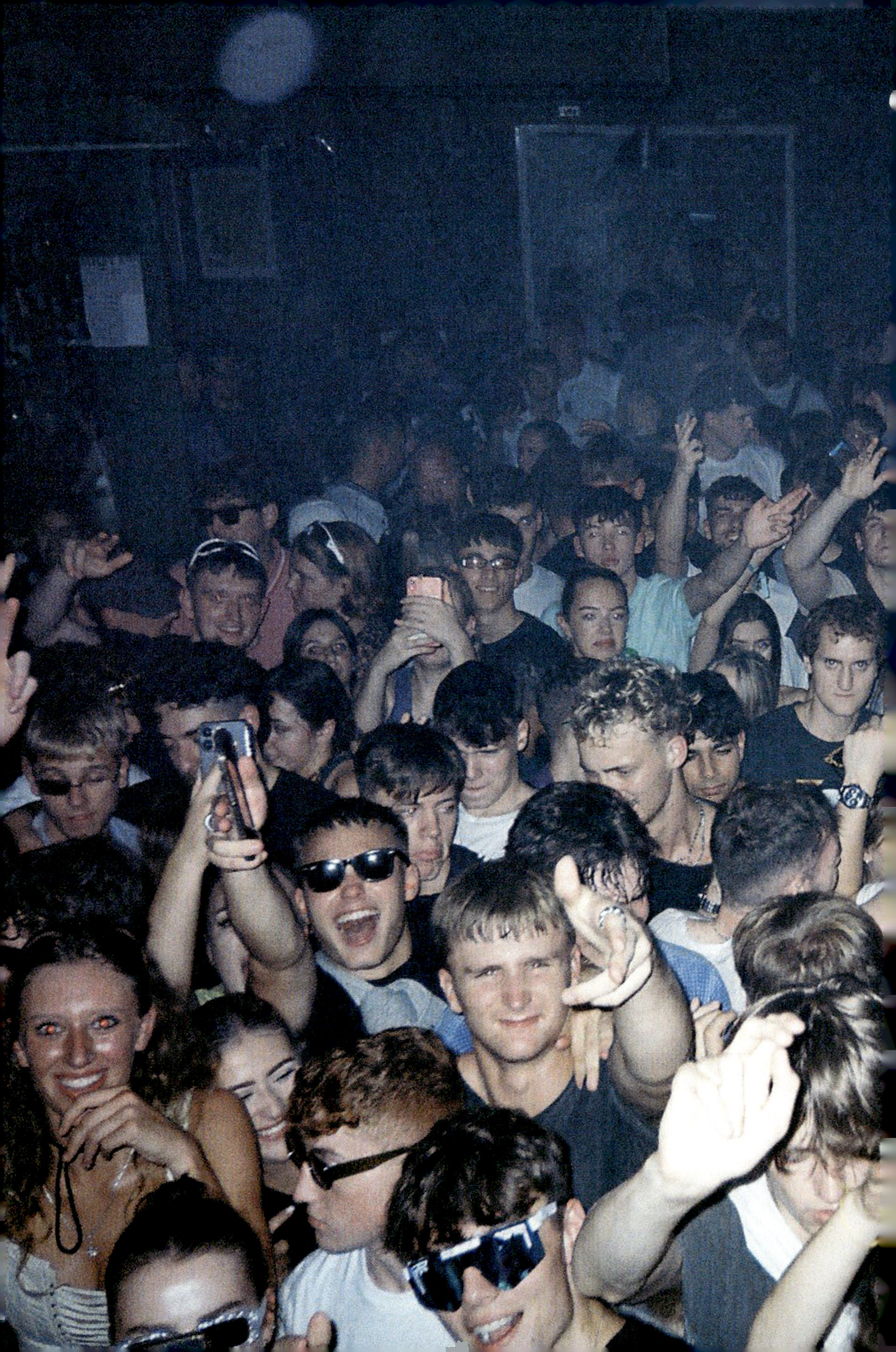

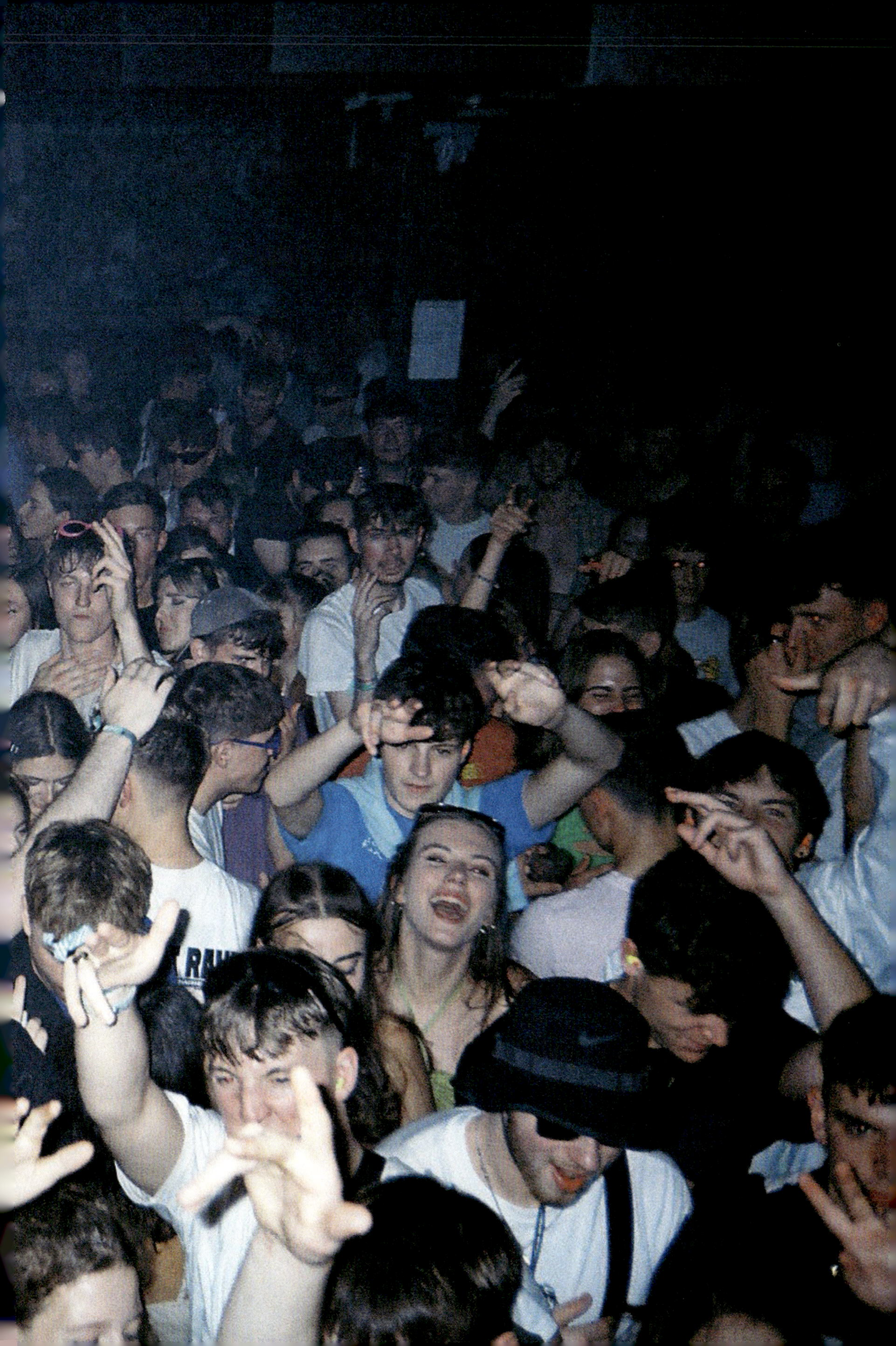

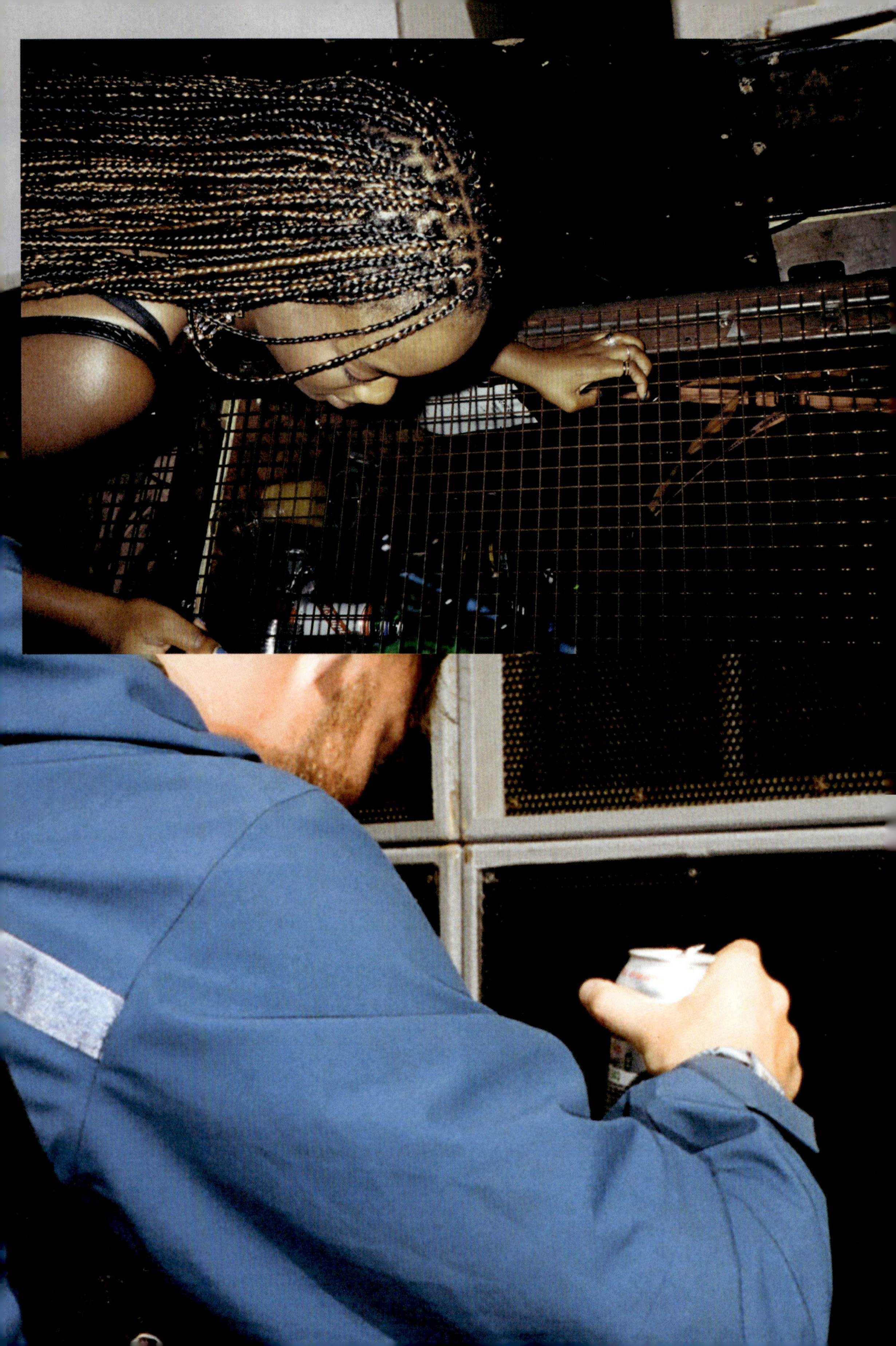

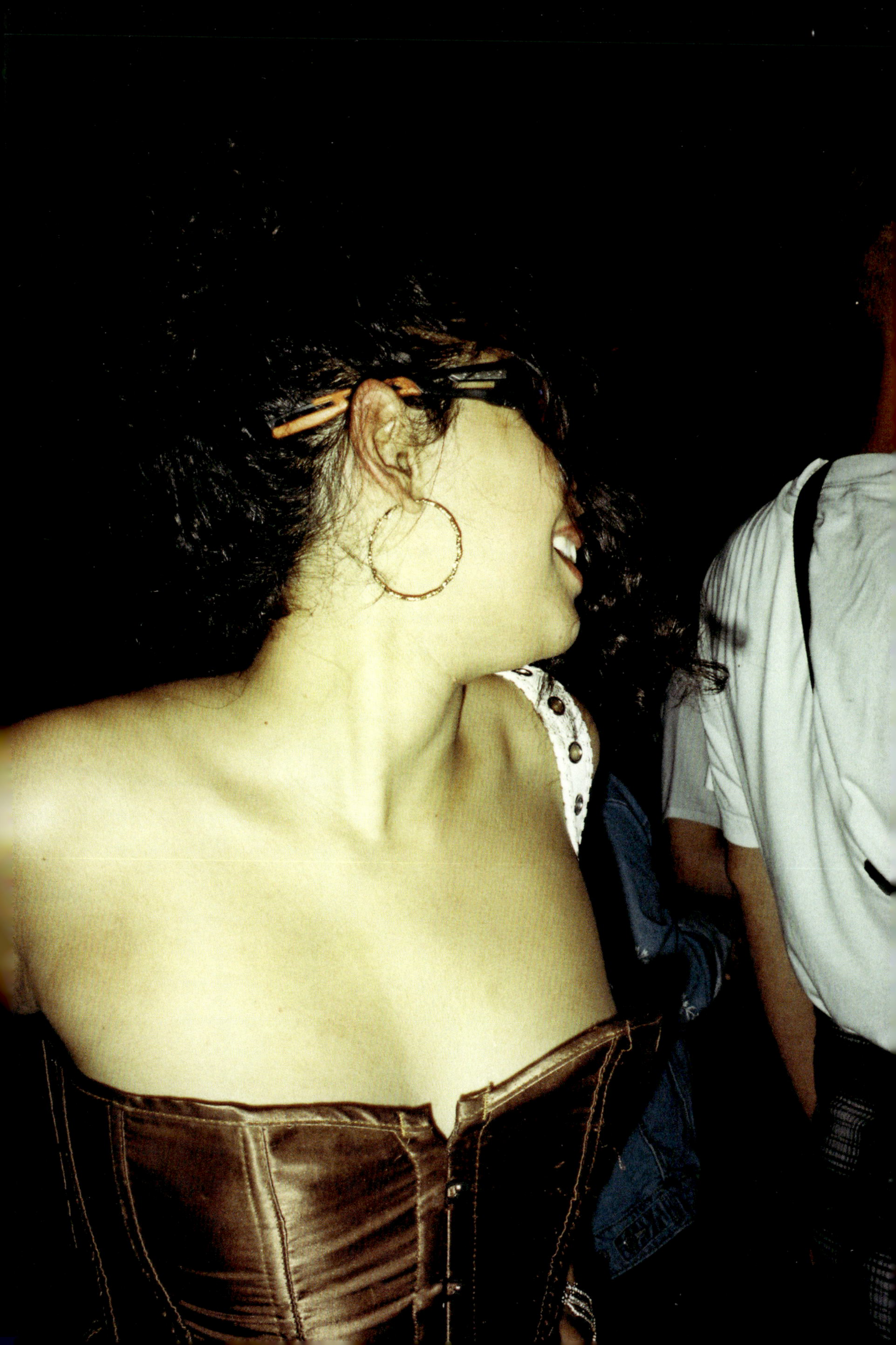

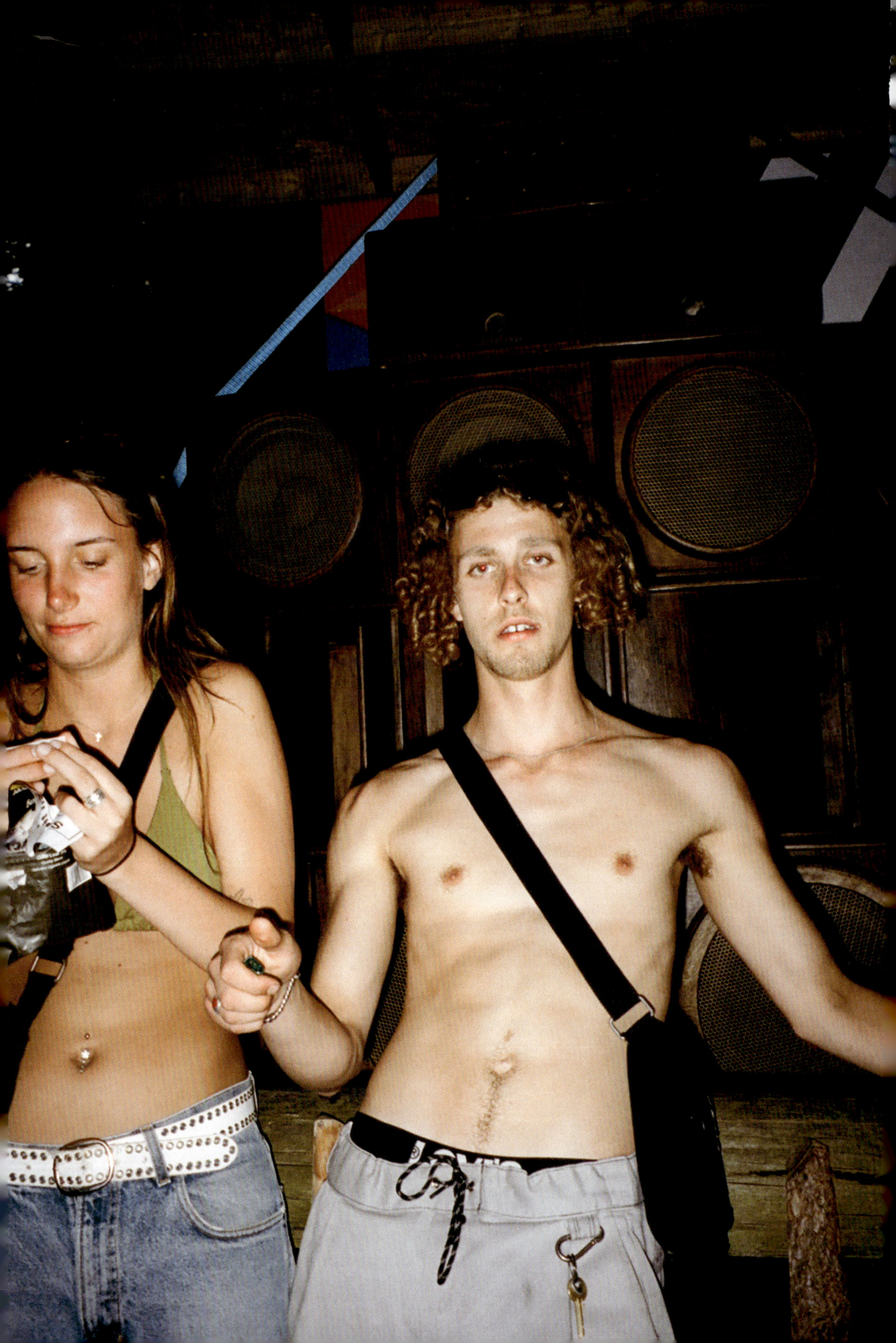

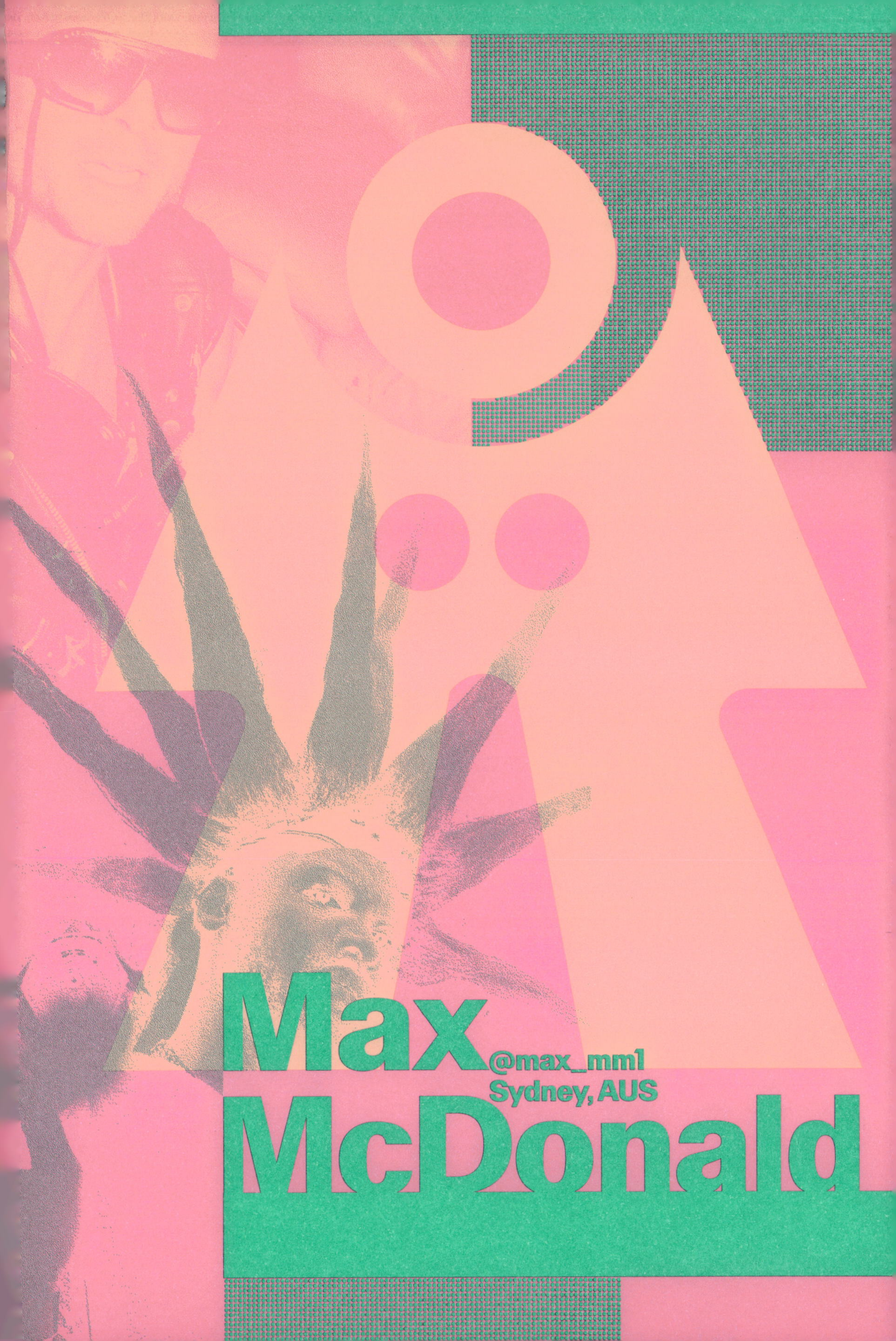
Max
@max_mm1
Sydney, AUS
McDonald

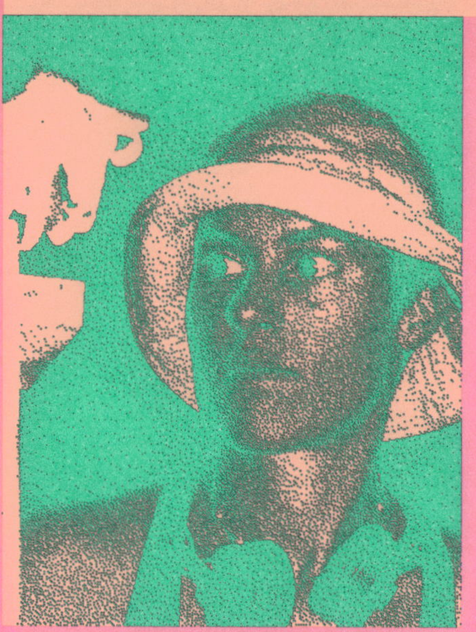

I'm a photographer immersed in the unpredictable energy of Sydney's clubbing and underground scene. Through my lens, I strive to capture the pulsating rhythm of bodies, eclectic personalities, and the mesmerising ambience that defines this culture. I hope to bridge the gap between the onlookers and the partygoers, inviting viewers to witness the beautiful, bizarre and ever-changing nature of Sydney's nightlife, in turn, encouraging them to experience and explore it for themselves.

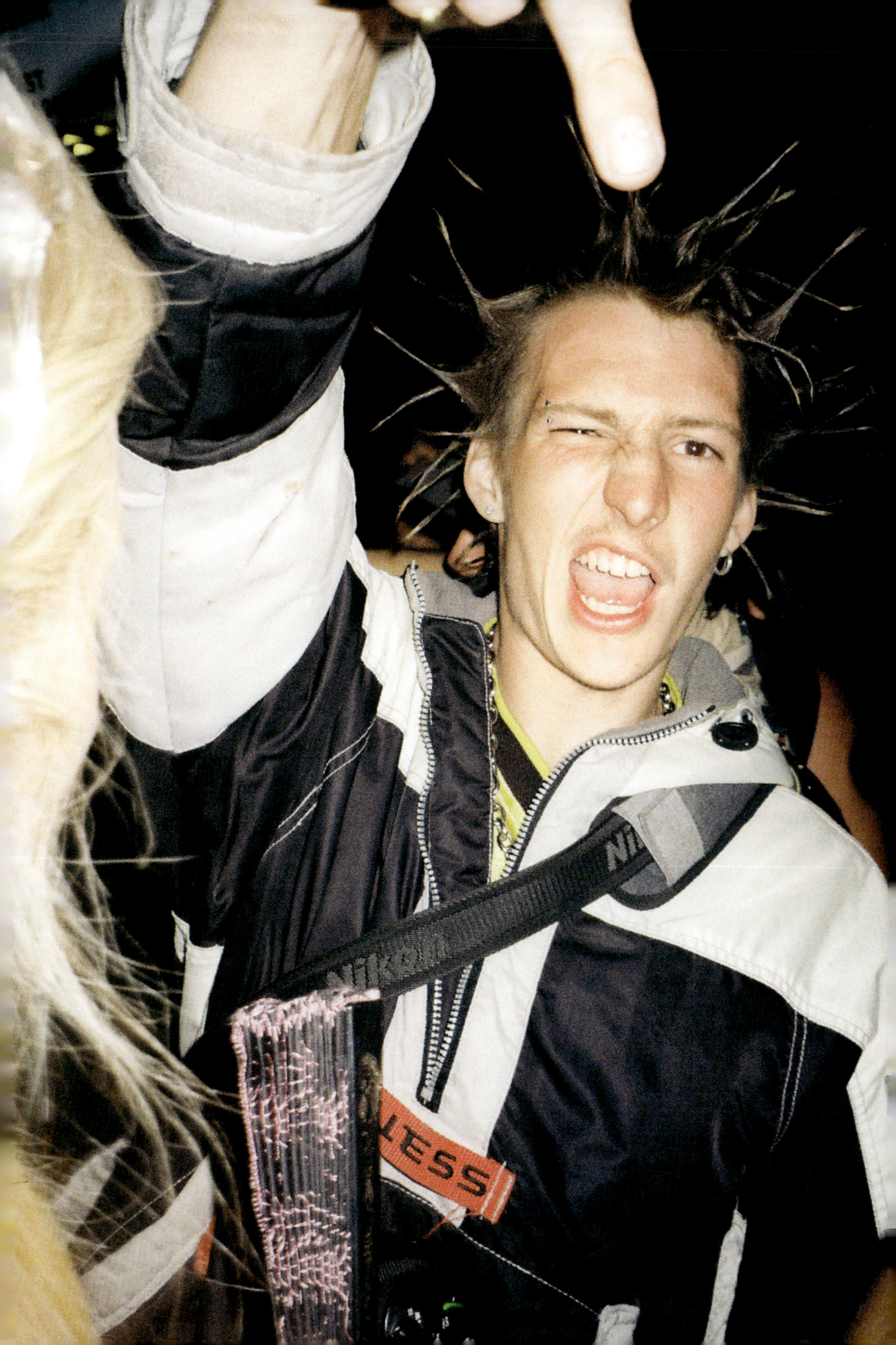

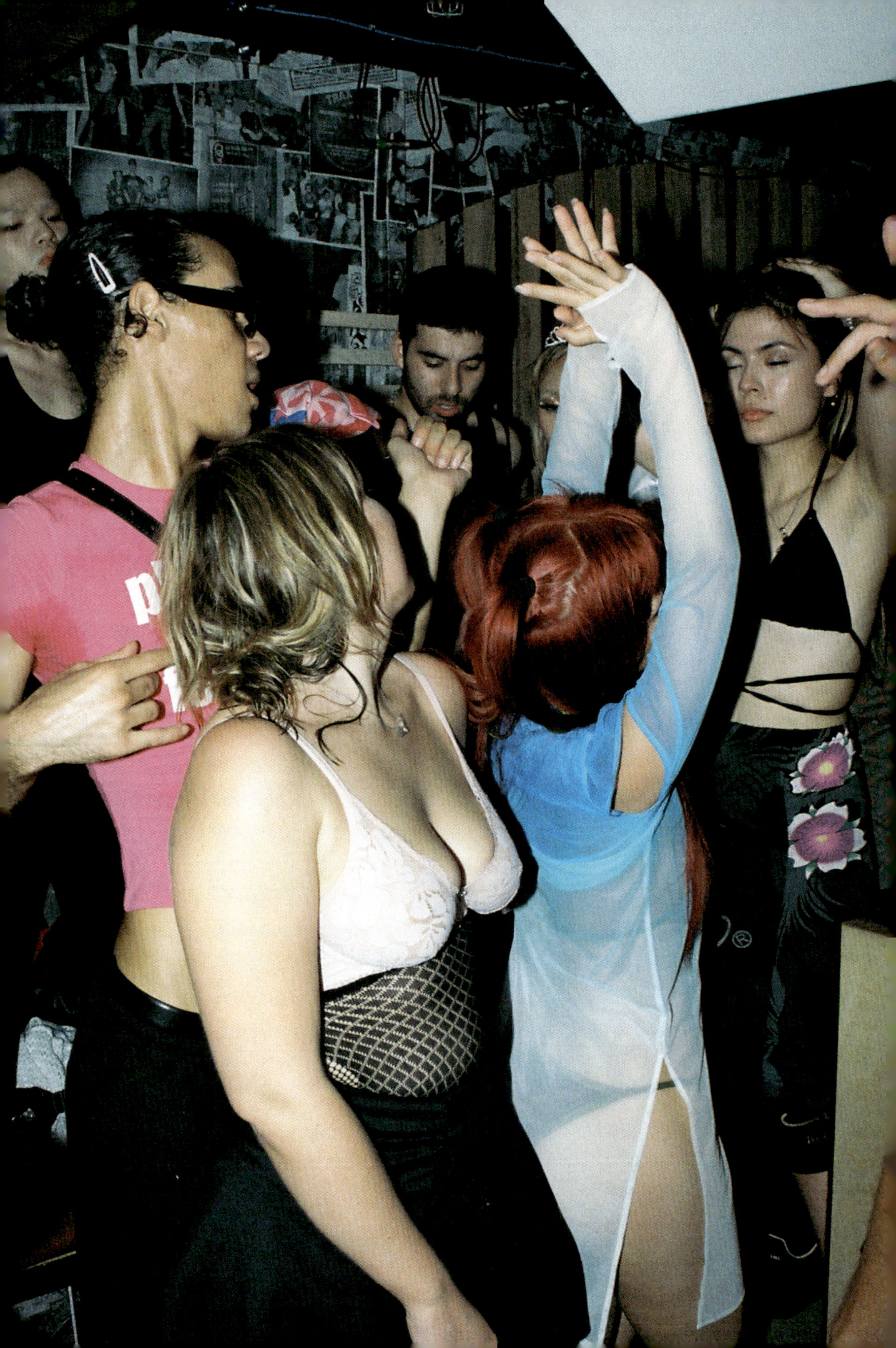

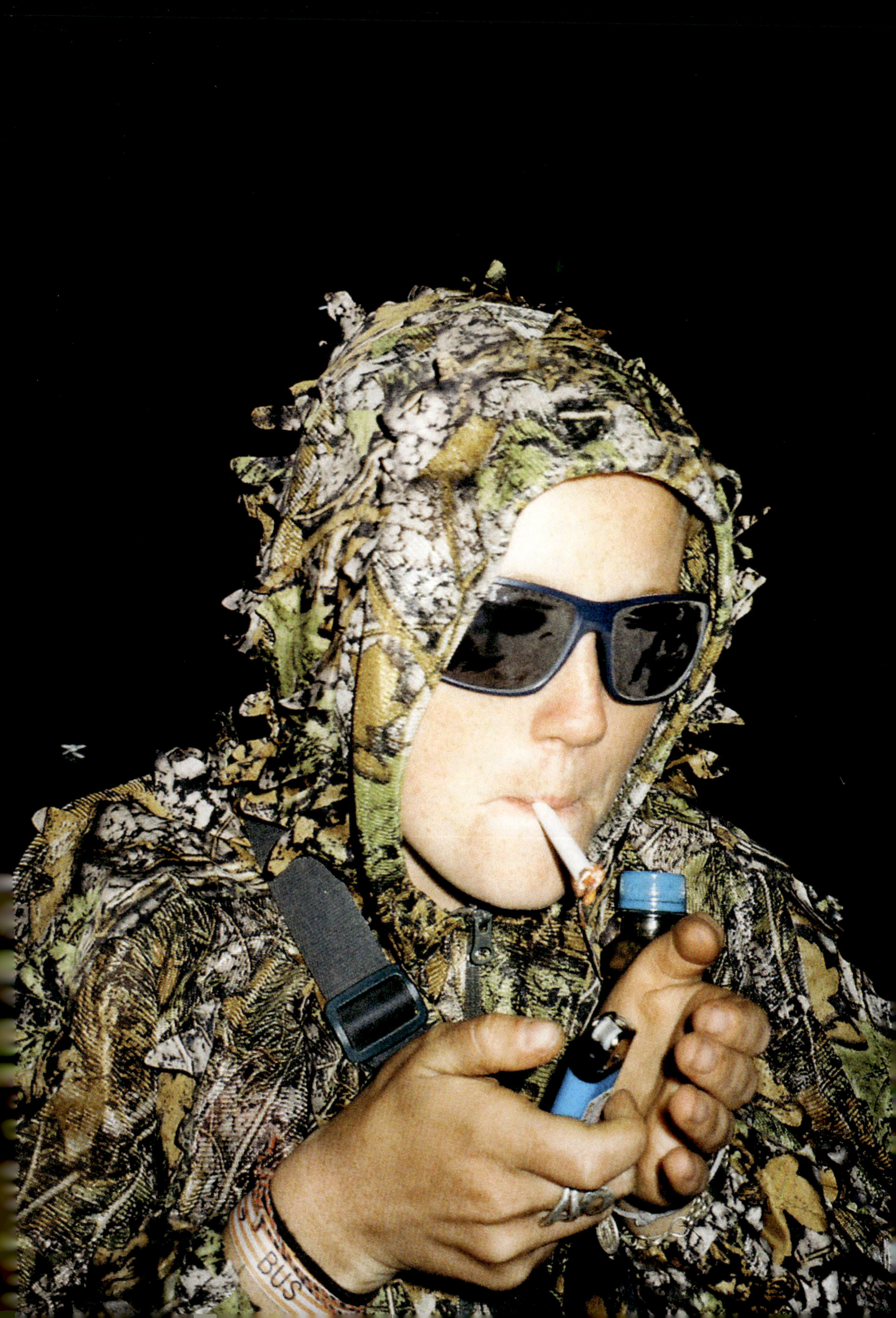

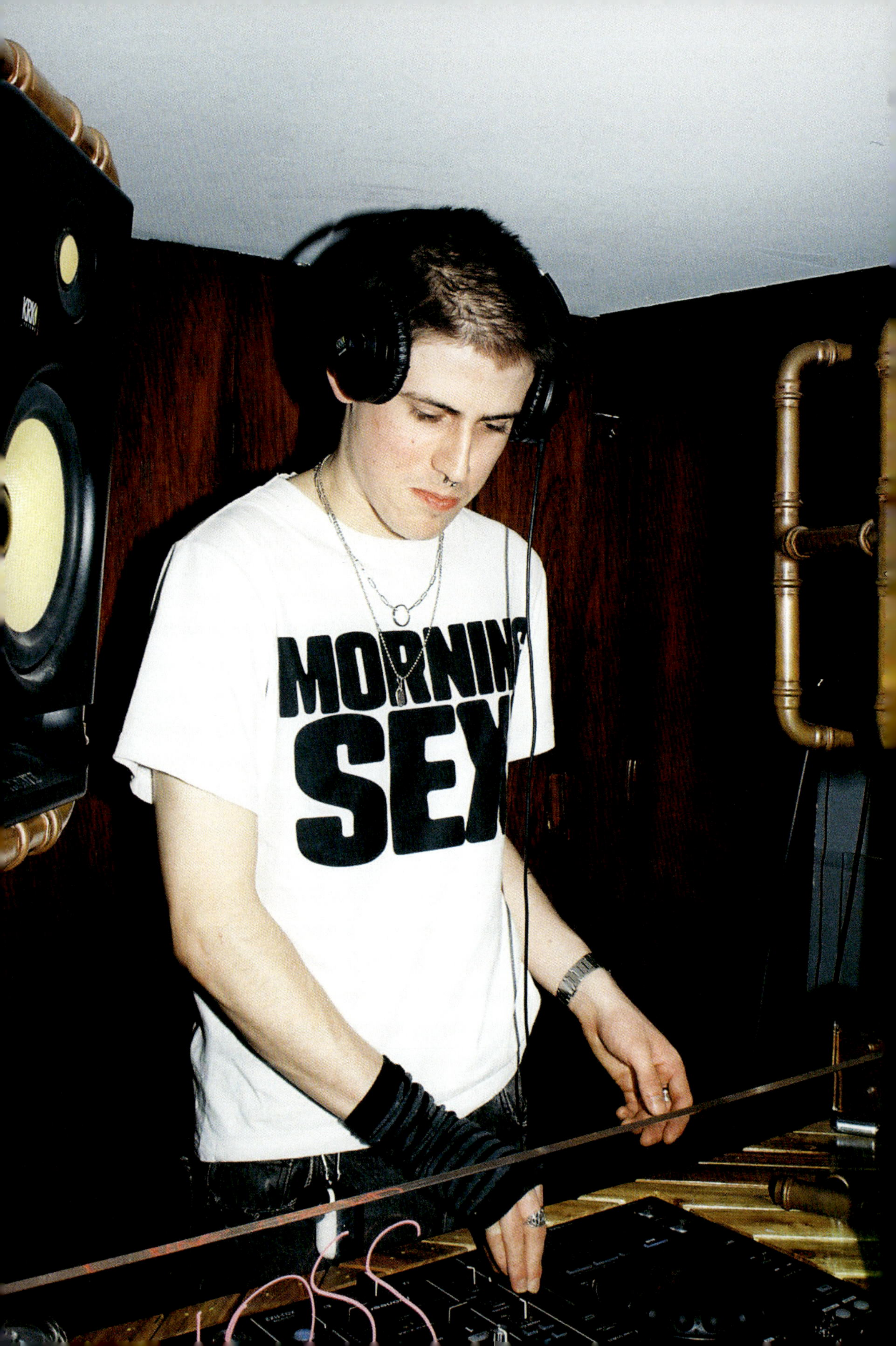
MORNING
SEX

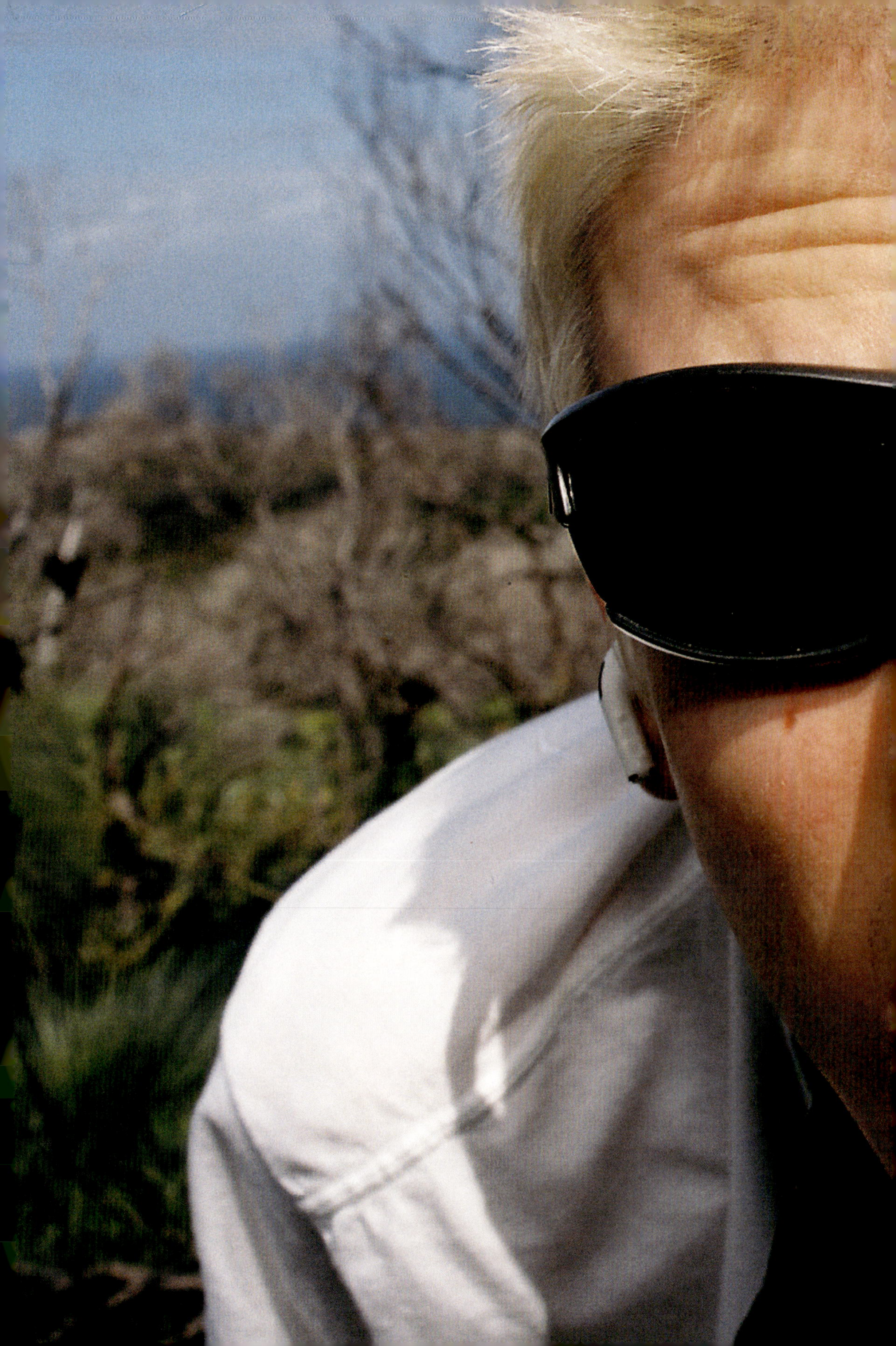

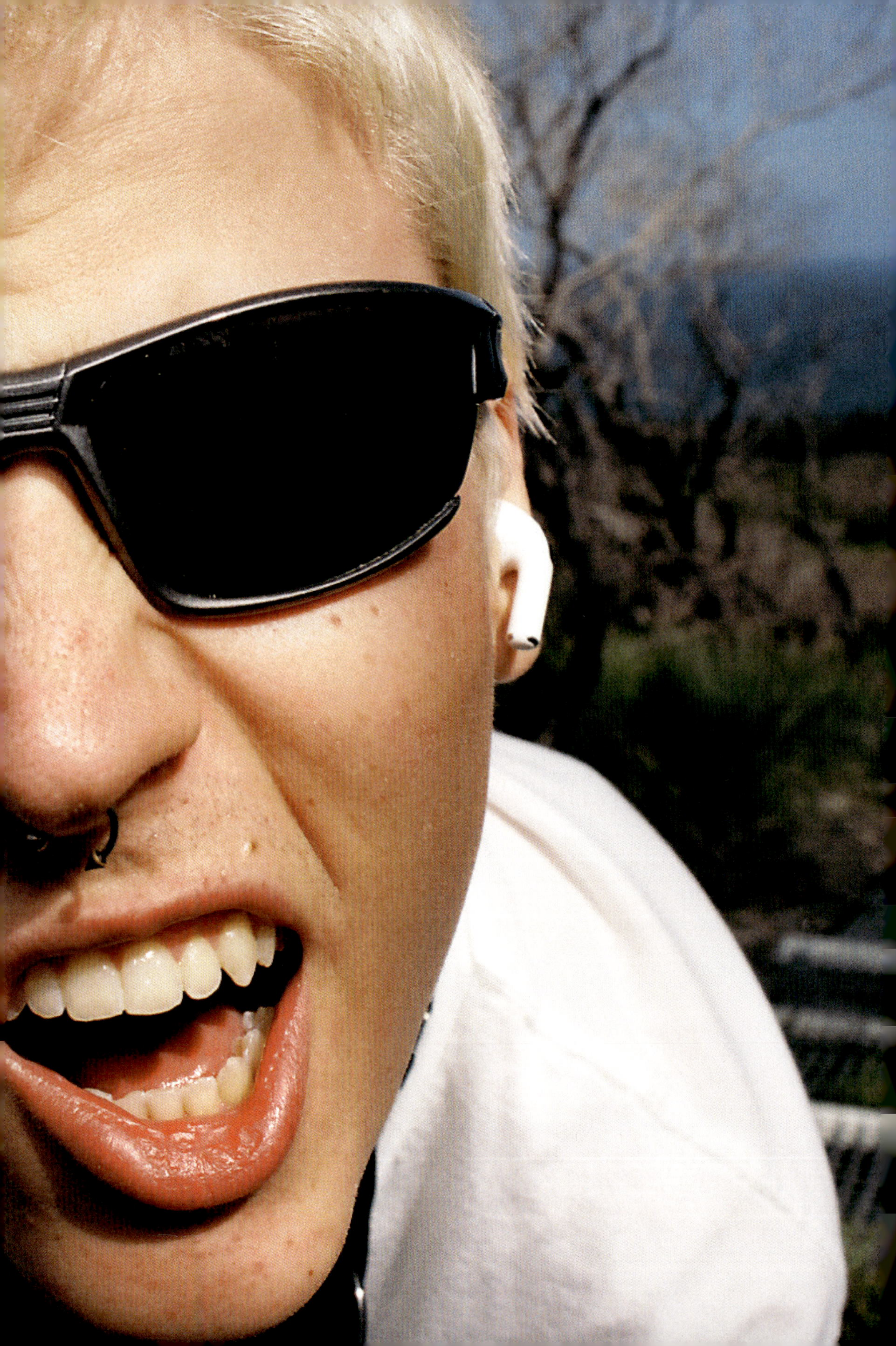

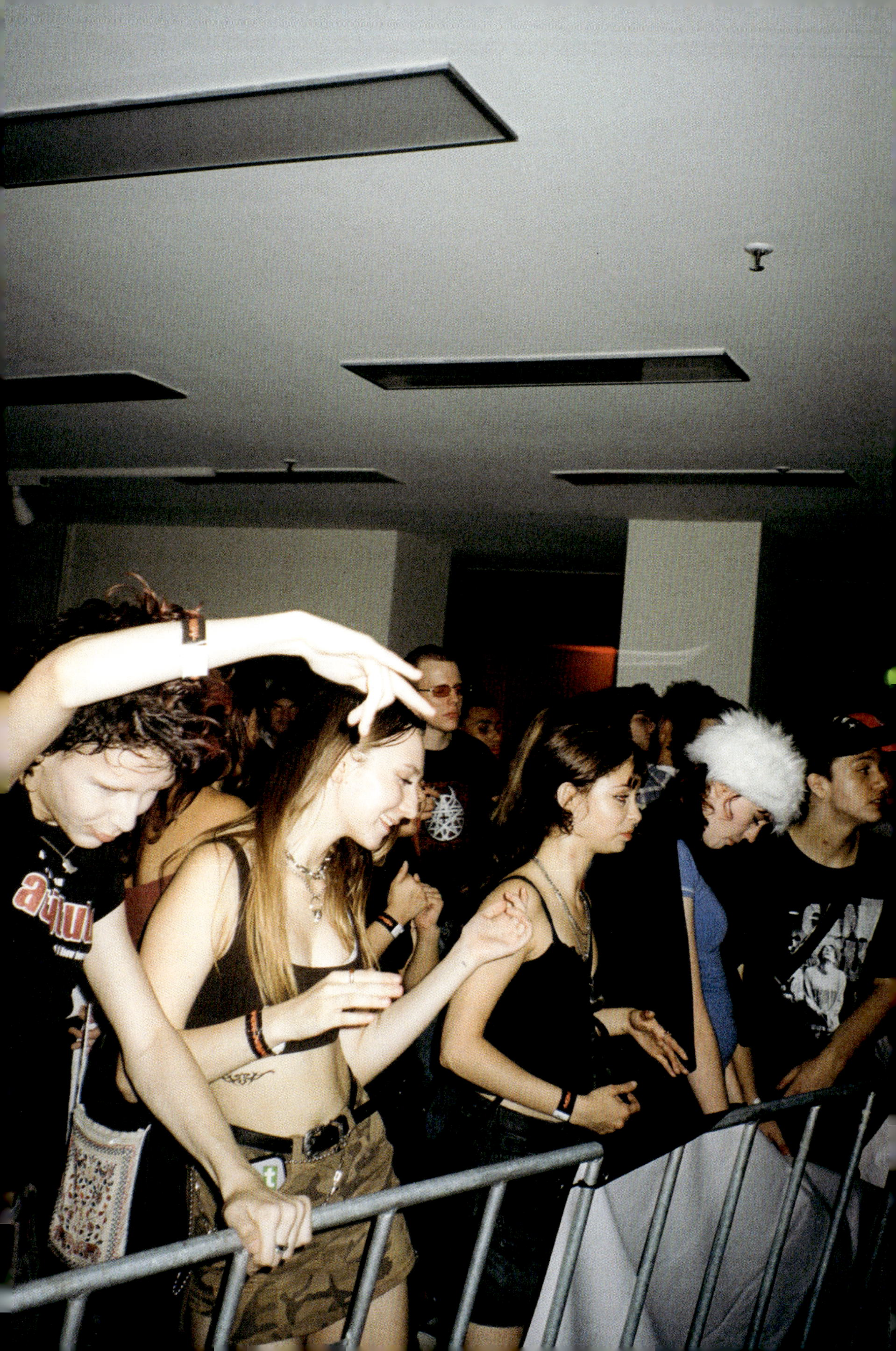

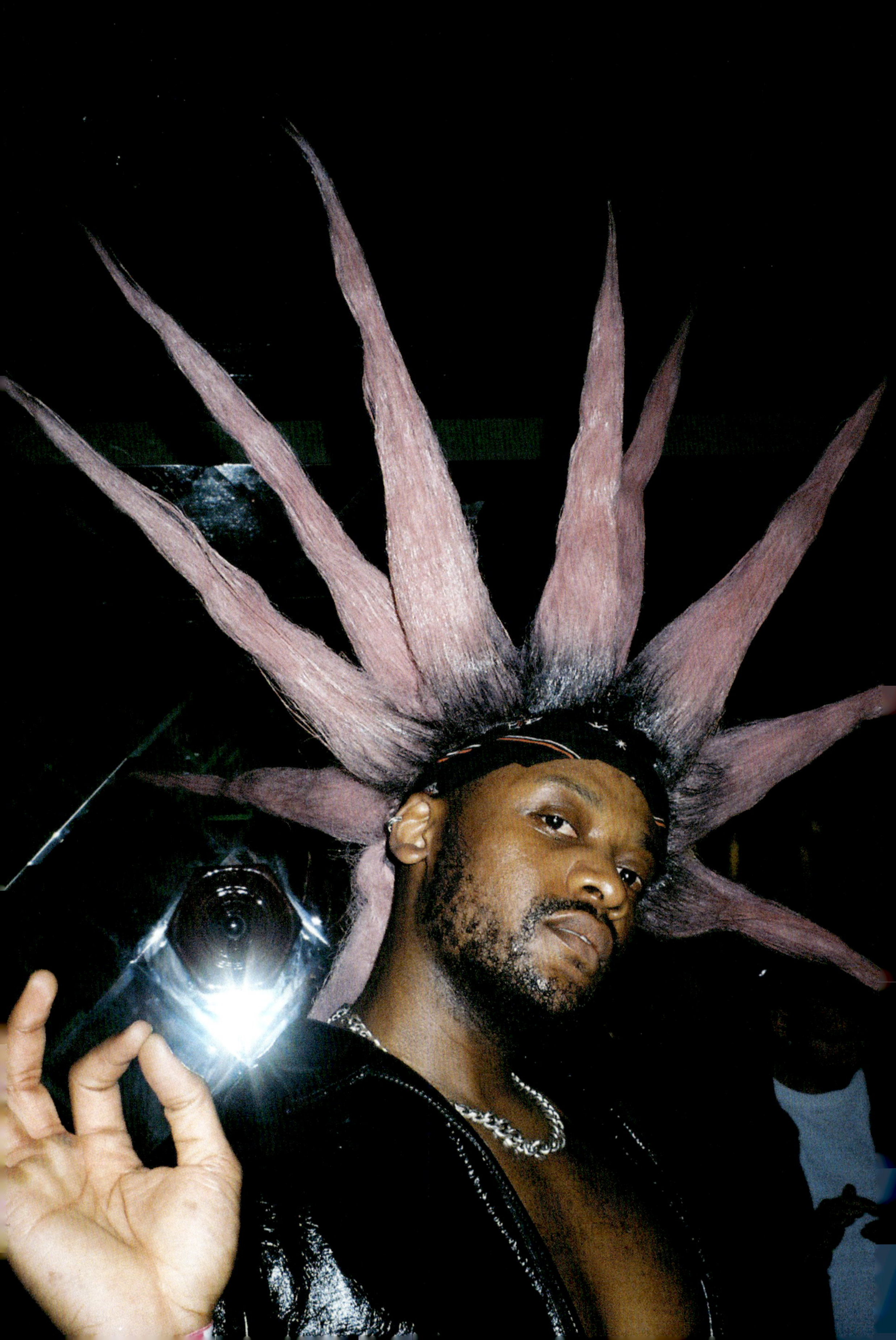

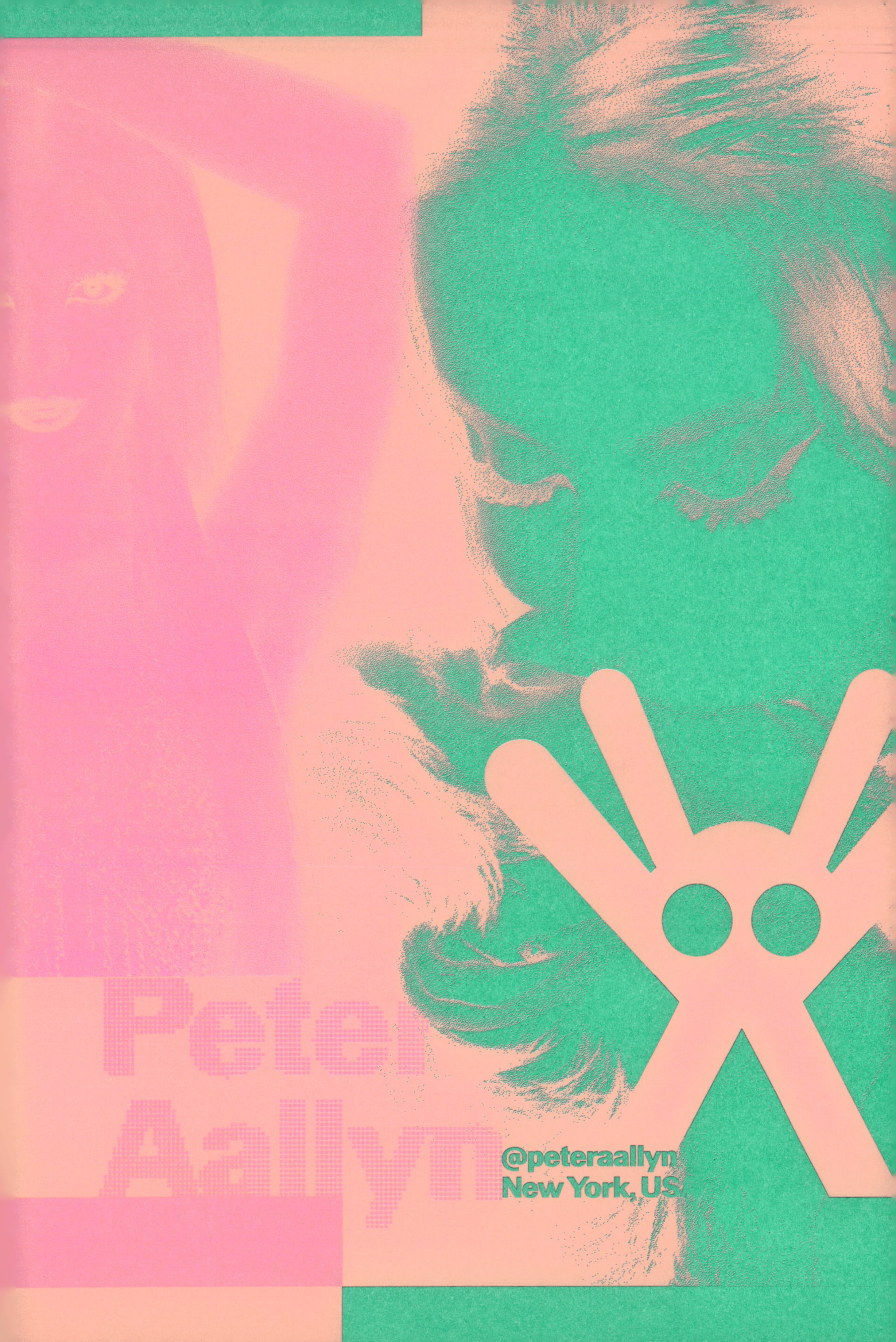
Peter
Aallyn
@peteraallyn
New York, US.

I'm Peter Aallyn, a 22-year-old photographer currently based in Brooklyn, New York. I've been taking part in capturing various nightlife events and parties here in the city since 2021. I've fallen in love with capturing how beautifully raw and how incredibly different partygoers are.

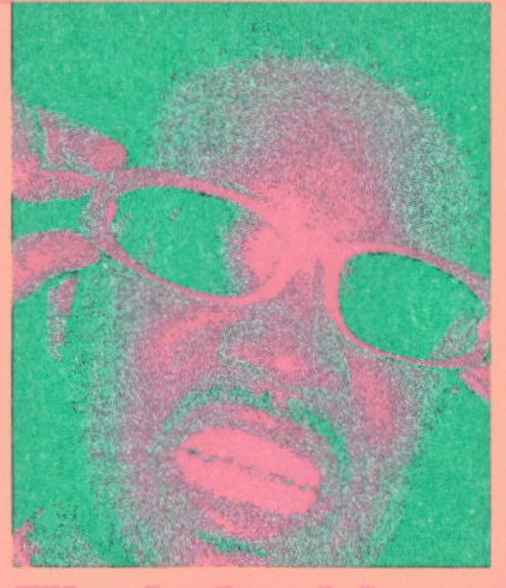

Their fashion, energy, and recklessness will stand testament to the glamour of the city's nightlife and inspire future generations of party pleasure seekers. Knowing that the photos I've taken will act as a part of the documentary that is actively being made of the scene here in NYC every day is an immense honour and delight.

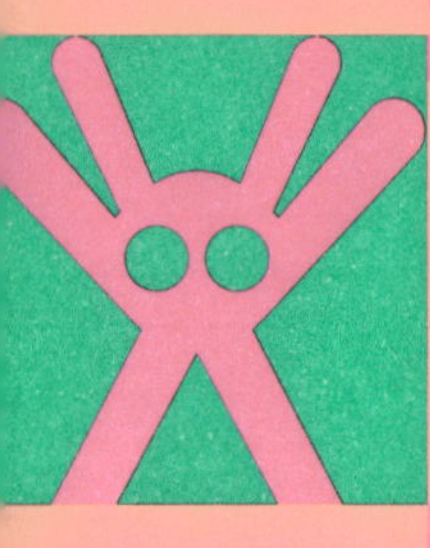

I'm Peter Aallyn, a 22-year-old photographer currently based in Brooklyn, New York. I've been taking part in capturing various nightlife events and parties here in the city since 2021. I've fallen in love with capturing how beautifully raw and how incredibly different partygoers are.

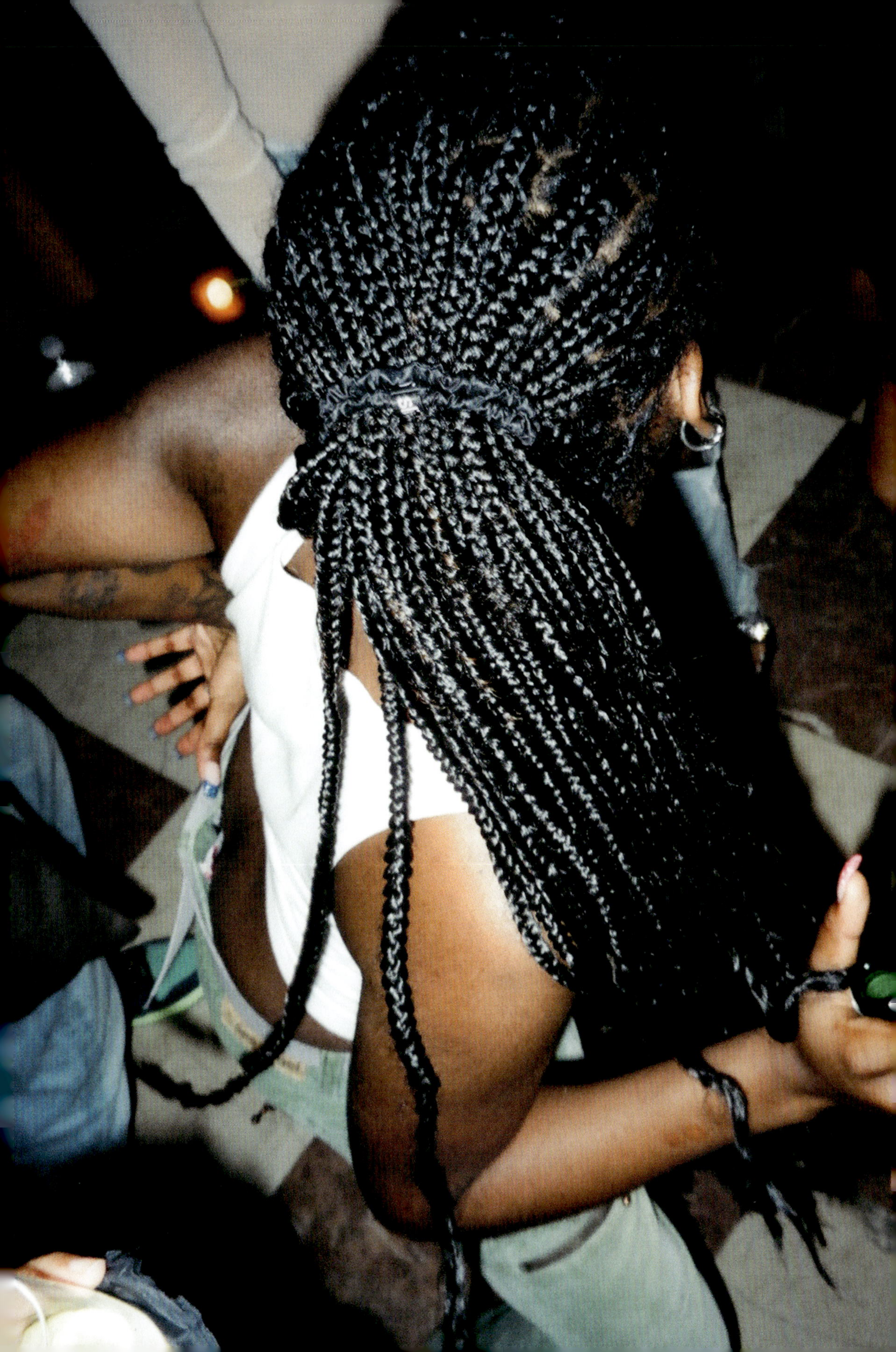

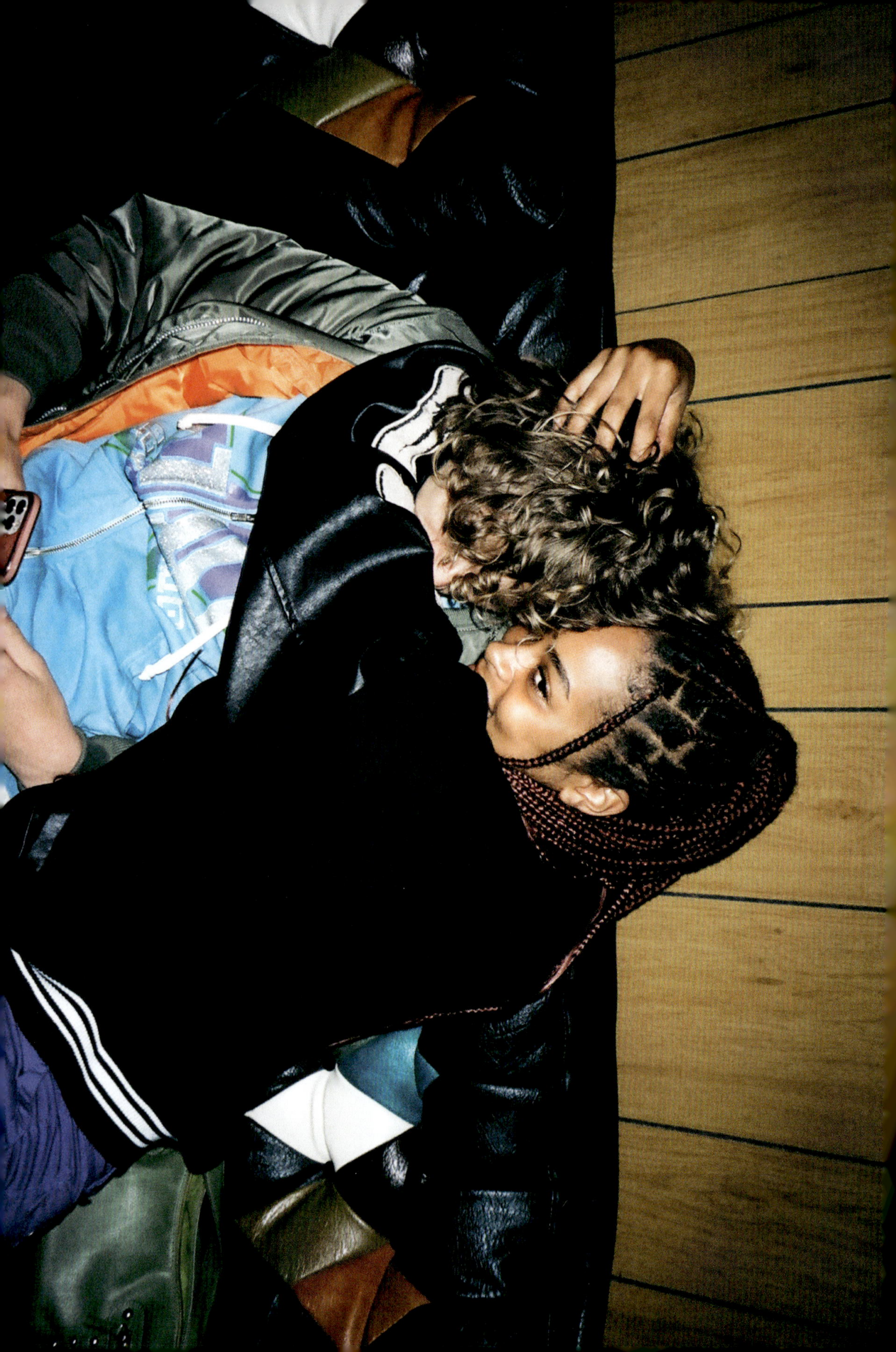

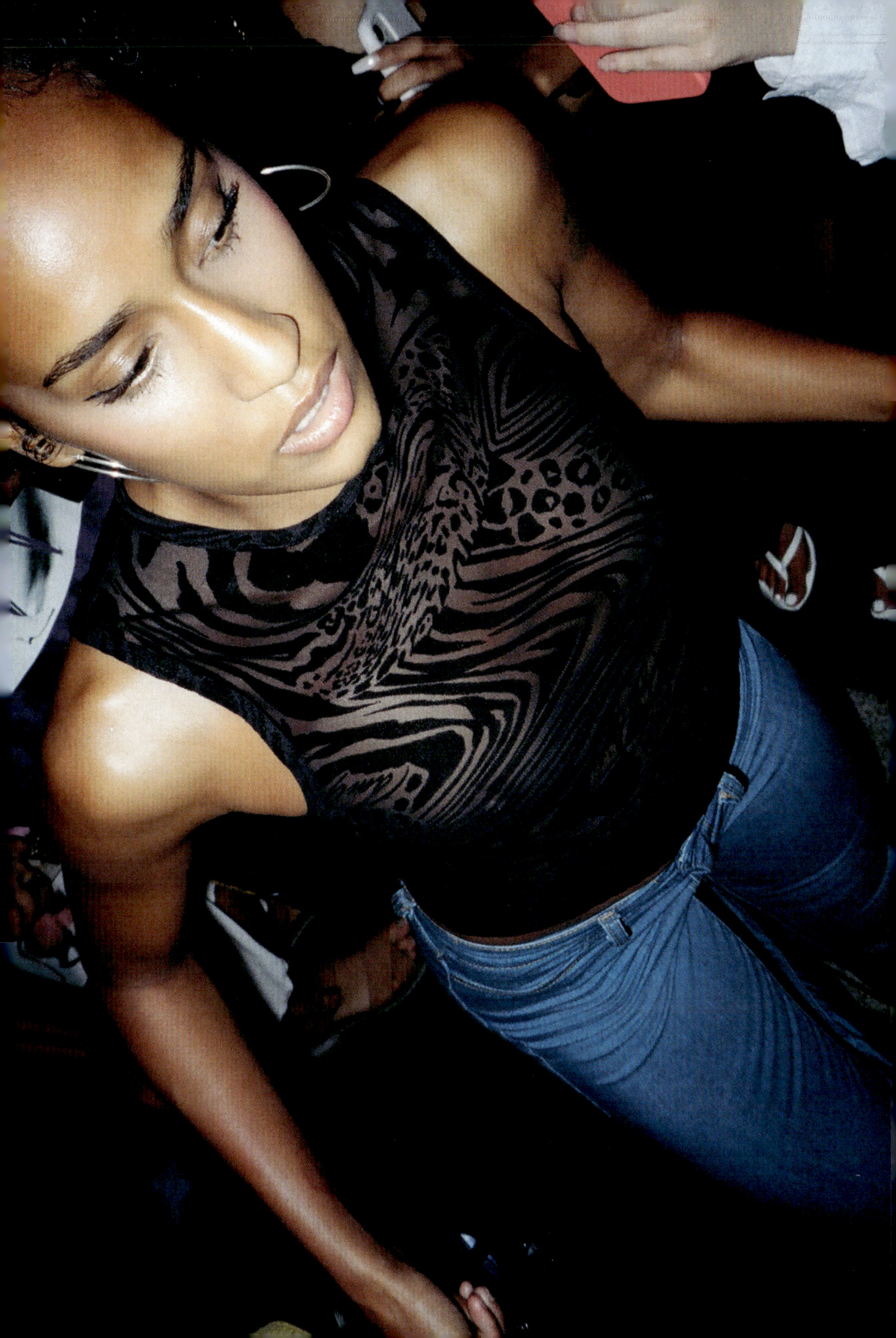

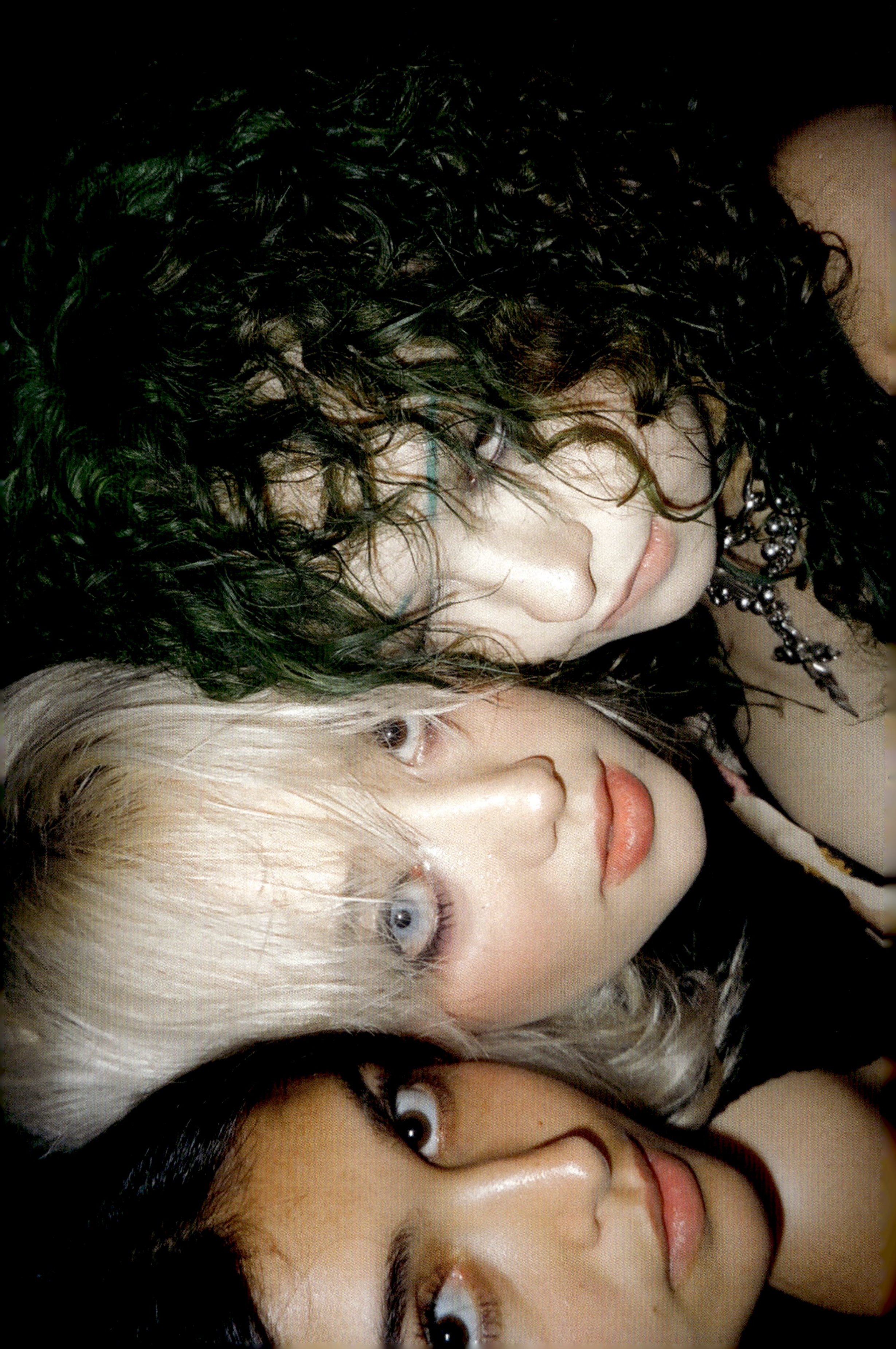

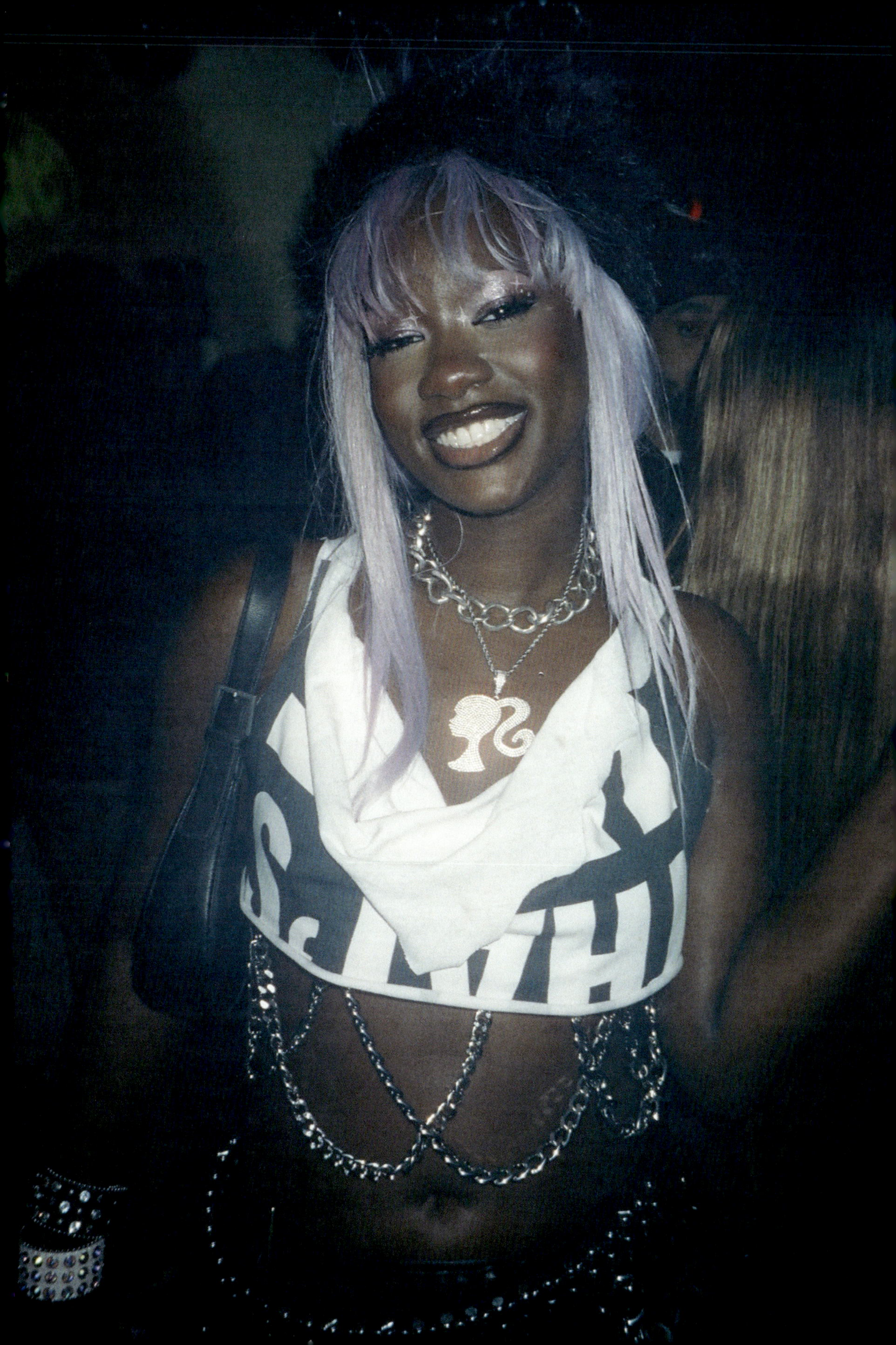

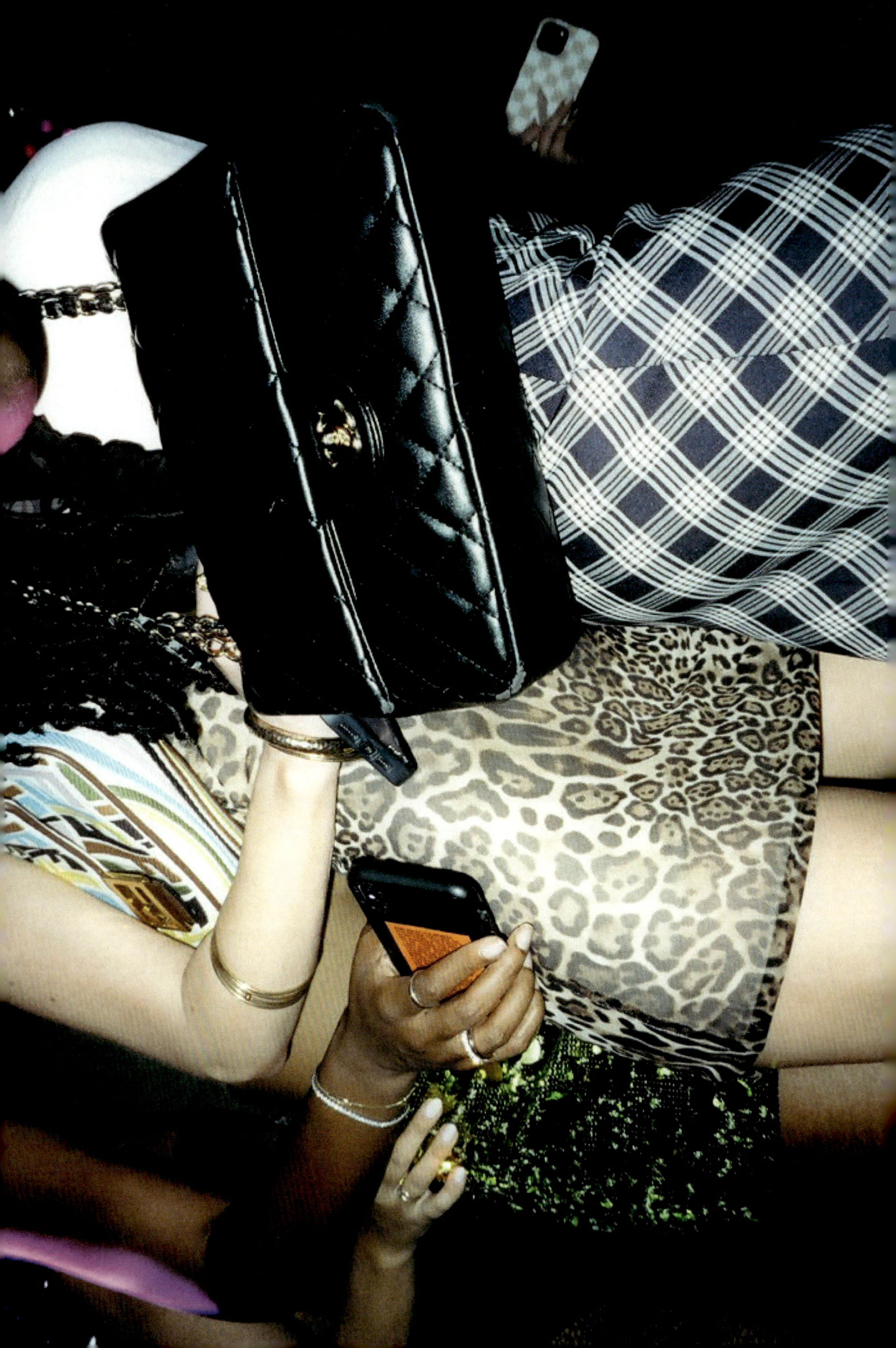

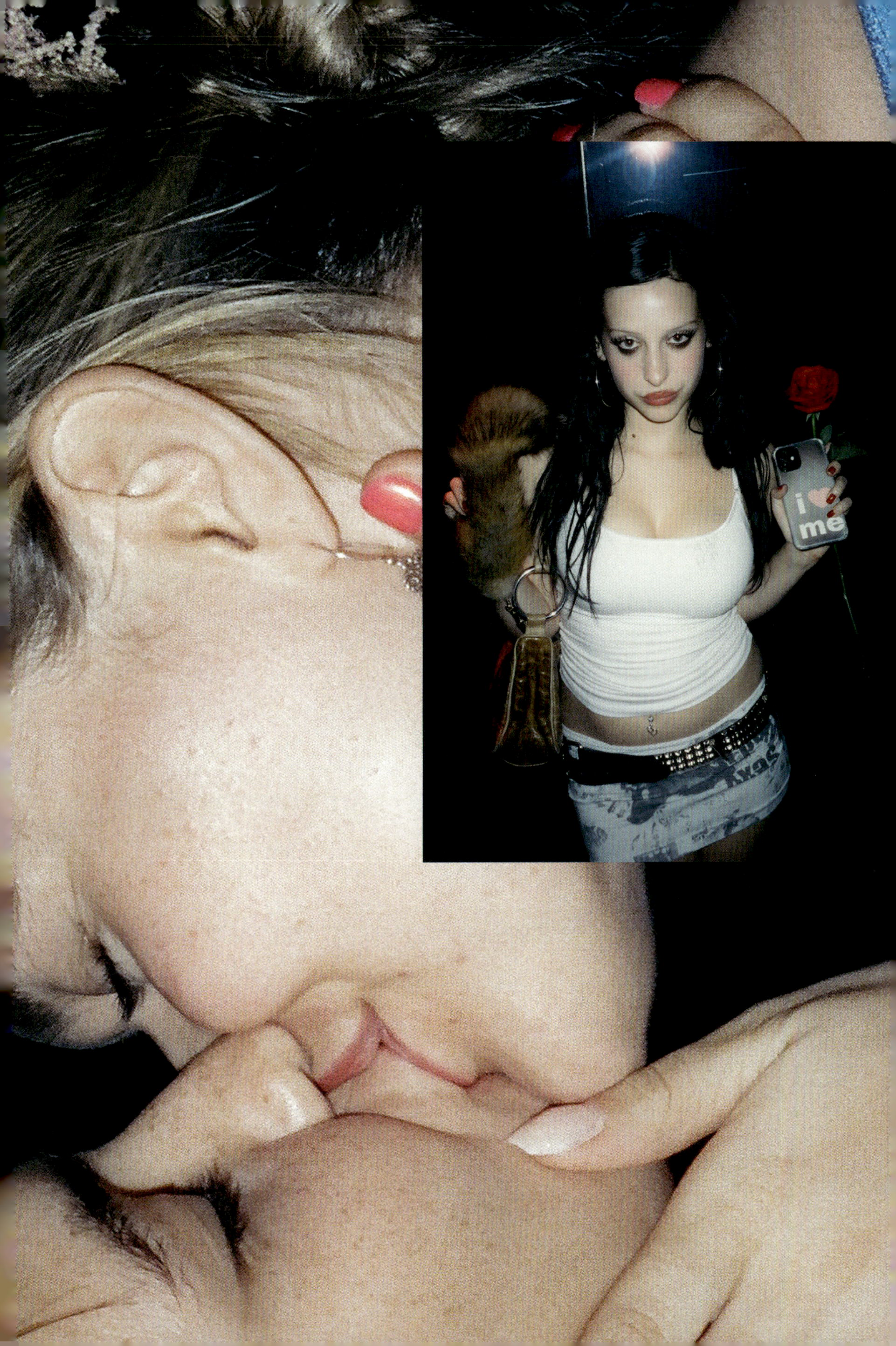

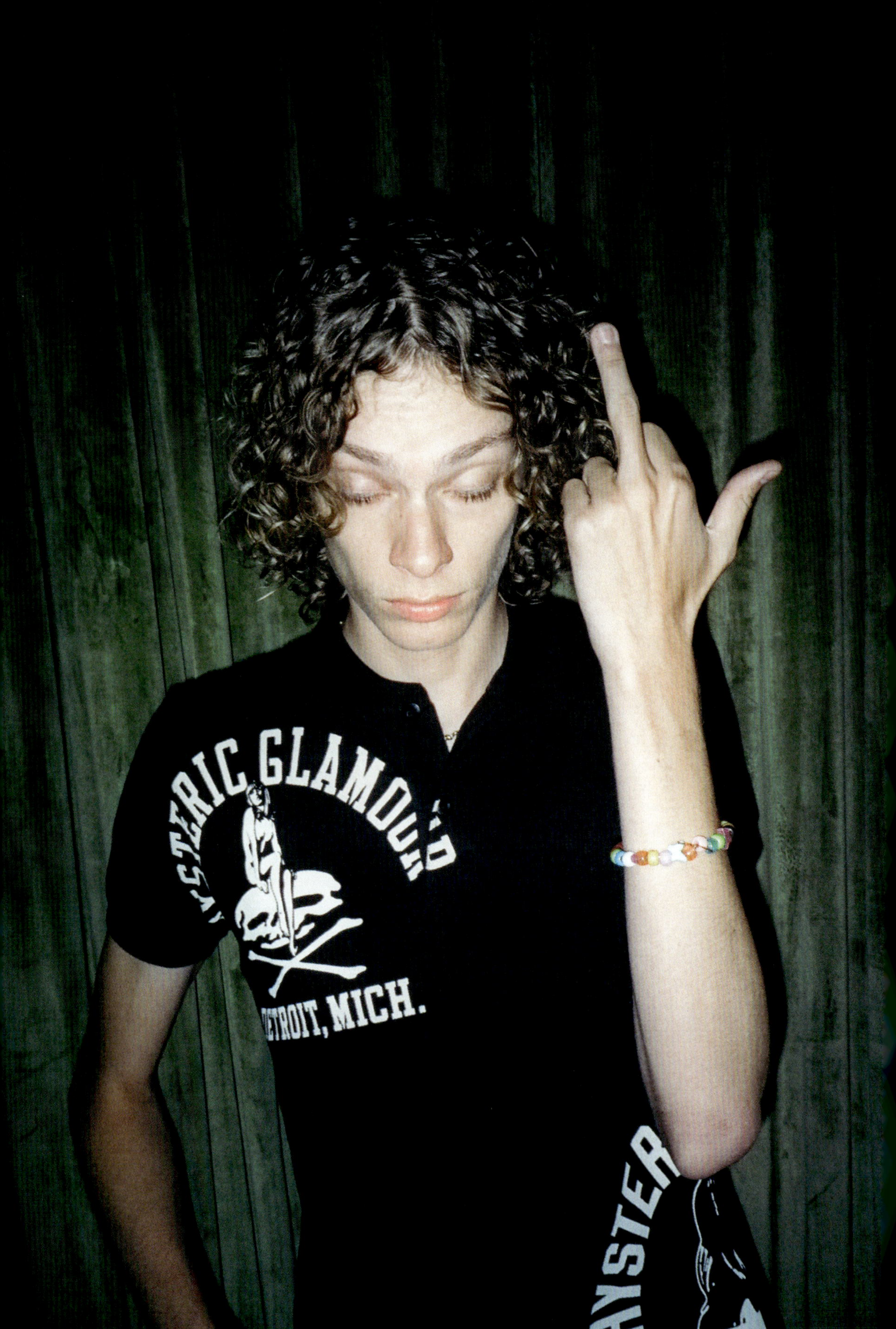
STERIC GLAMOUR
DETROIT, MICH.
YSTER

@roffa_archive
Rotterdam, NL
Roffa
Archive

We are Mara, Franka and Annemoon - three photography students born and raised in Rotterdam. Almost two years ago we started Roffa Archive. The project was initially started because of an assignment for school where we had to create a photography project that would support a community. At this time, all nightlife had been shut down for two years because of Covid. We decided that as soon as the clubs would open again we would visit the parties and take pictures there to show how beautiful Rotterdam nightlife really is. We believe that this city has a lot to offer and that it's something that we should treasure.

While building this archive we try to show the diversity and evolution that's currently going on within the nightlife, new concepts that are being born, nightlife fashion trends that are evolving and, of course, the people that come to these events.

While capturing this we also built an archive that can continue to live on beyond our generation.

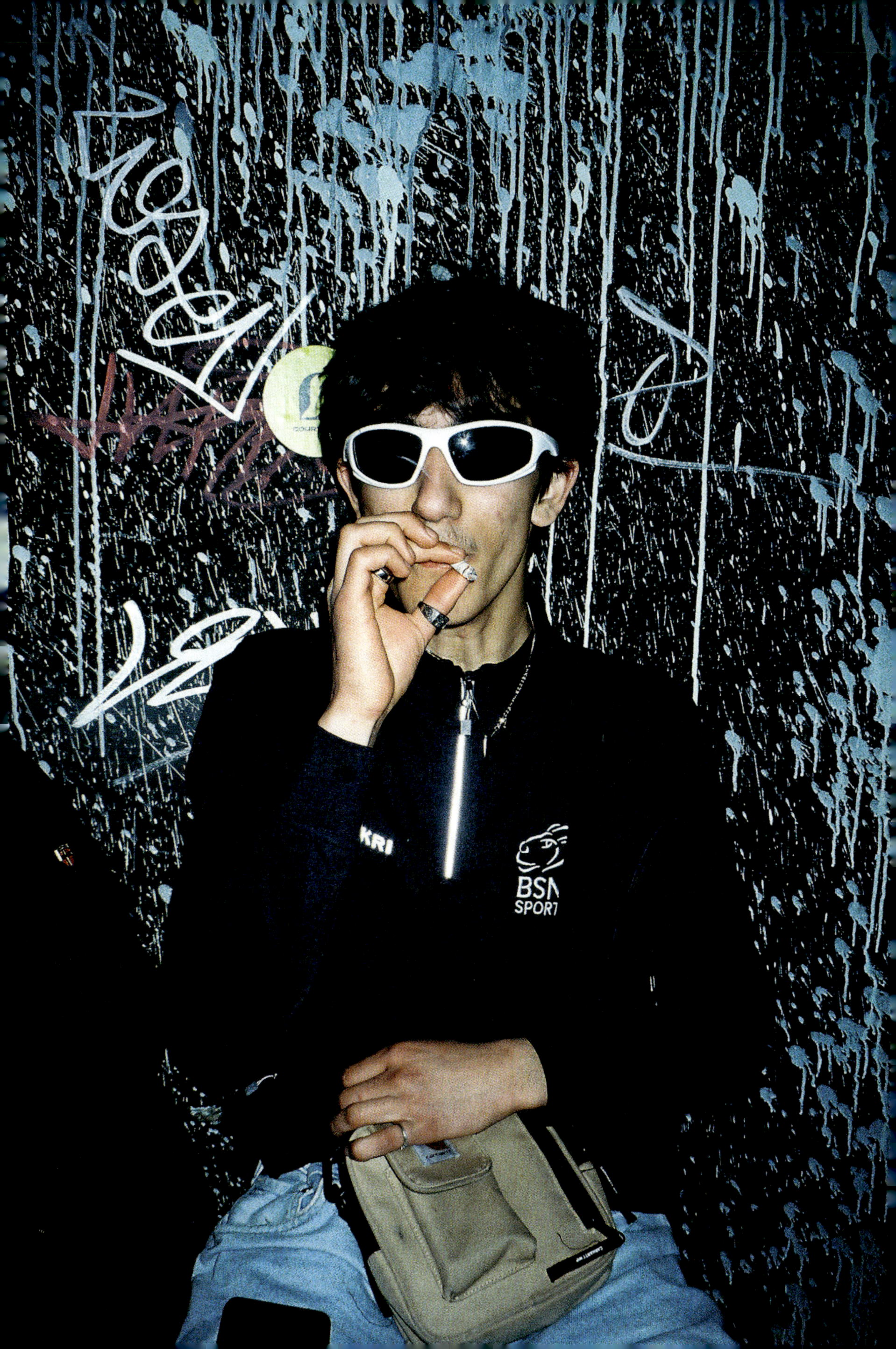

KRI
BSN
SPORT

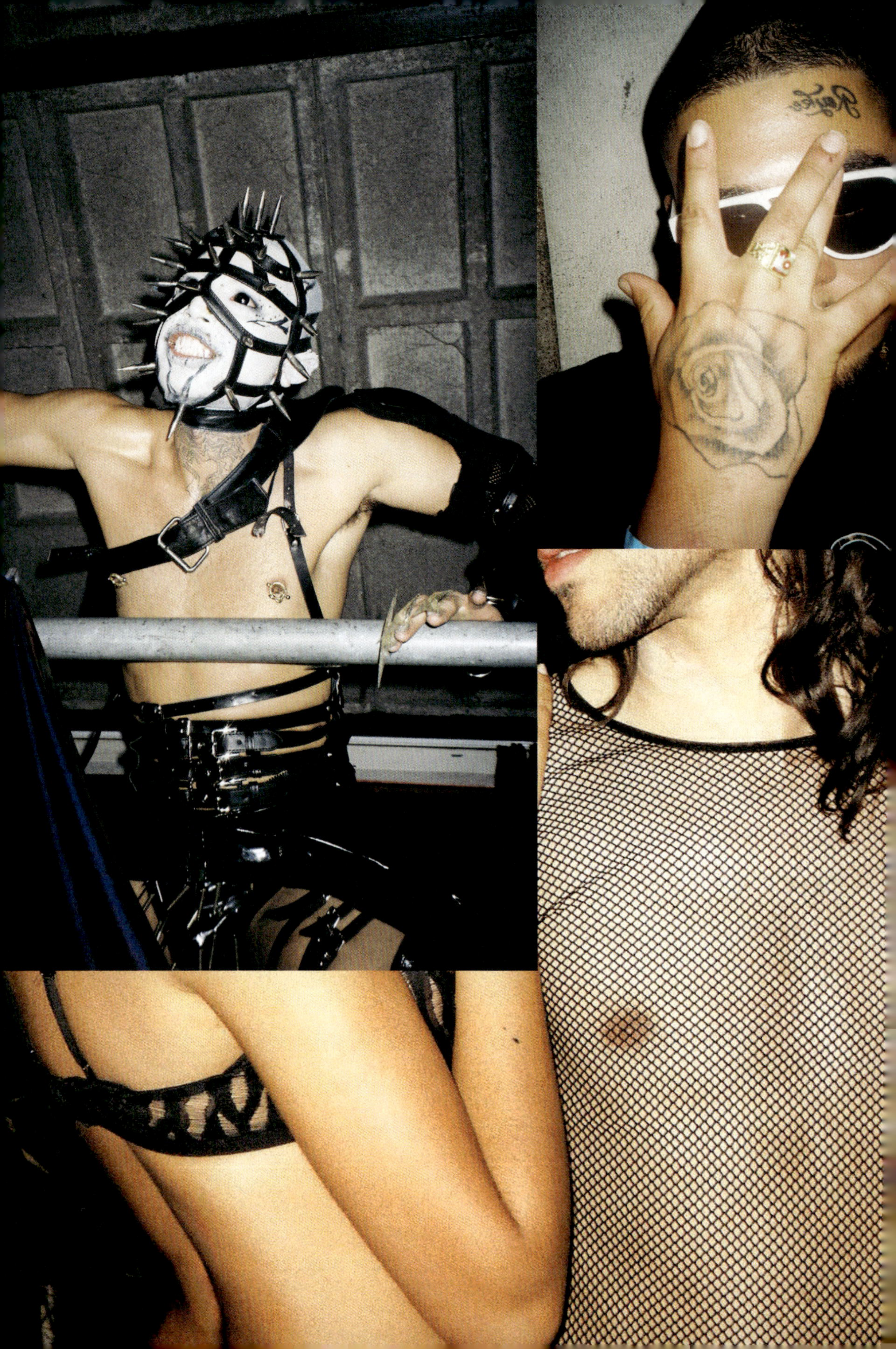

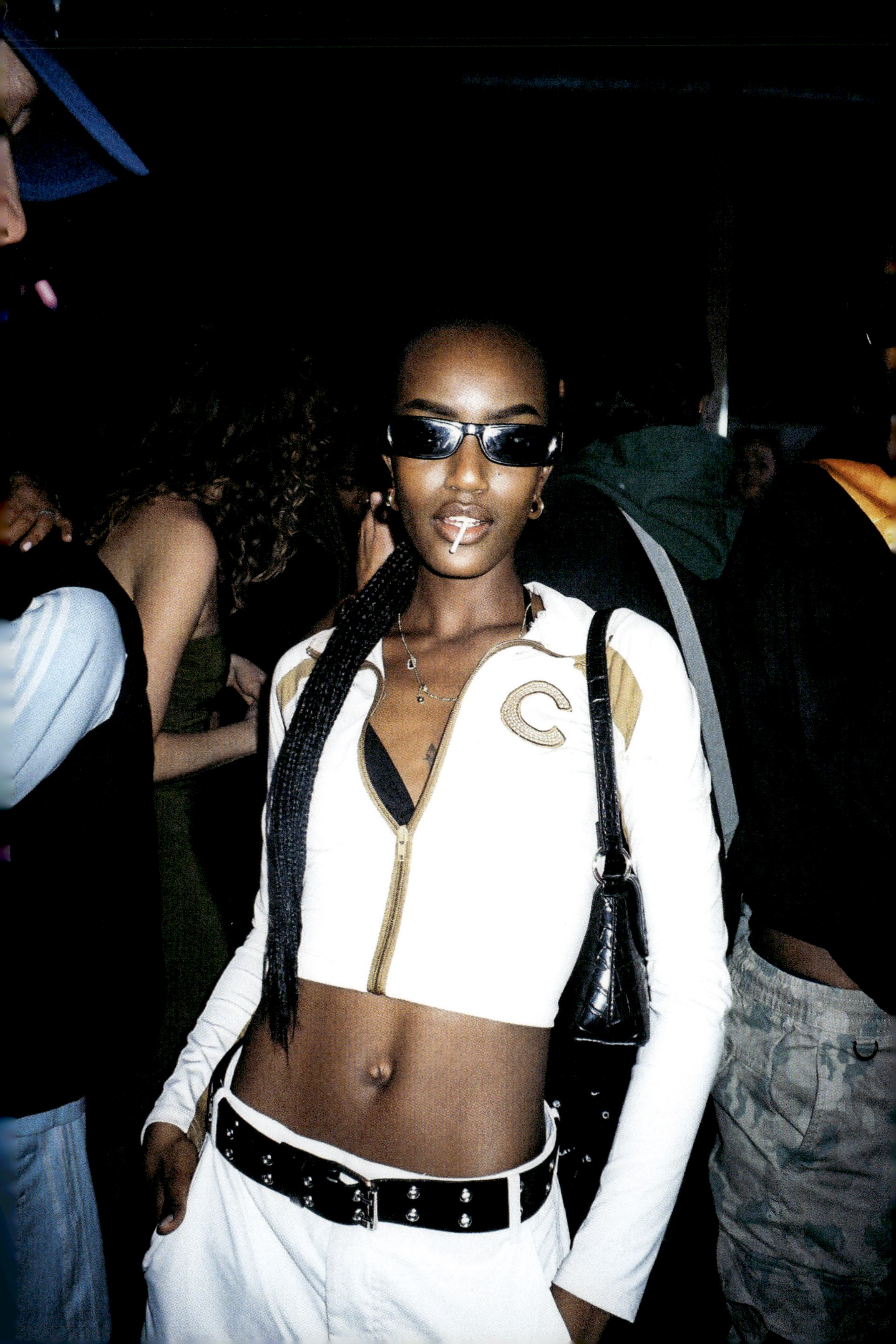

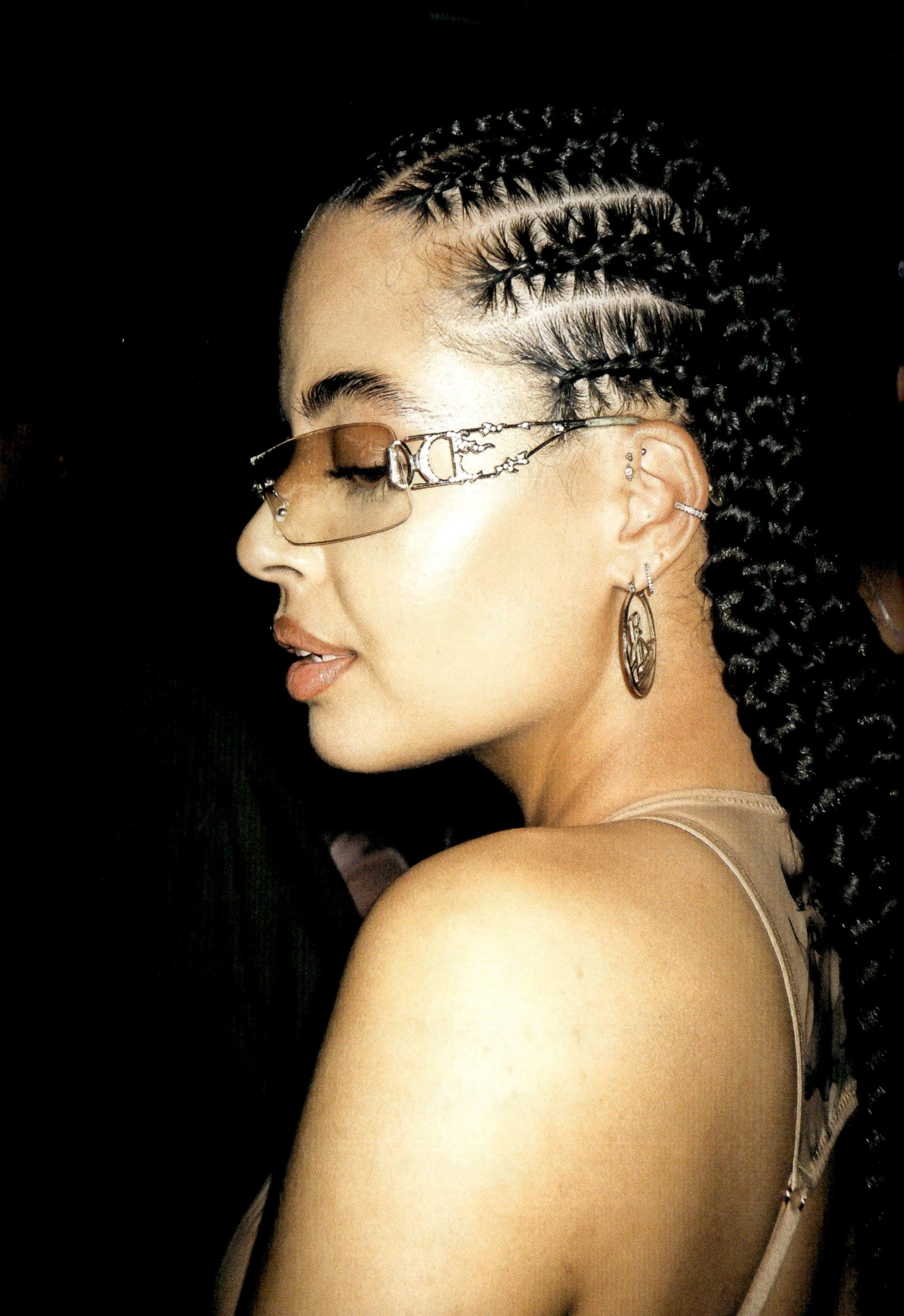

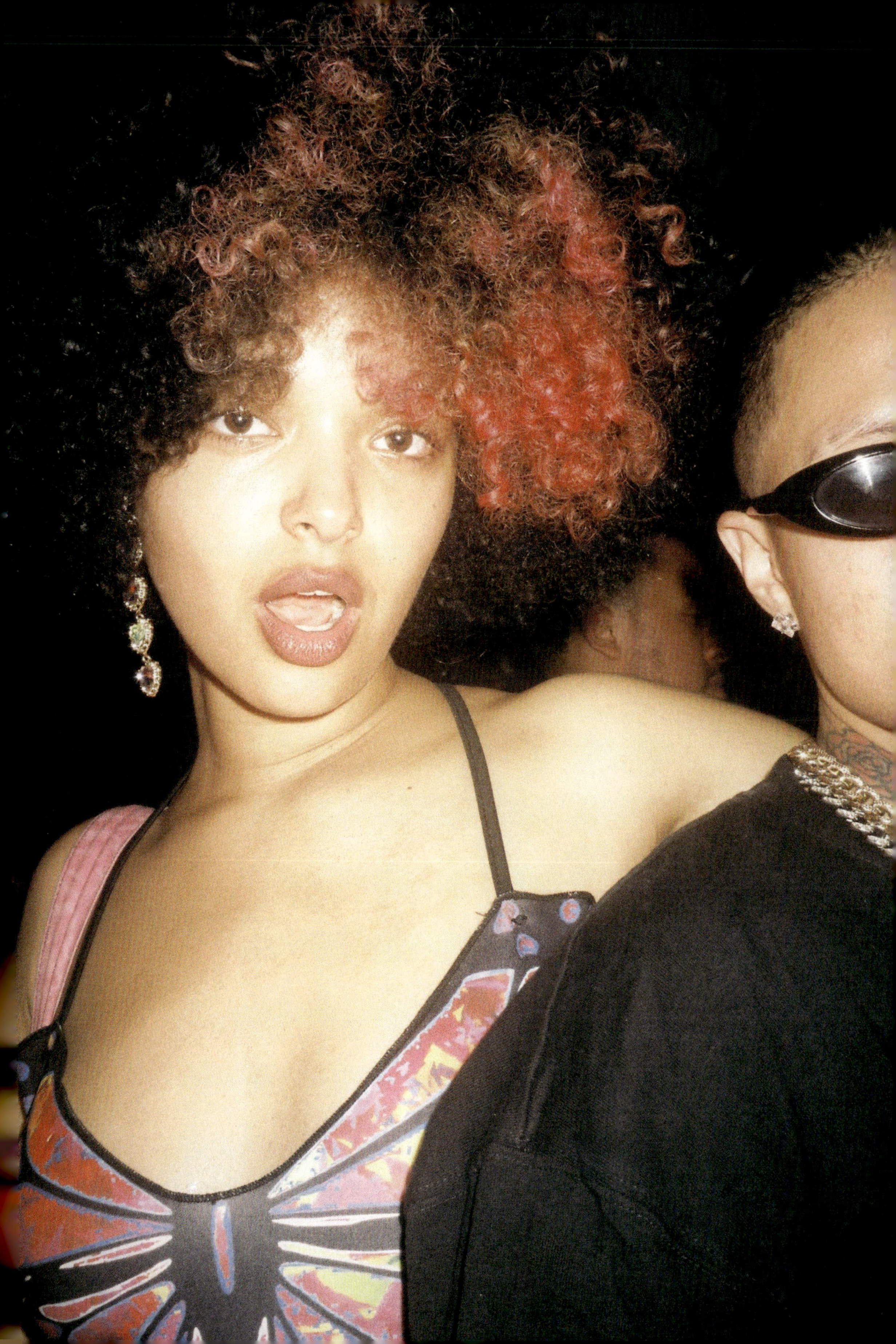

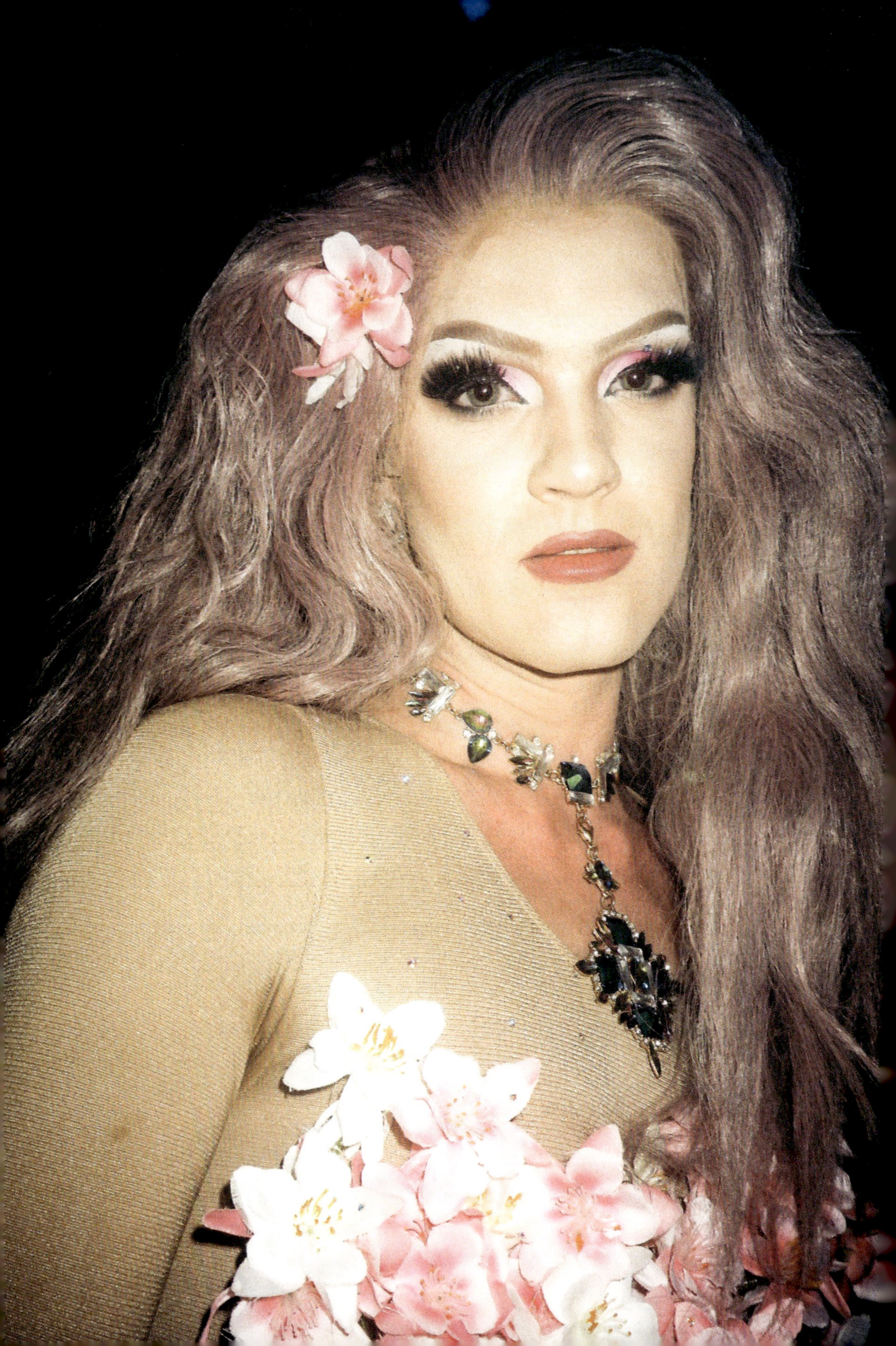

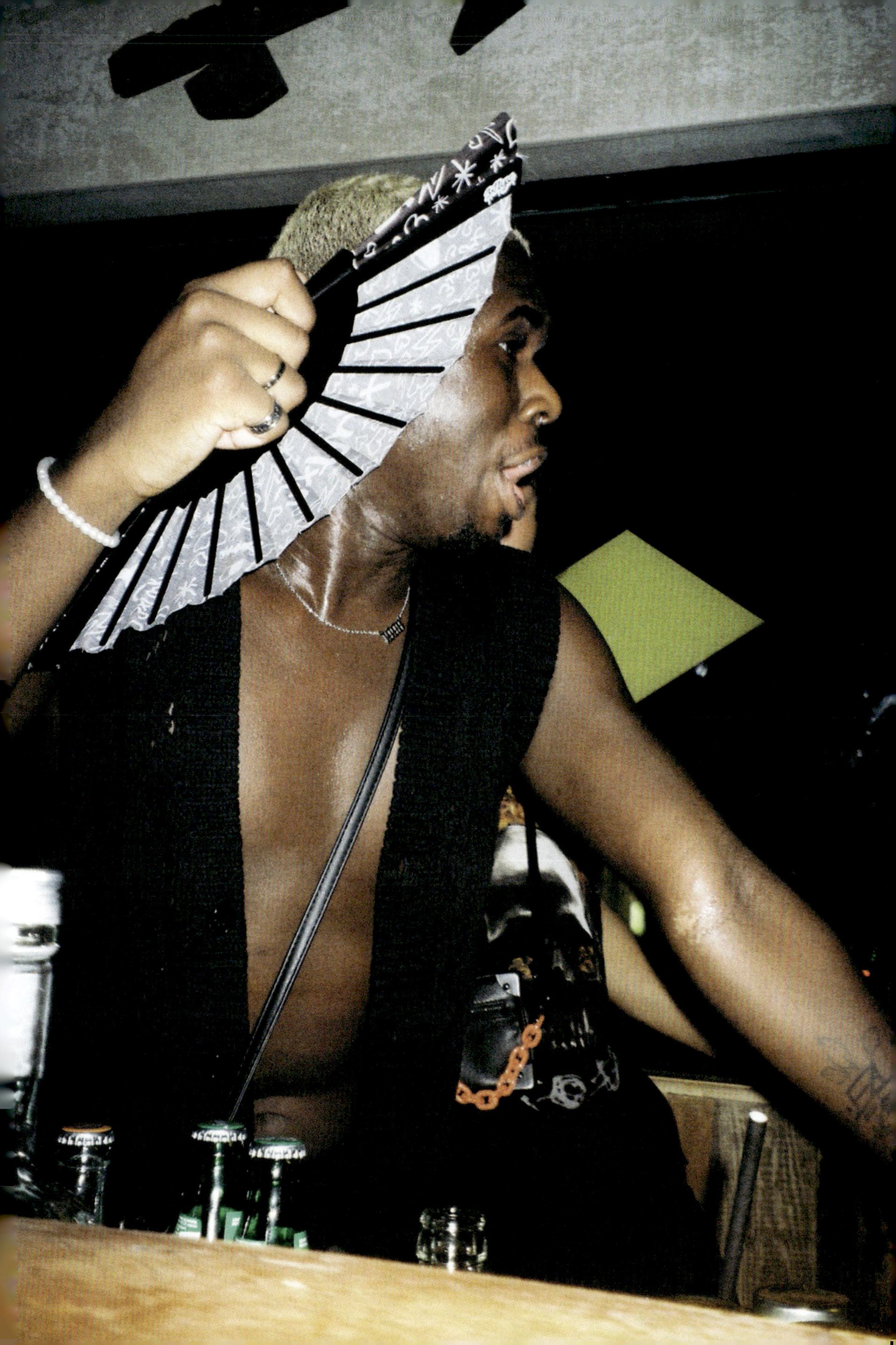

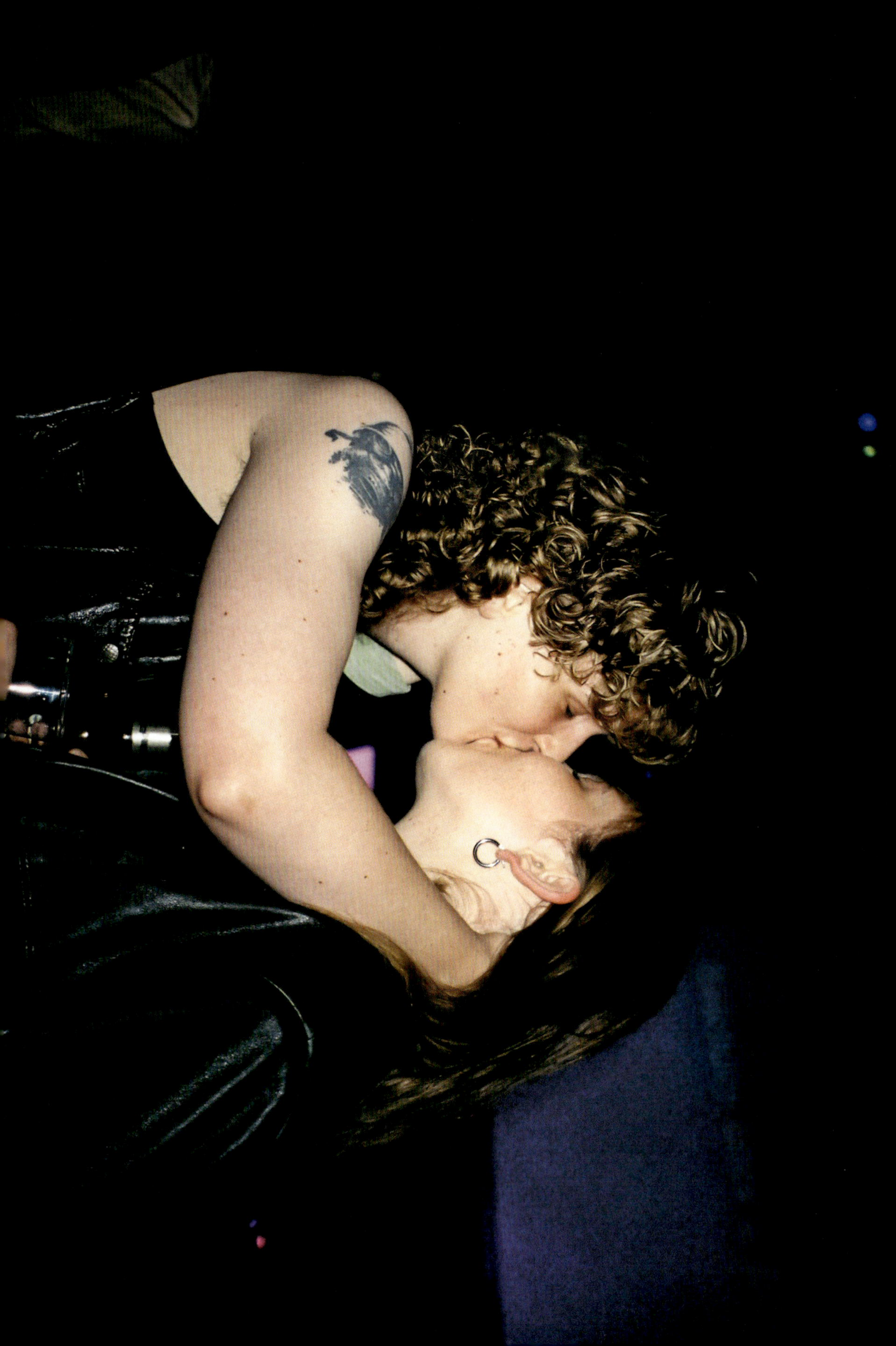

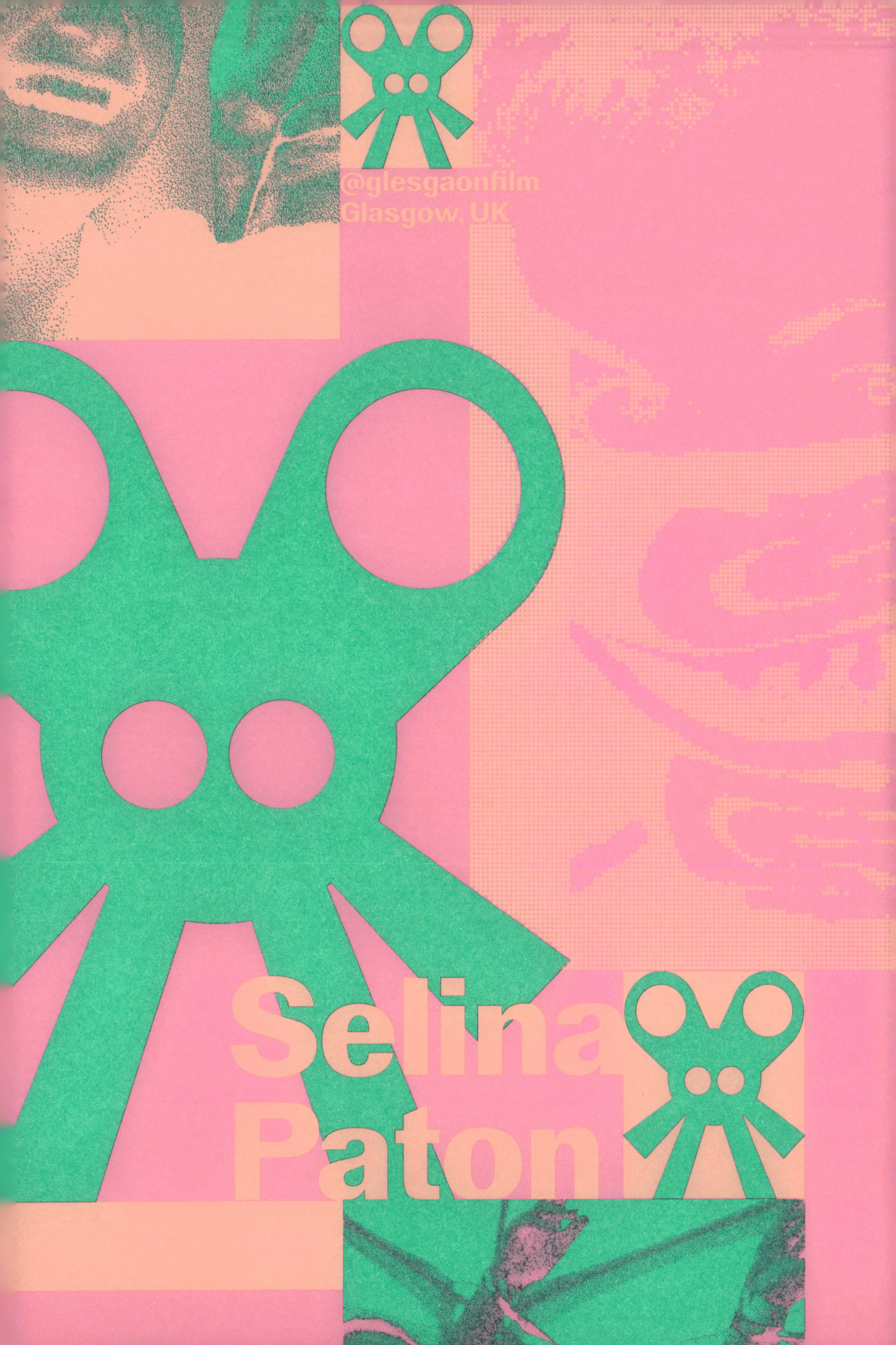
@glesgaonfilm
Glasgow, UK
Selina
Paton

I'm Selina, a Glaswegian photographer. I began documenting Glasgow's pulsating nightlife scene after lockdown, with the aim of capturing the electric energy in Glasgow's best underground clubs. I started my journey photographing the Sub Club, as I was drawn to the special atmosphere of this iconic space.

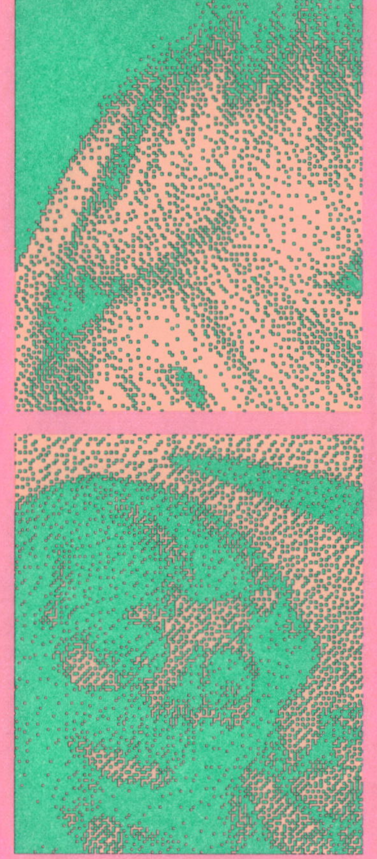

Through my photography, I aim to capture the raw authenticity of DJs and dancefloors, freezing in time those intimate connections between artist and crowd, moments of euphoria, and the pure passion and community that is felt in Glasgow's clubs. Capturing this goes beyond photography, I feel completely immersed in a community and scene that is so important to me. My work has become a documentation of clubs, festivals and underground rave scenes across Scotland. Electronic music unites all and is core to Glasgow's culture, which I will continue to document until the music stops.

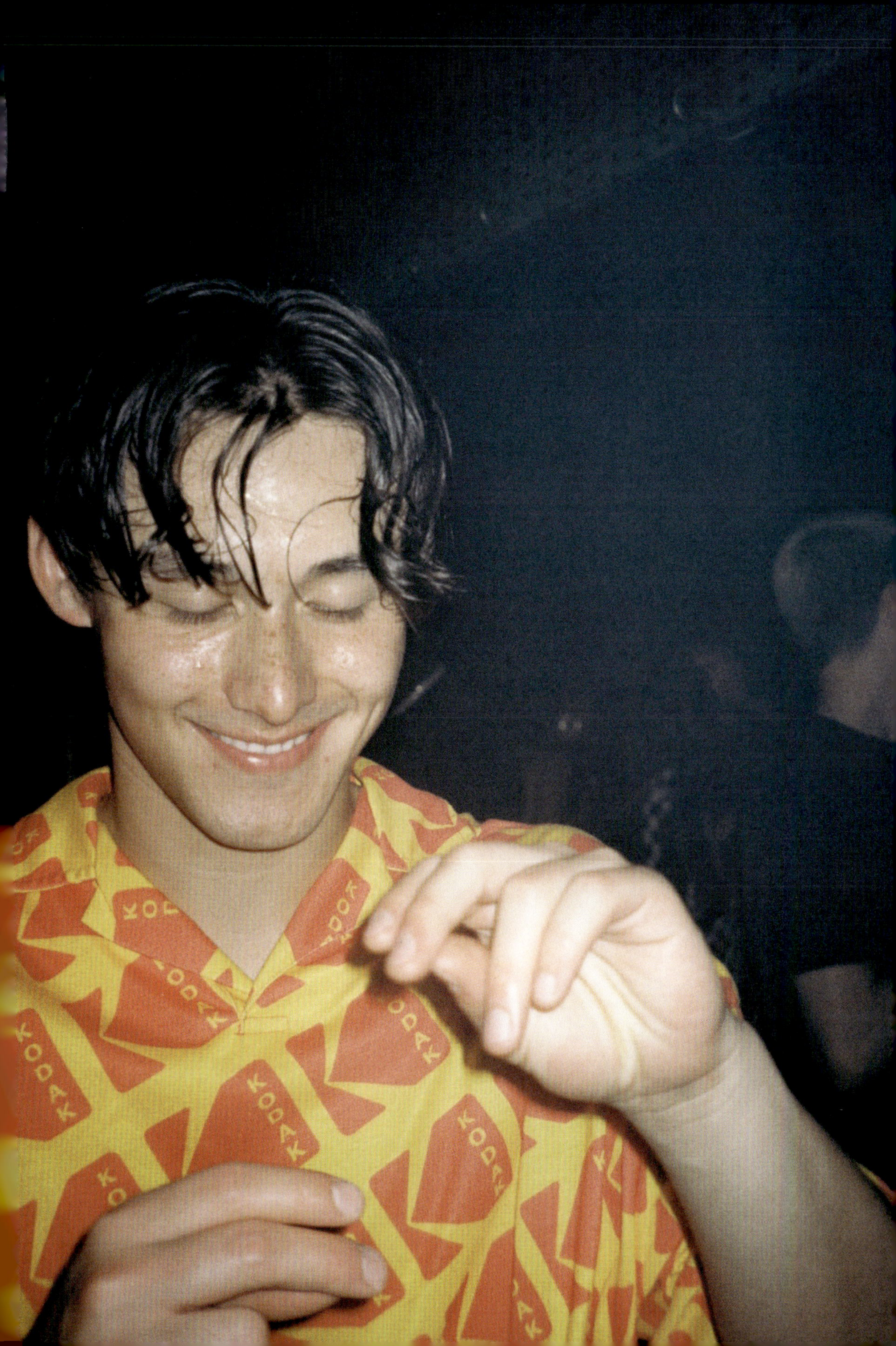

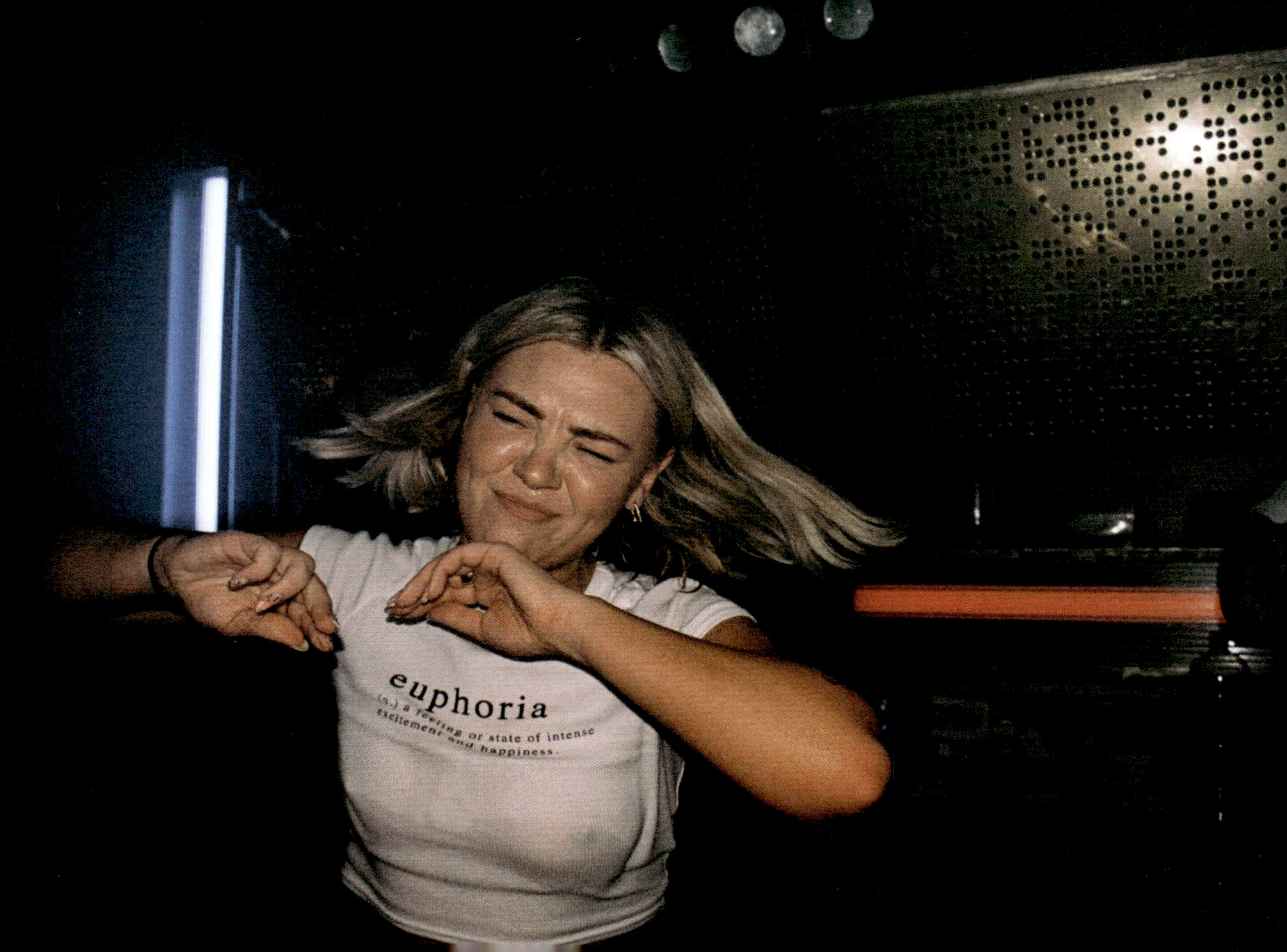
euphoria
(n.) a feeling or state of intense
excitement and happiness.

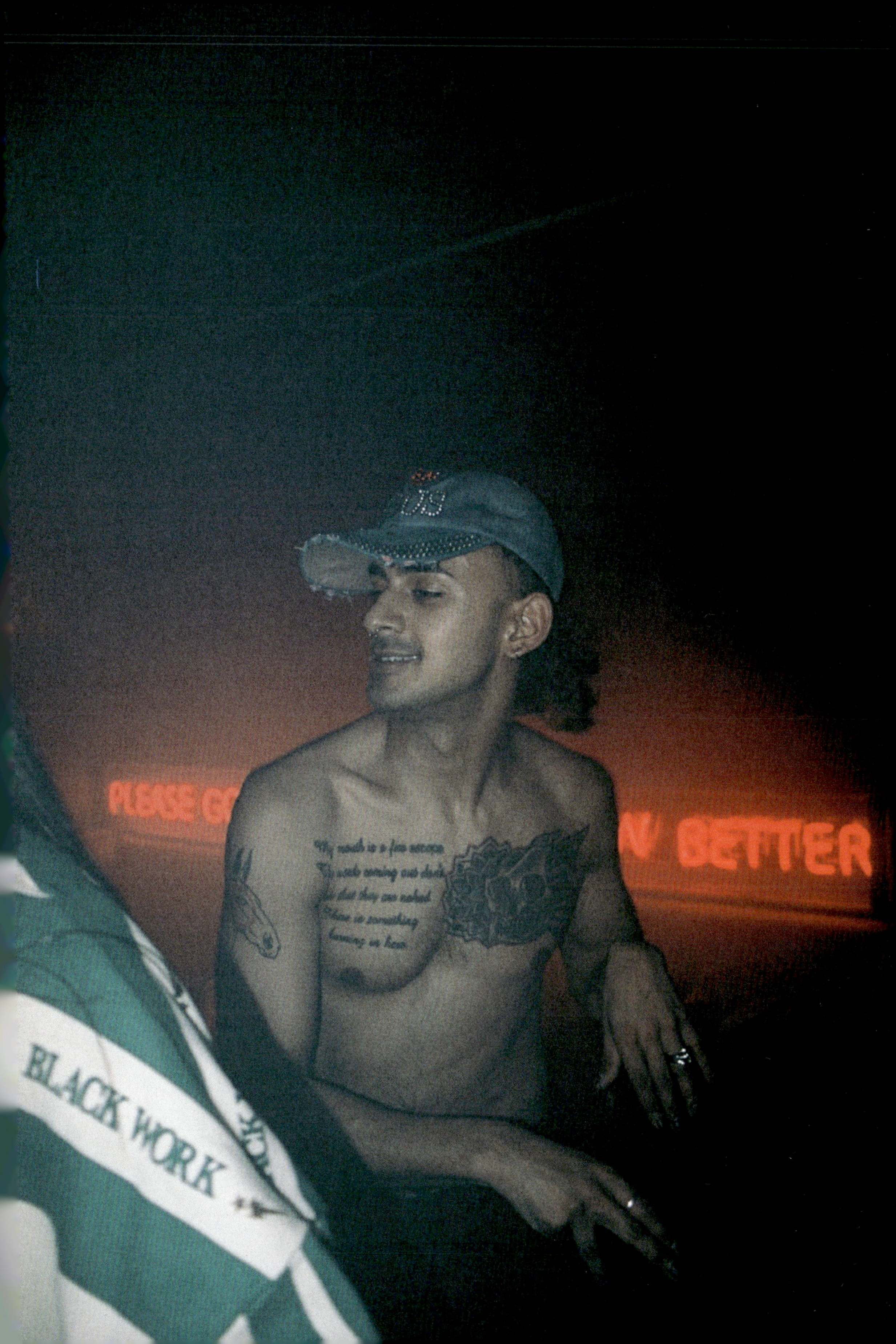

PLEASE CO
N' BETTER
BLACK WORK

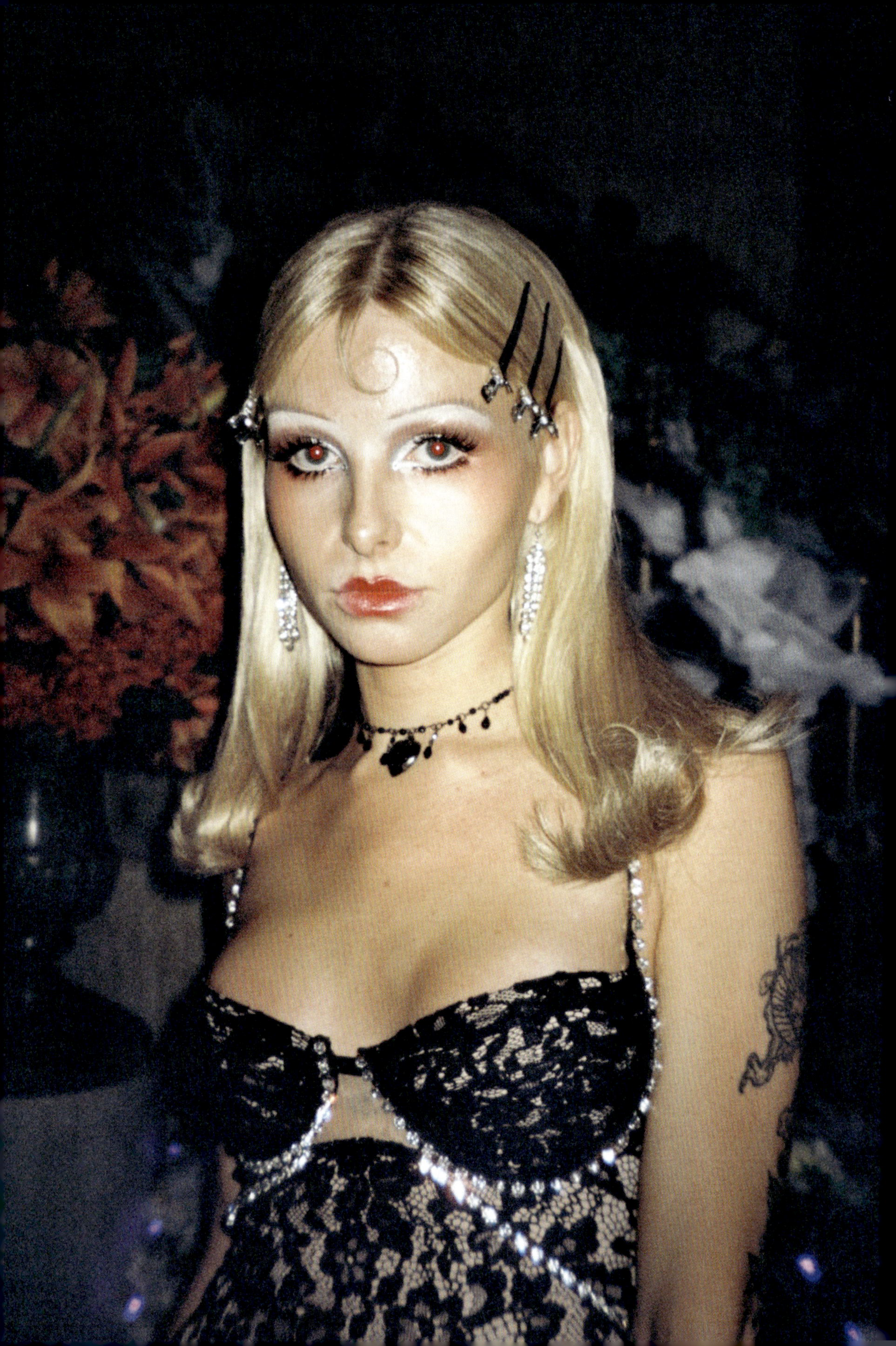

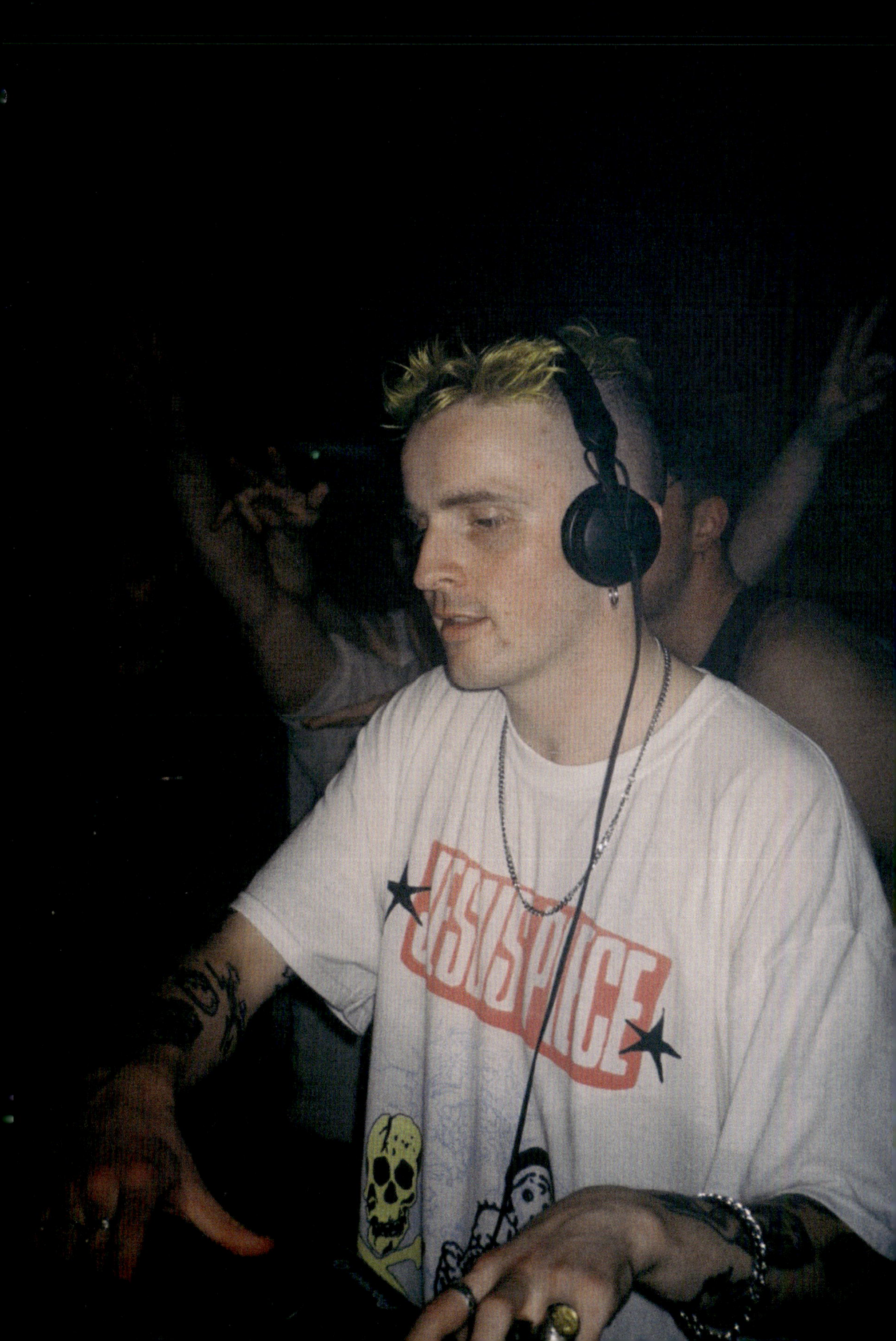
JESUSPIECE

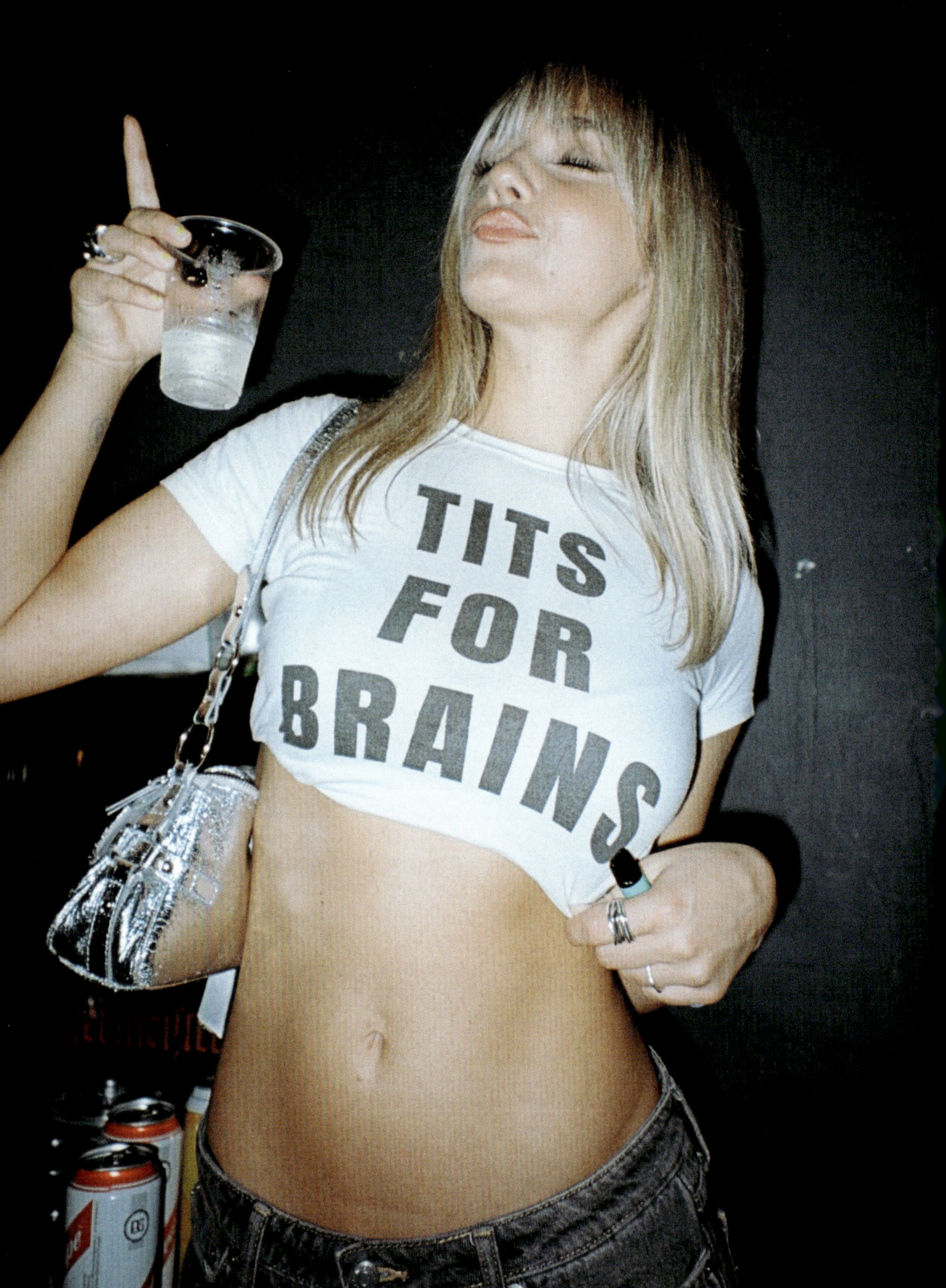
TITS
FOR
BRAINS

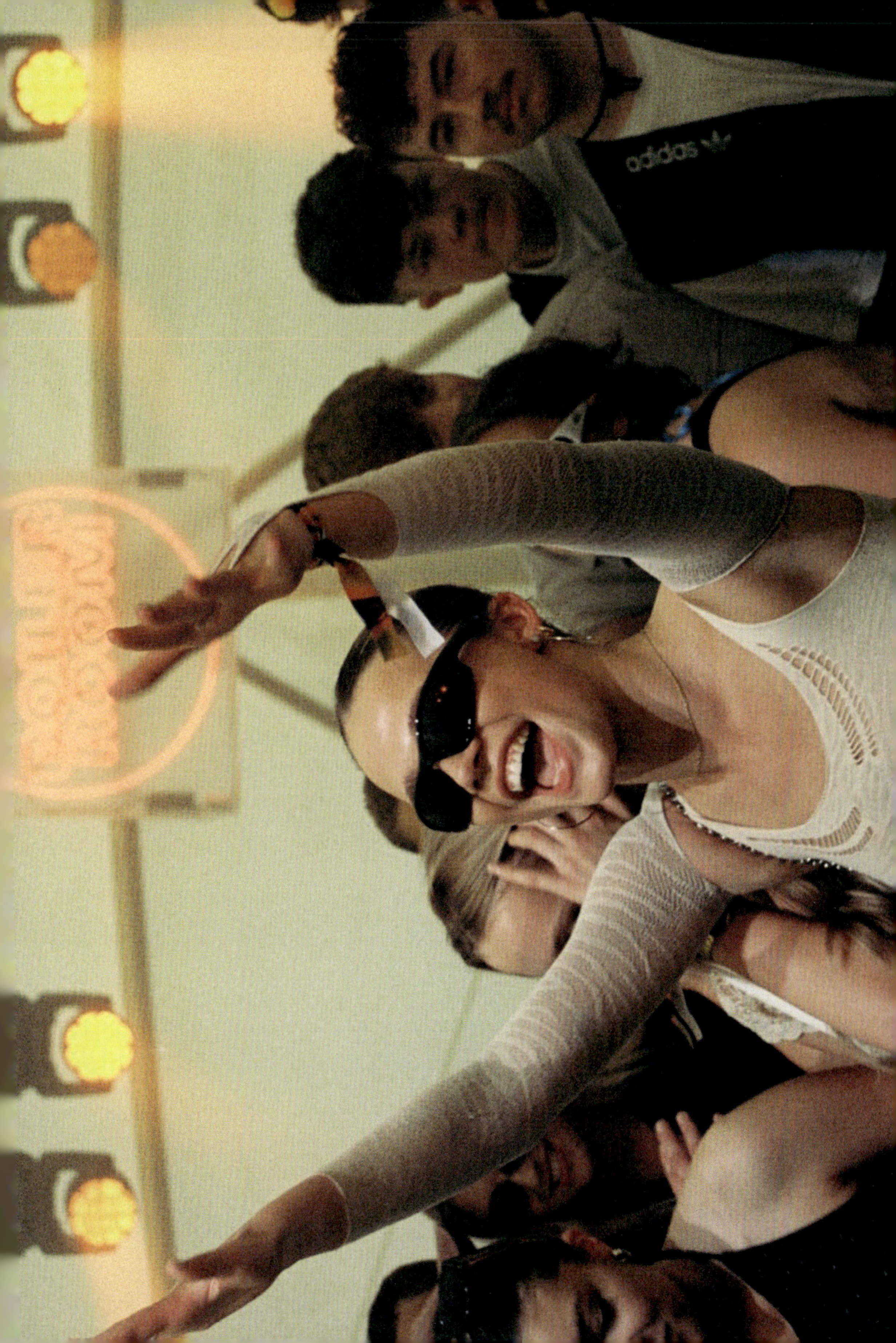

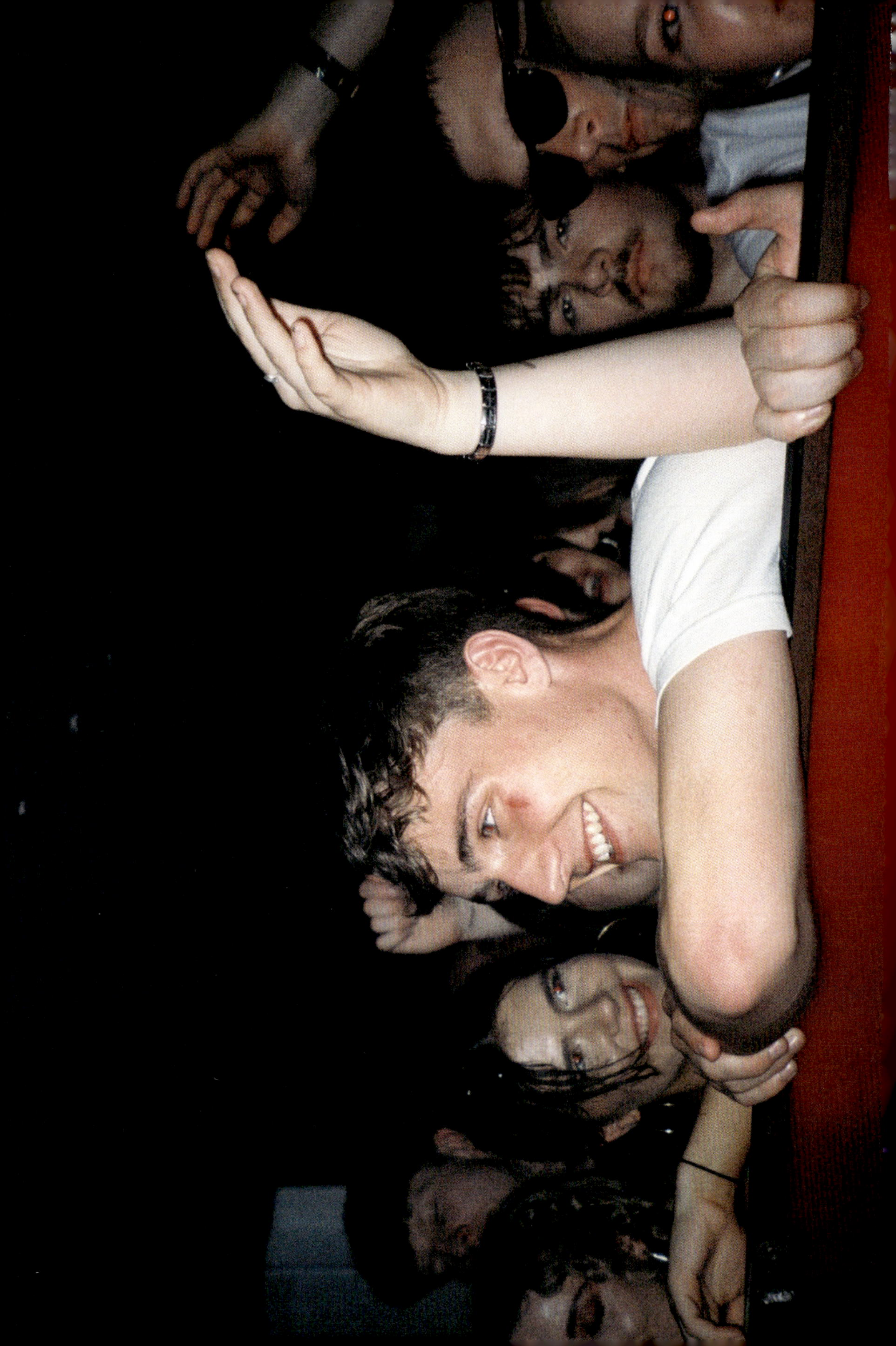

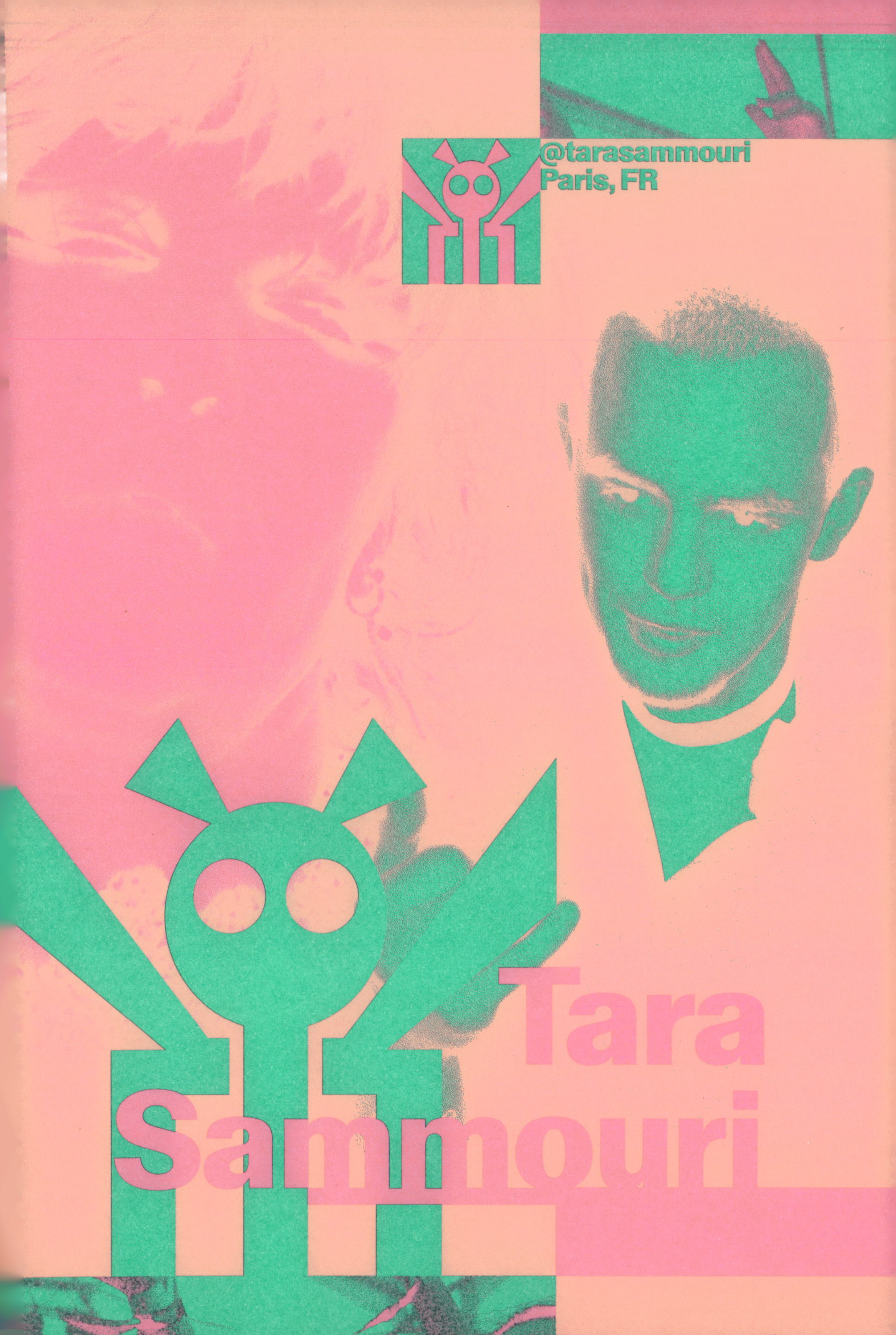

@tarasammouri
Paris, FR
Tara
Sammouri

I'm Tara, a Paris-born photographer living in Paris, and I started taking pictures back in 2019.

From the beginning what I enjoyed the most was simply this action I had on life, being able to capture my environment and ephemeral moments, and kind of building archives of my life. As my practice and my desire grew, I finished the bachelor in law I was doing and I decided to focus my time on a creative path, so I'm currently a student at the Beaux Arts School of Paris. While I expanded my creative processes by finding other mediums like videos, sounds or writings, photography has remained a preferred way of expression.

The coexistence of collectiveness and individualities is really something that I found vibrant and important, and sometimes, nights become a utopian space where love and pure life energy flow. Notions of presence and experiences in space and time are central in my work; from people and portraits allowing representations, to trying to catch pure moments, emotions and flows of energies, to portraying spaces that tell stories even when no humans are visible.

I think memory is important and as the only thing constant in life is change, I find it magical that I can freeze movements that will never happen again, making them eternal in a certain way.

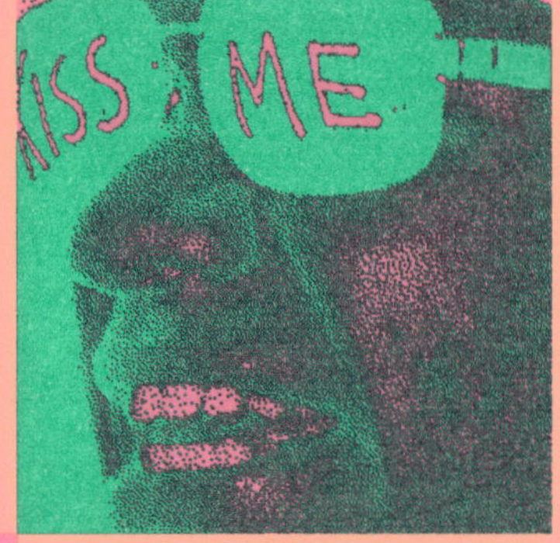

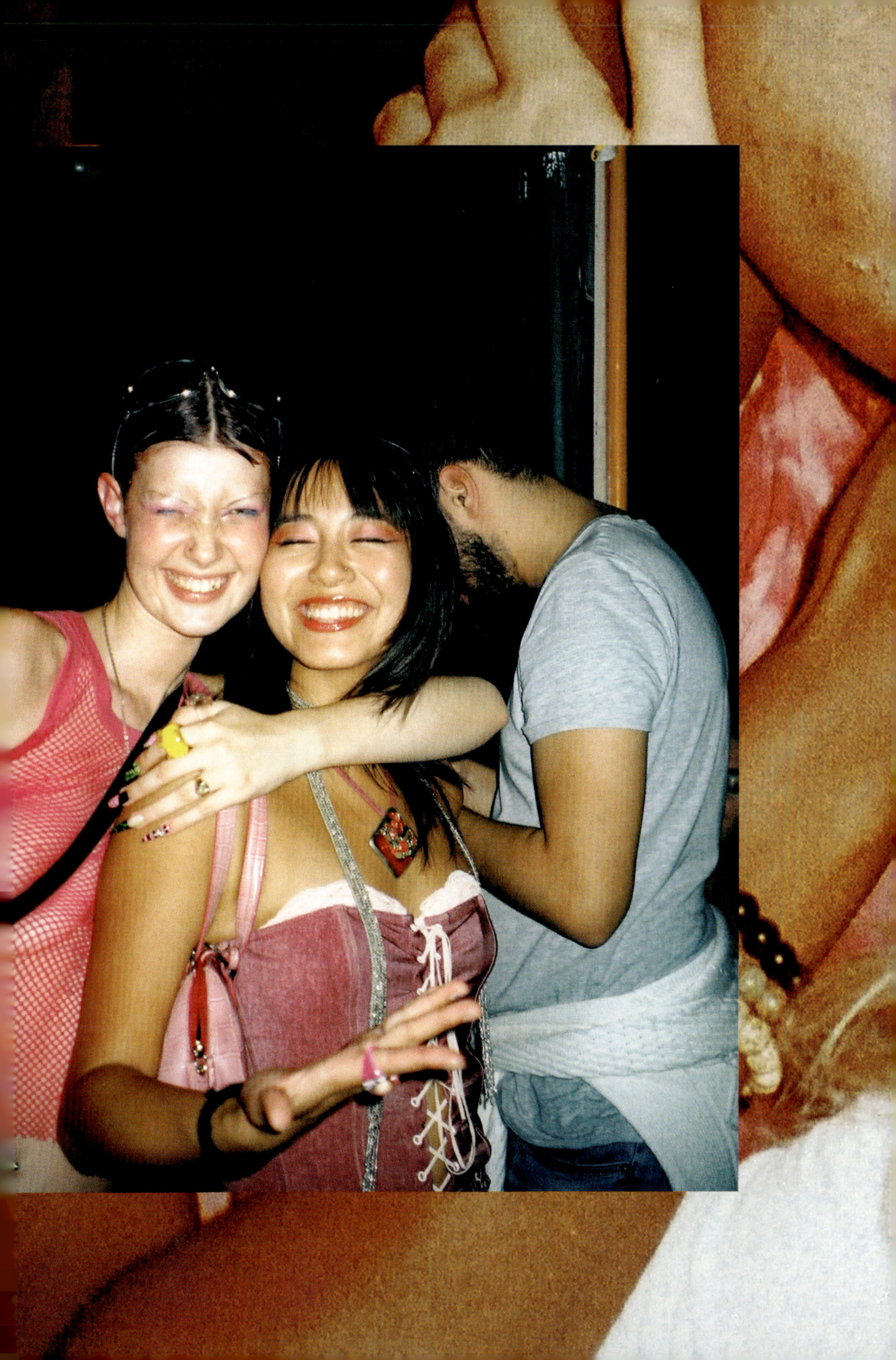

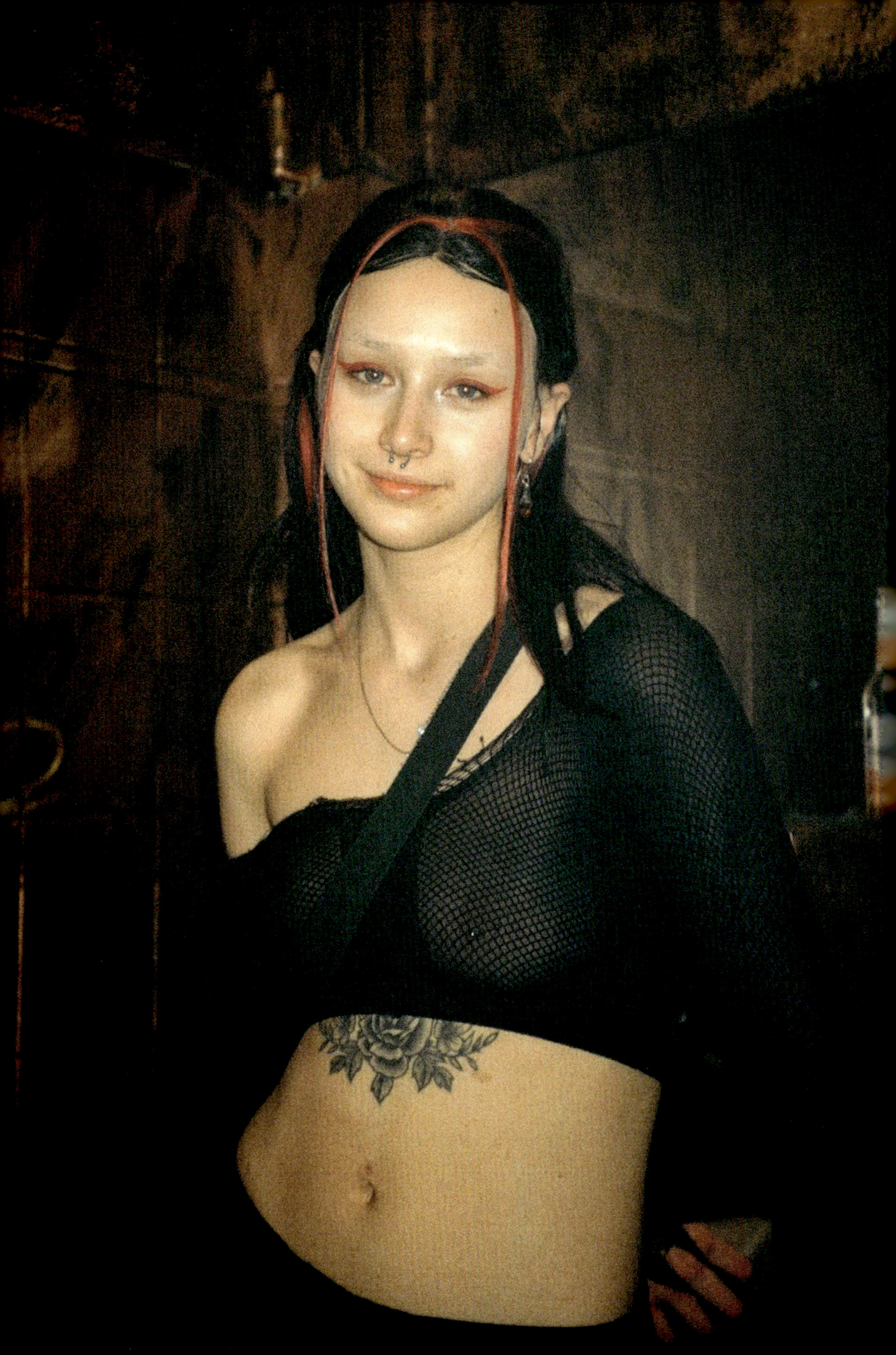

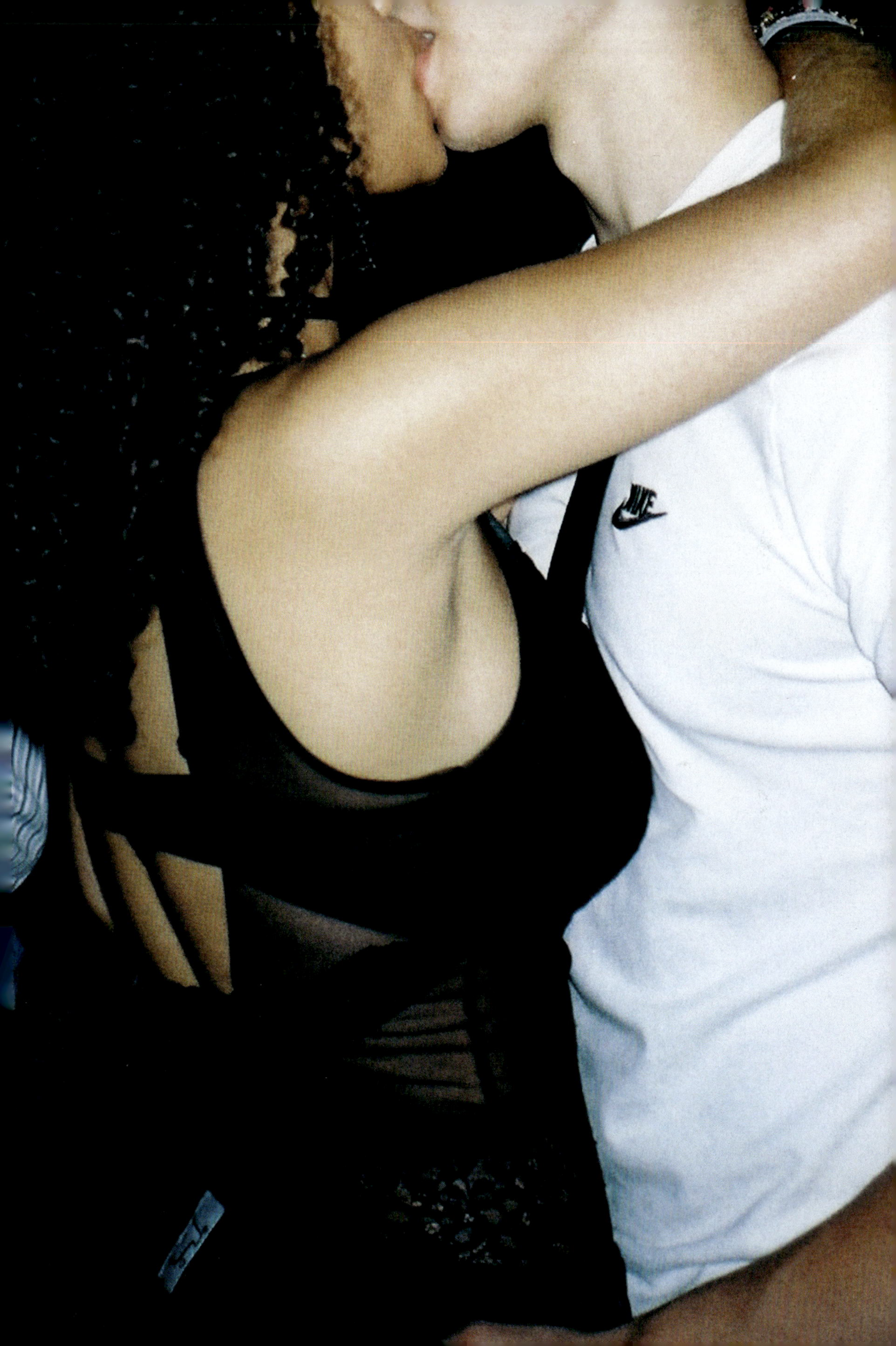

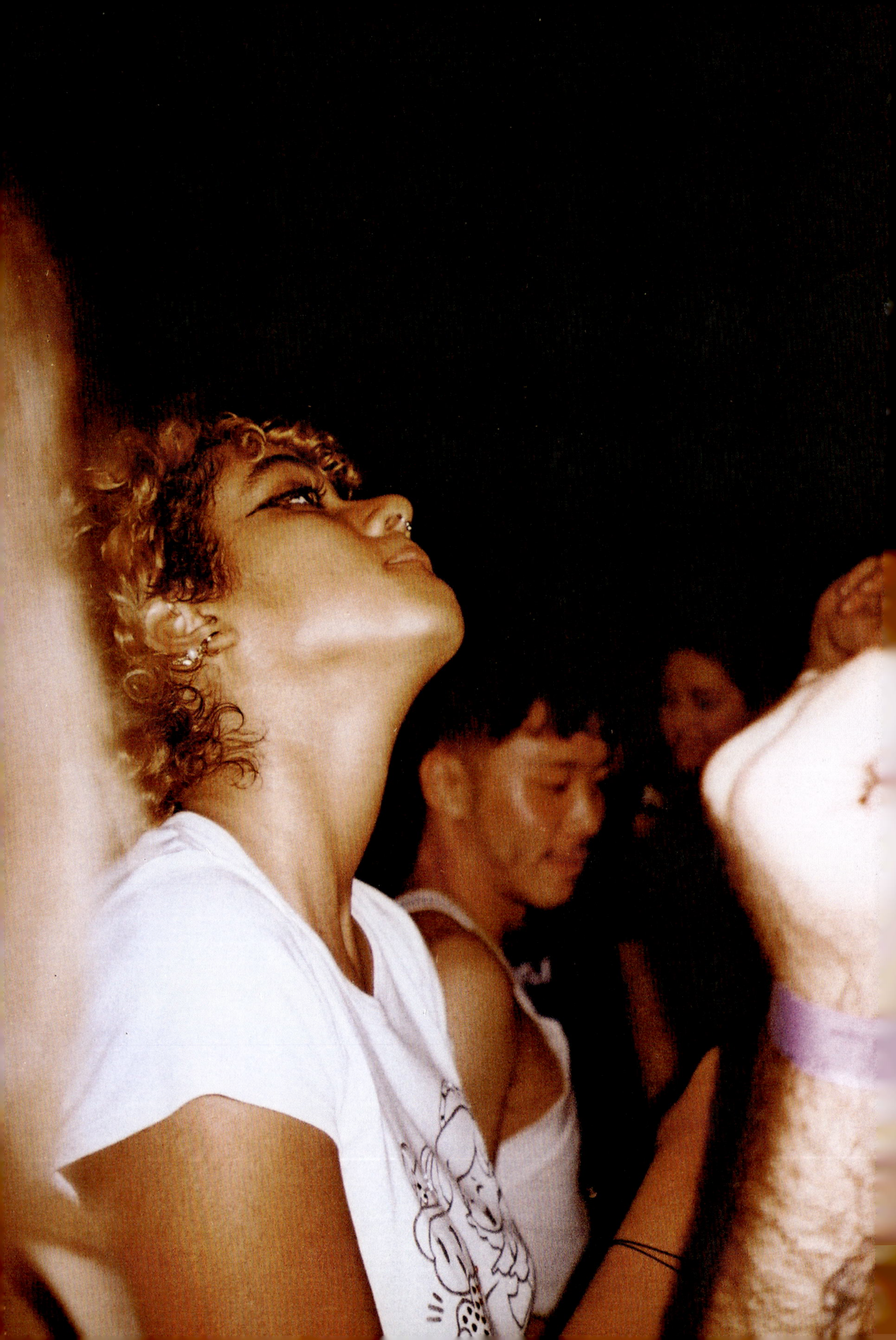

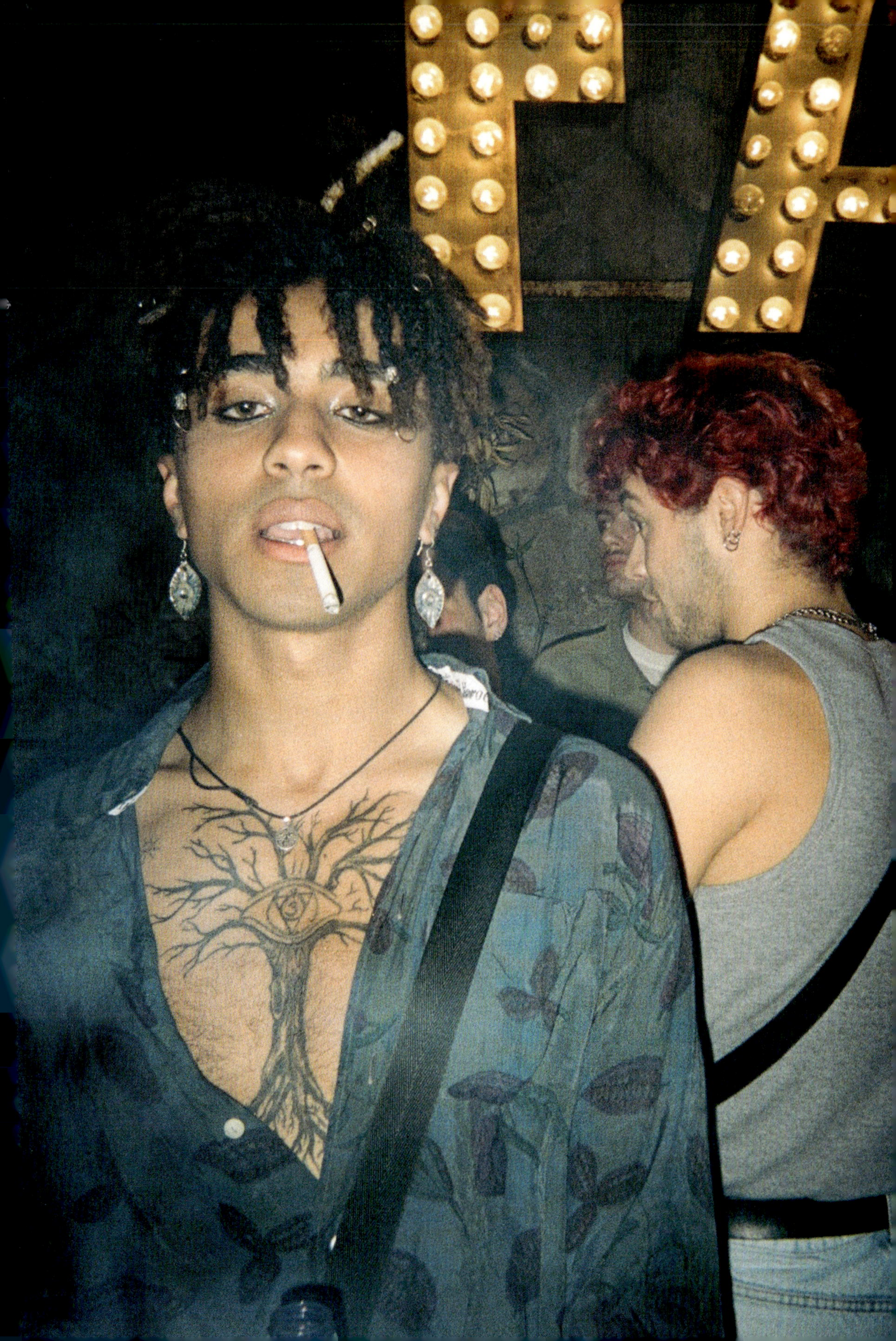

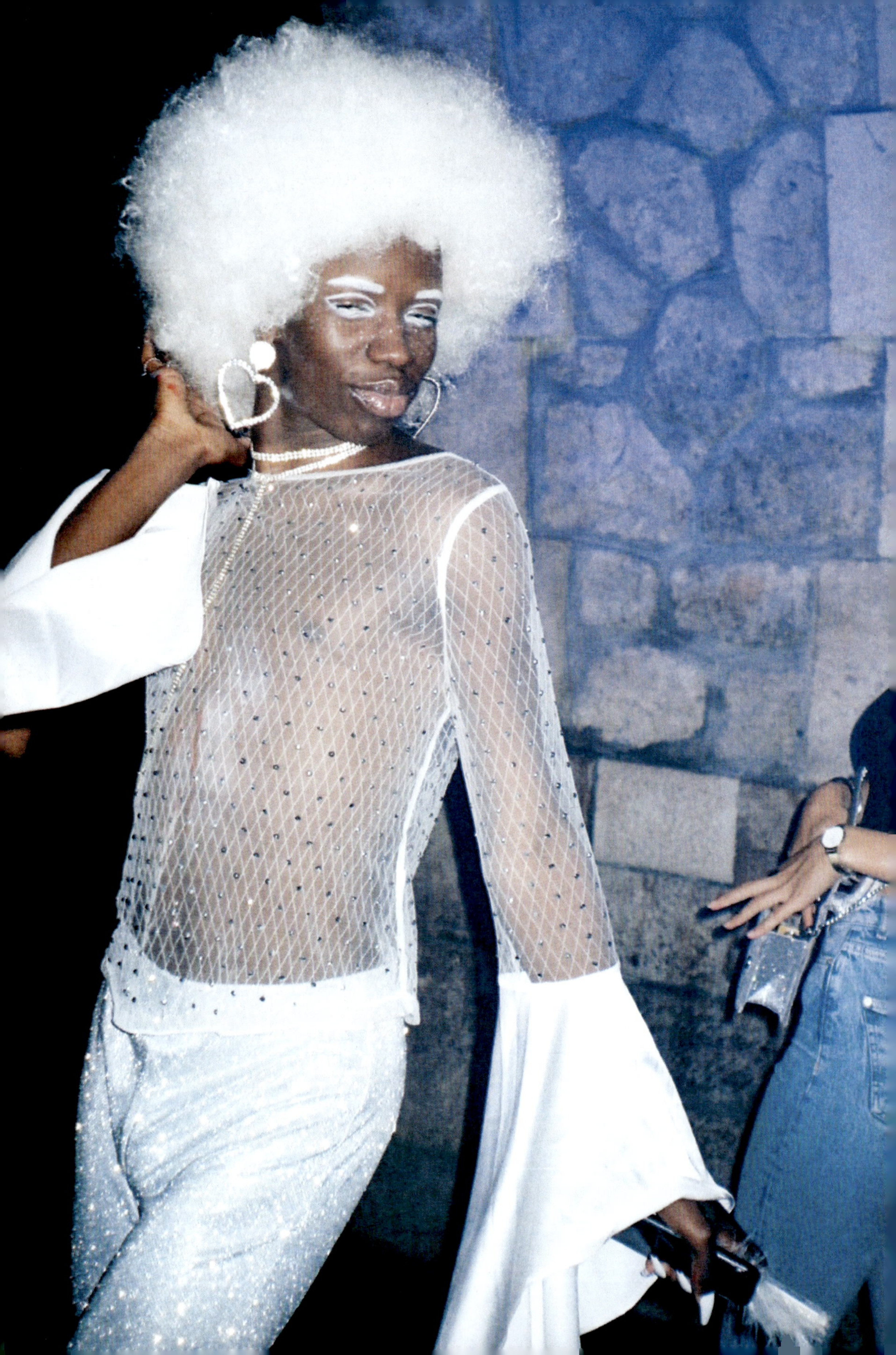

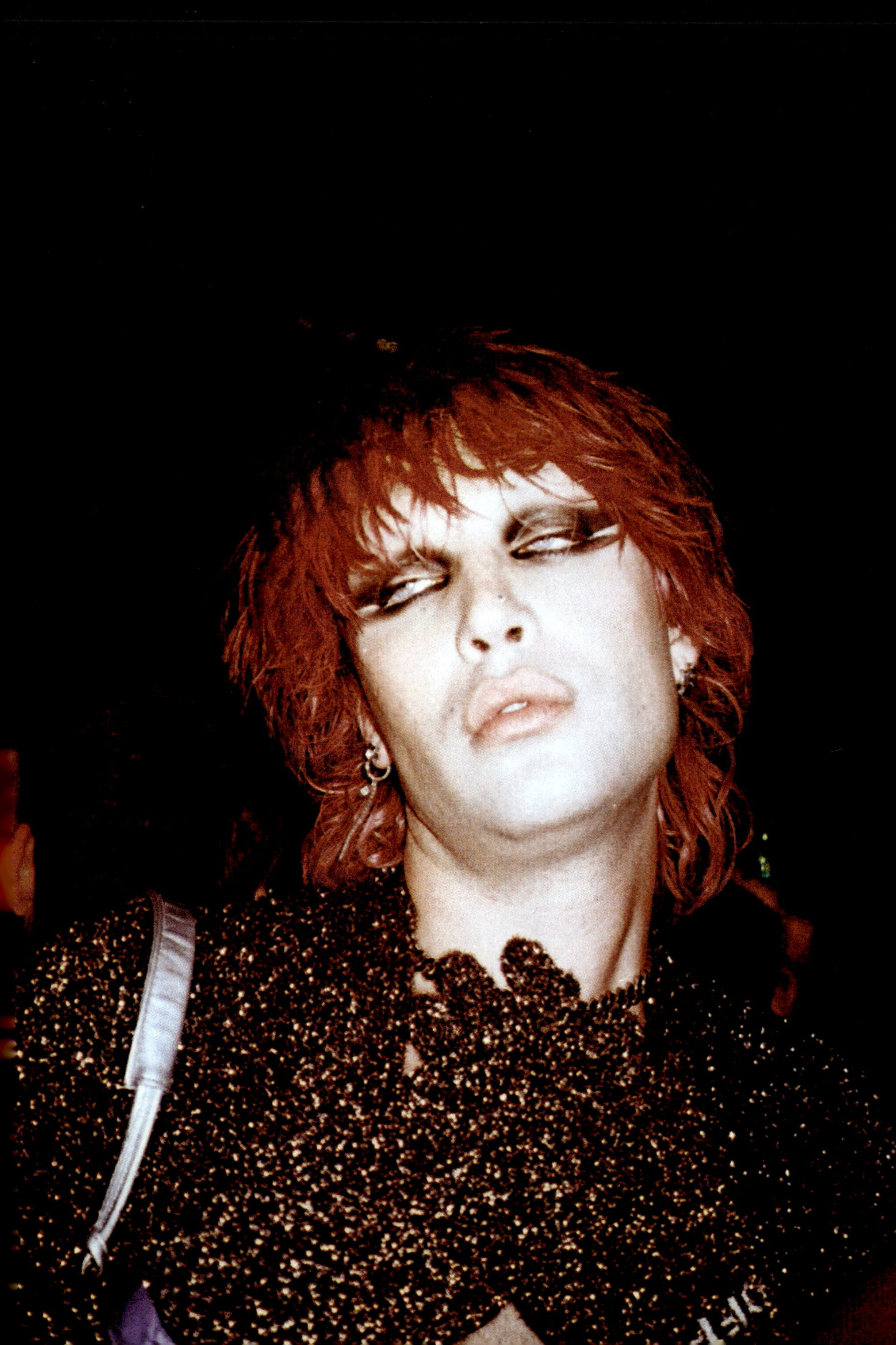

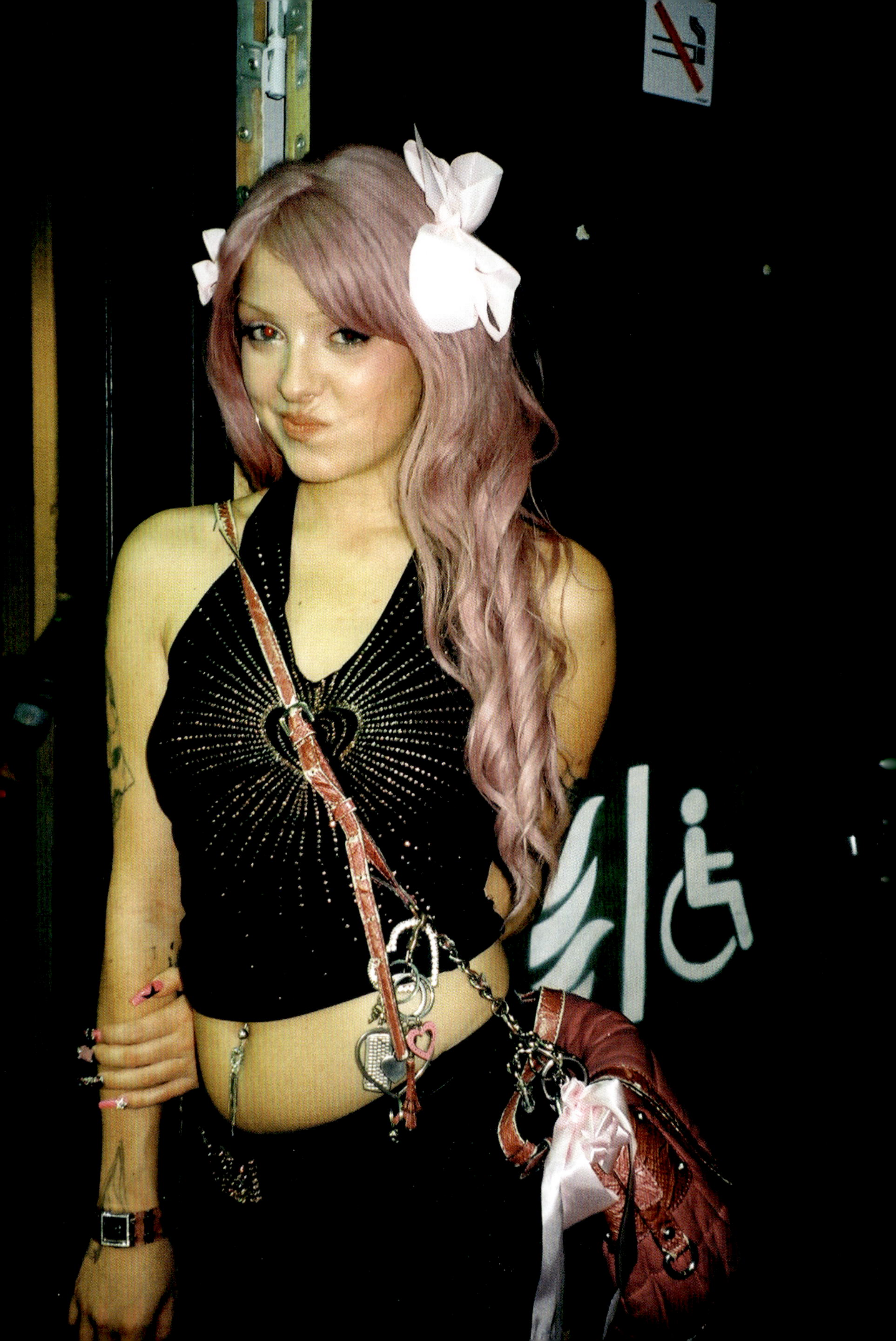

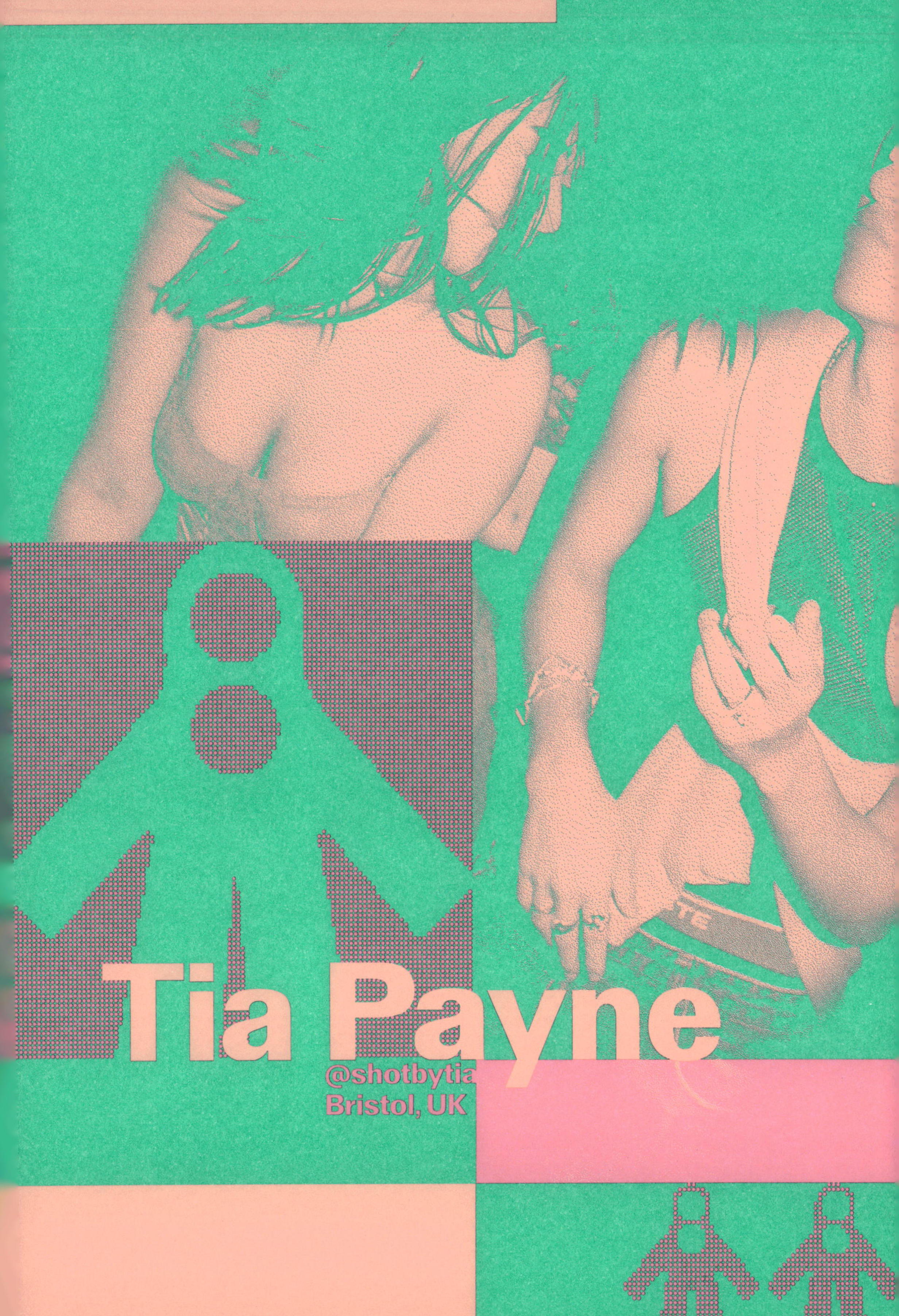

Tia Payne
@shotbytia
Bristol, UK

I'm Tia, a film photographer now based in Bristol, originally from Portsmouth. My work has always focused on music and the surrounding culture, specifically dance music and the vibrant settings and spaces local to me. I guess it wasn't my intention for it to develop into my work the way it has now - it happened naturally.

Capturing those moments of people's genuine reactions, their expression of style/fashion and trying to capture the overall mood in the room is just something that has always appealed to me. It gives me a personal attachment to the photos and is something I've been trying to do since I was old enough to get into a club. Before living in Bristol, I had a strong affection for the nightlife here and used to spend a lot of my weekends travelling up for events and anything music related, really. This city has had a big impact on my journey and is such a key part of my life now. The Bristol scene is so unique - such a lovely community of individuals, and I can't imagine myself anywhere else. I see it as an extension of my identity and I'm forever grateful for the places it has taken me.

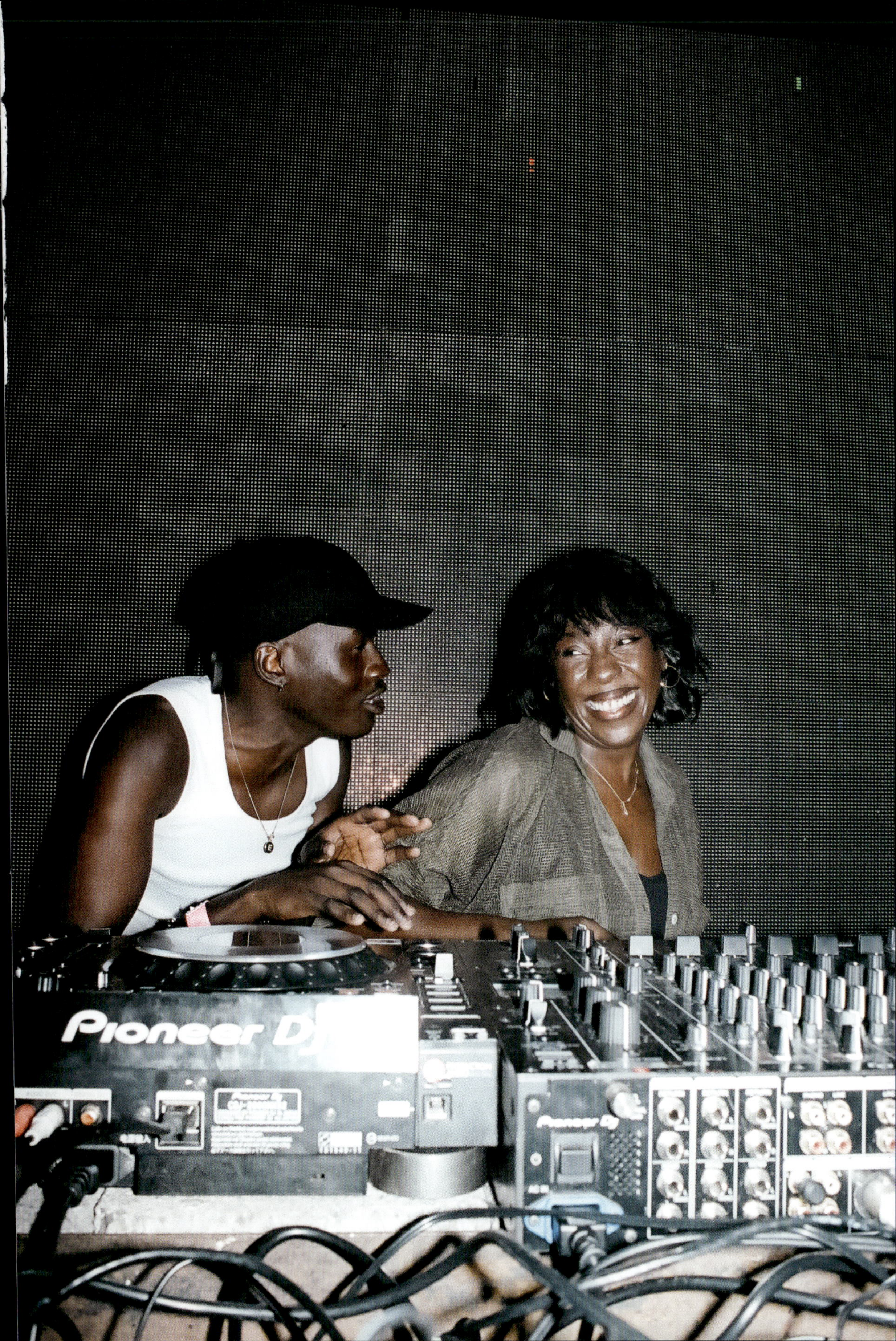

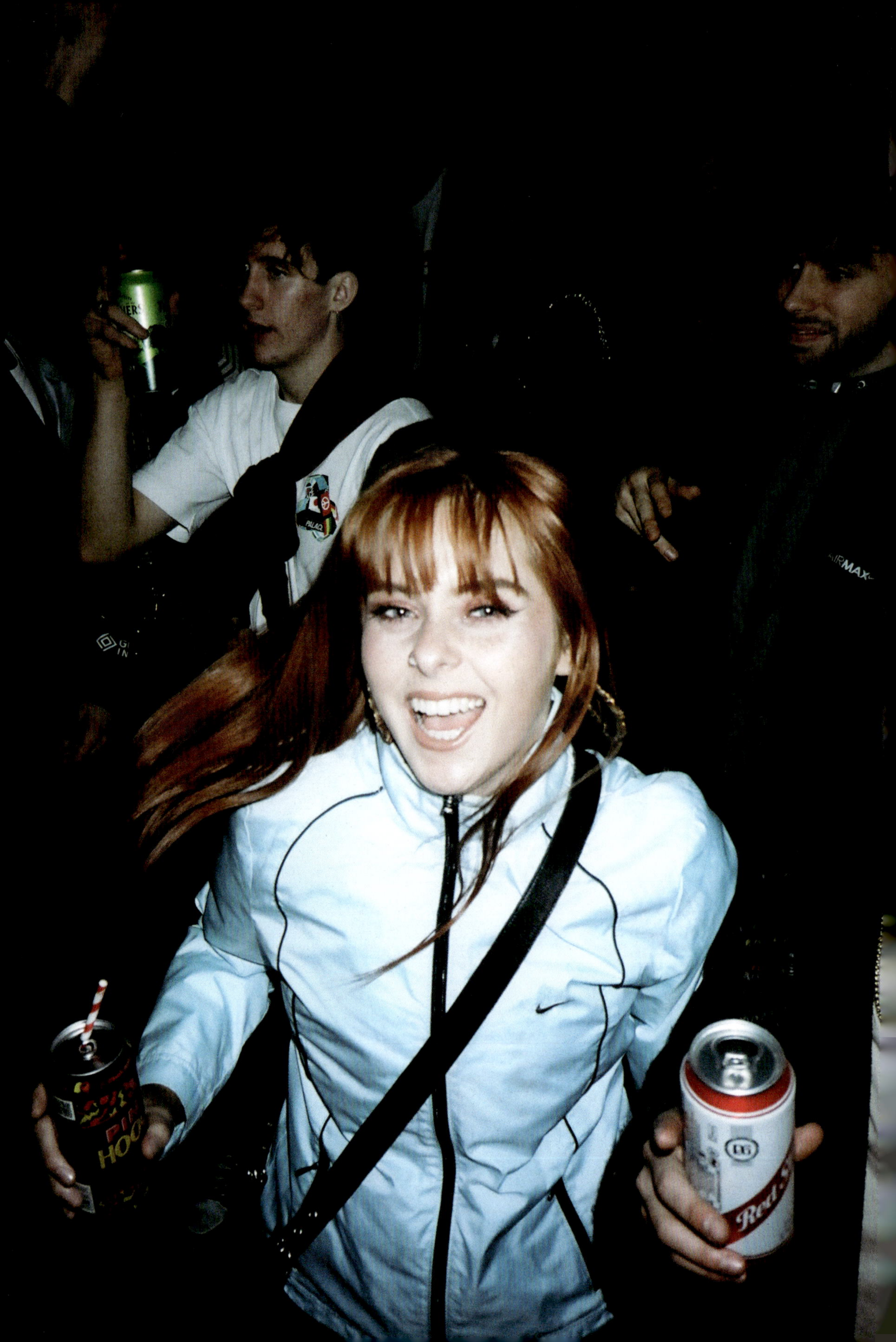

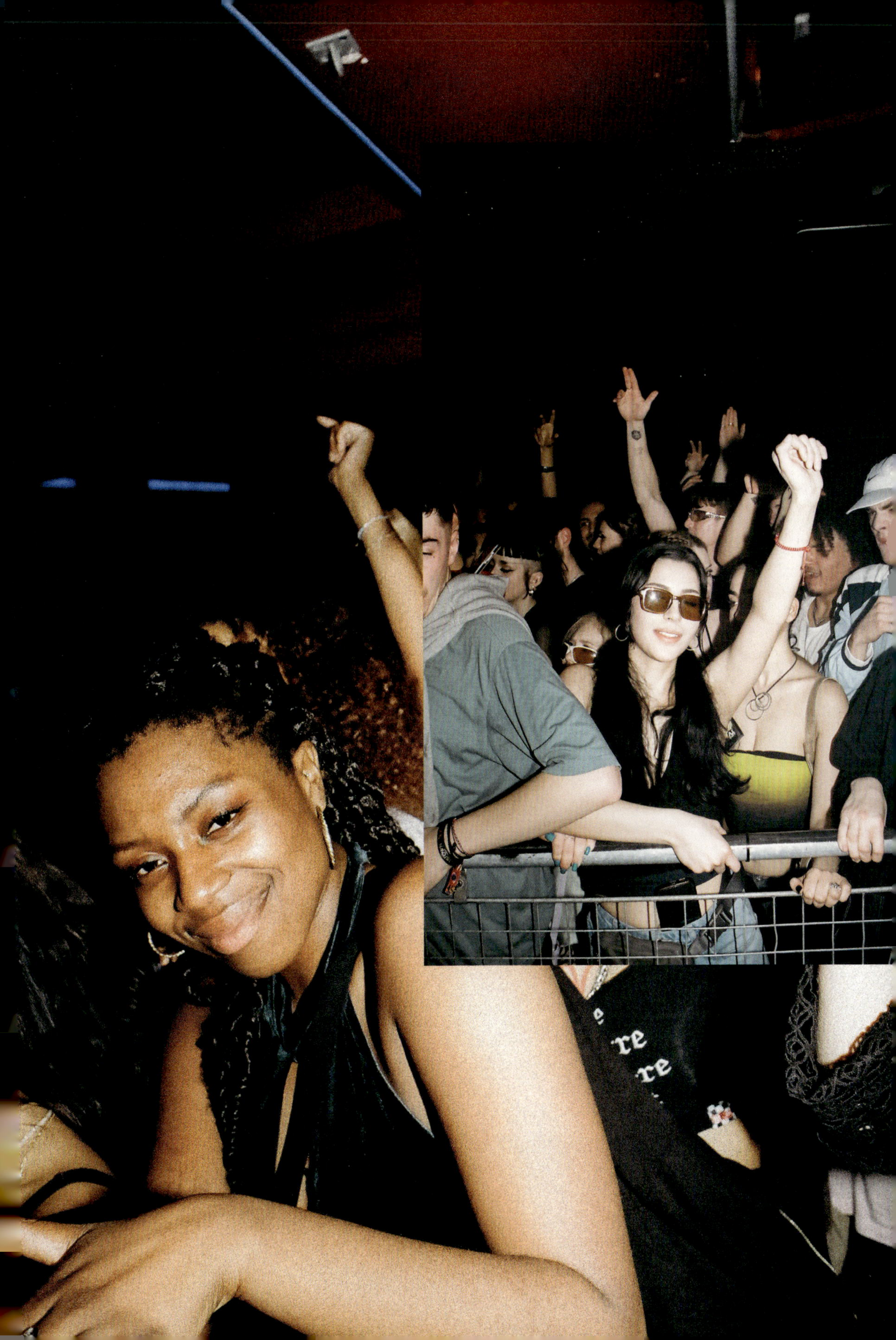

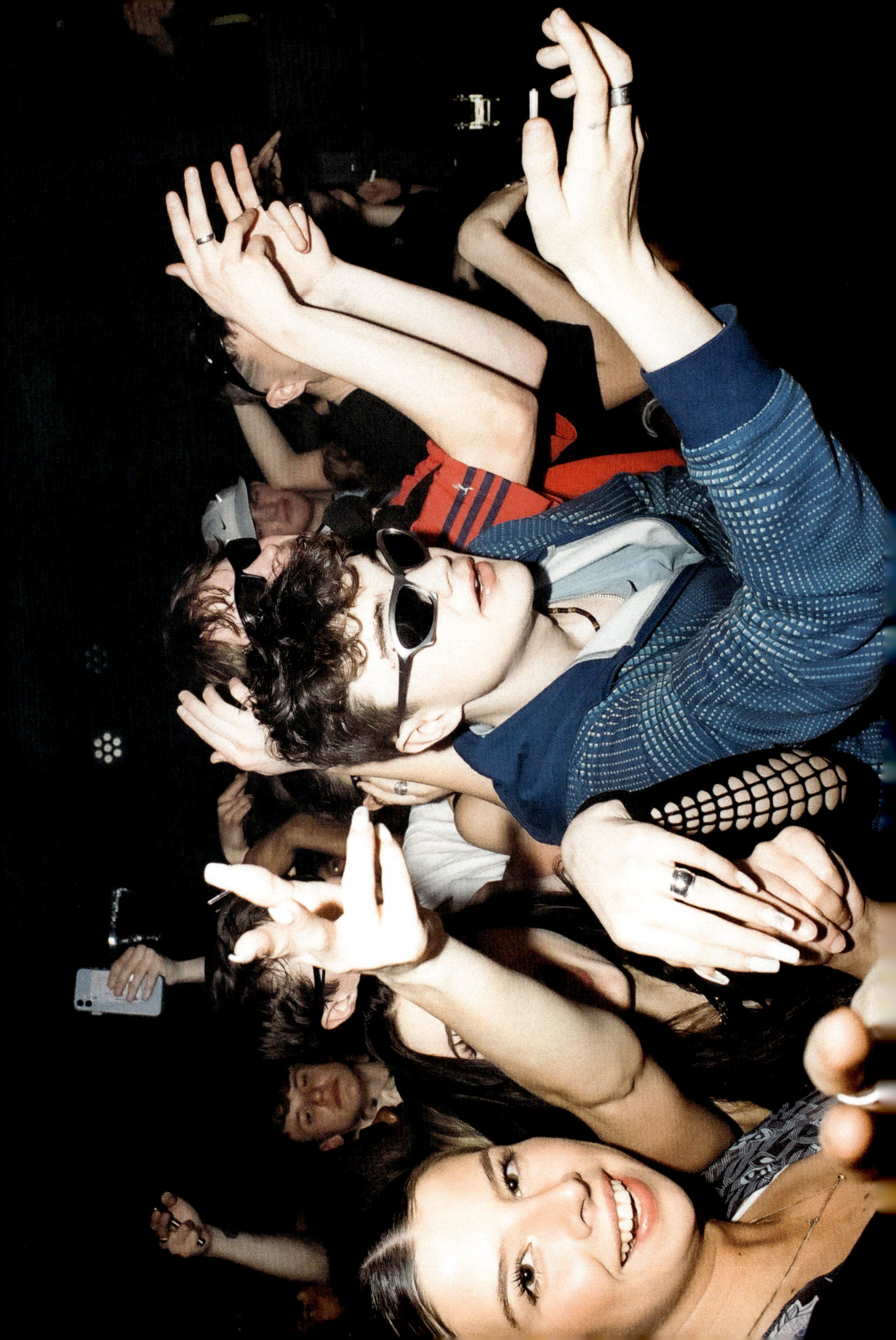

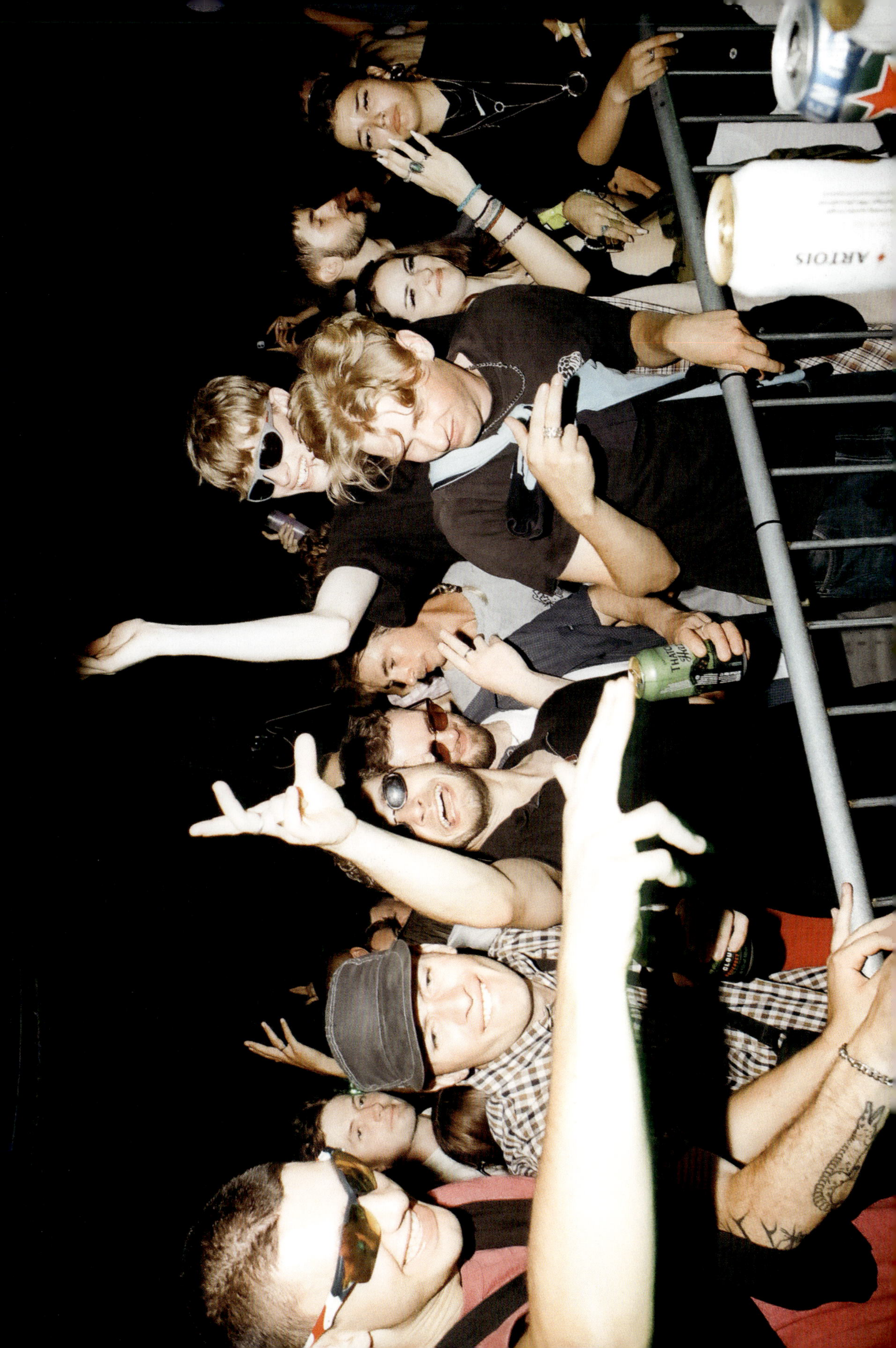

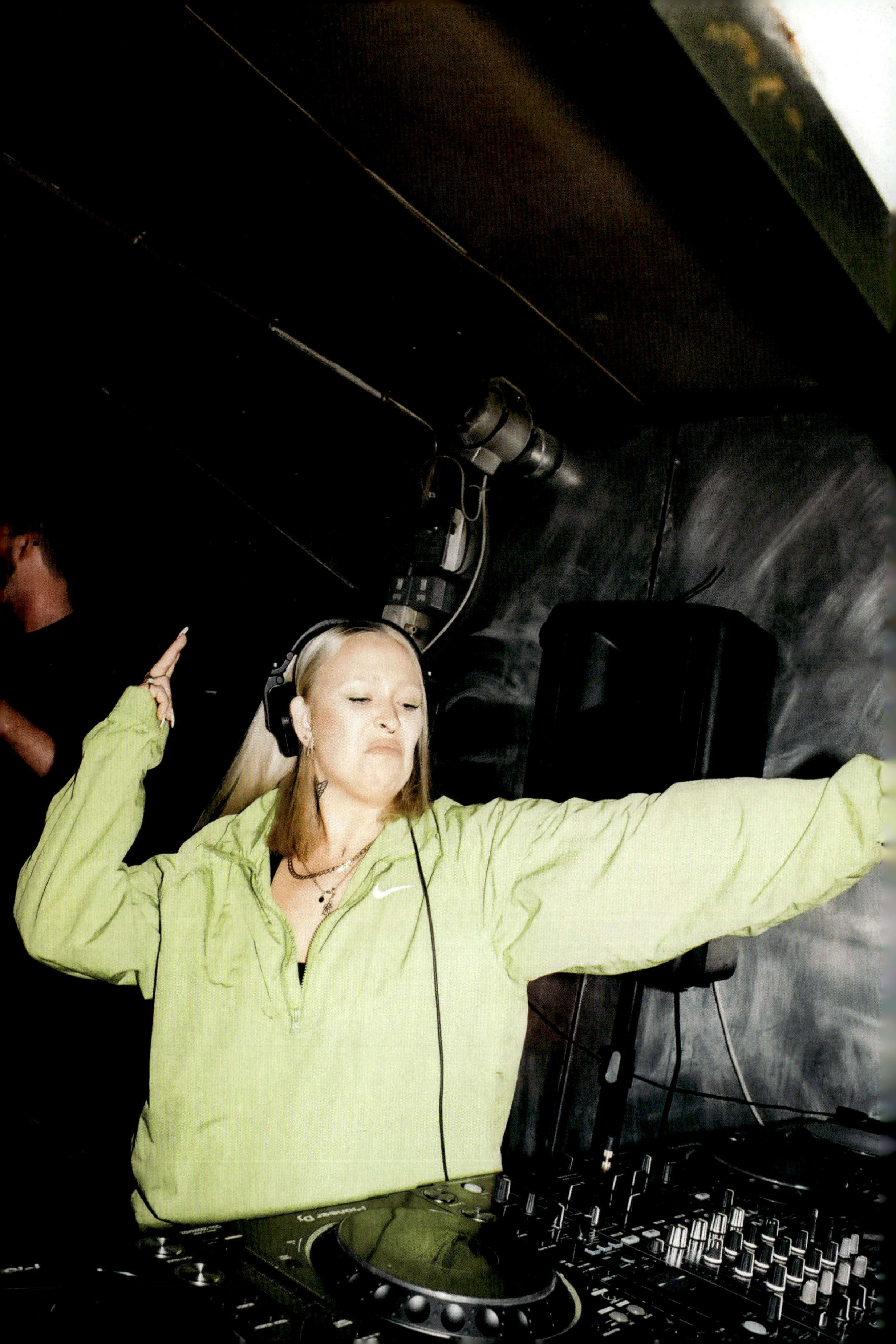

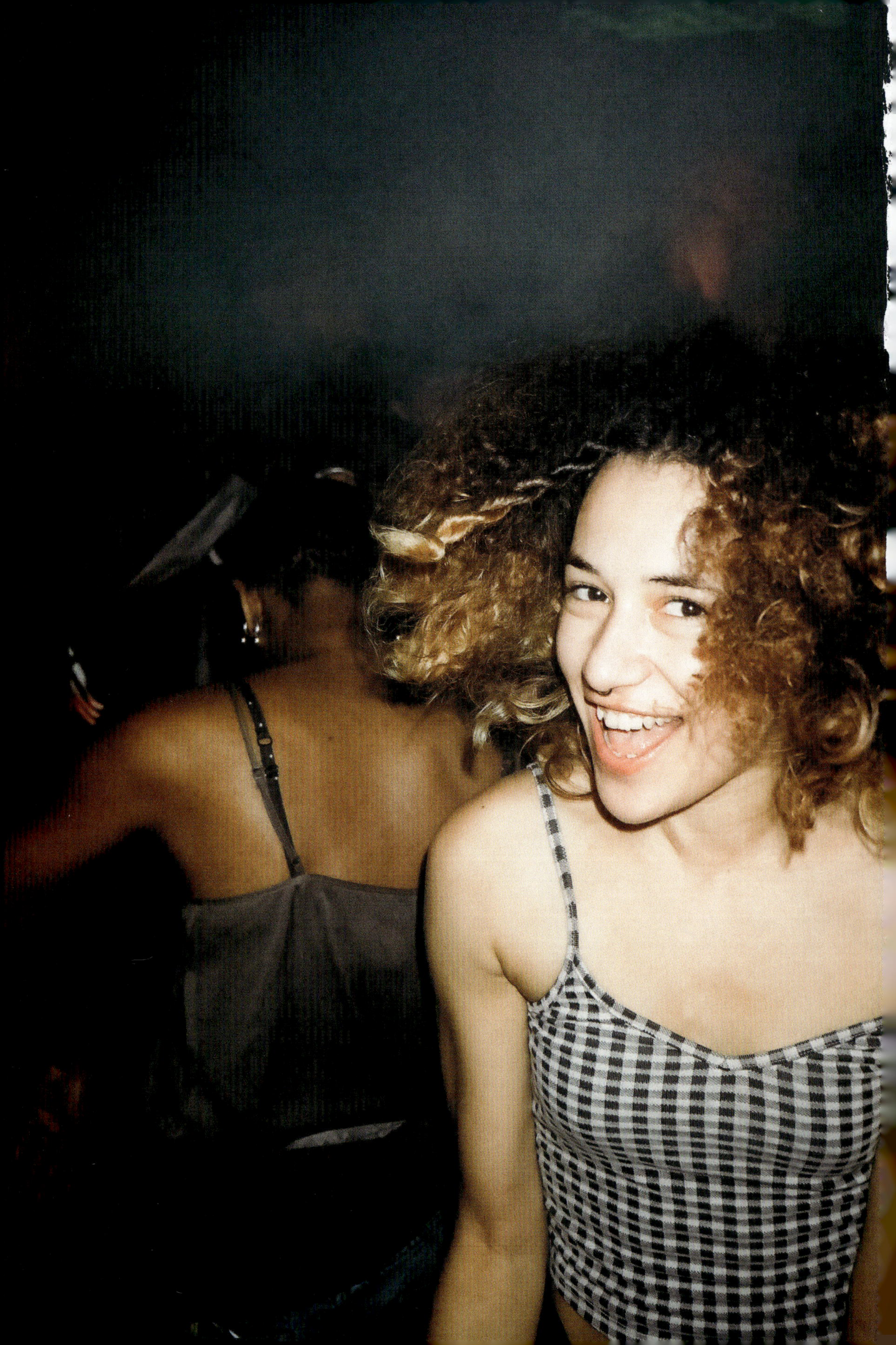

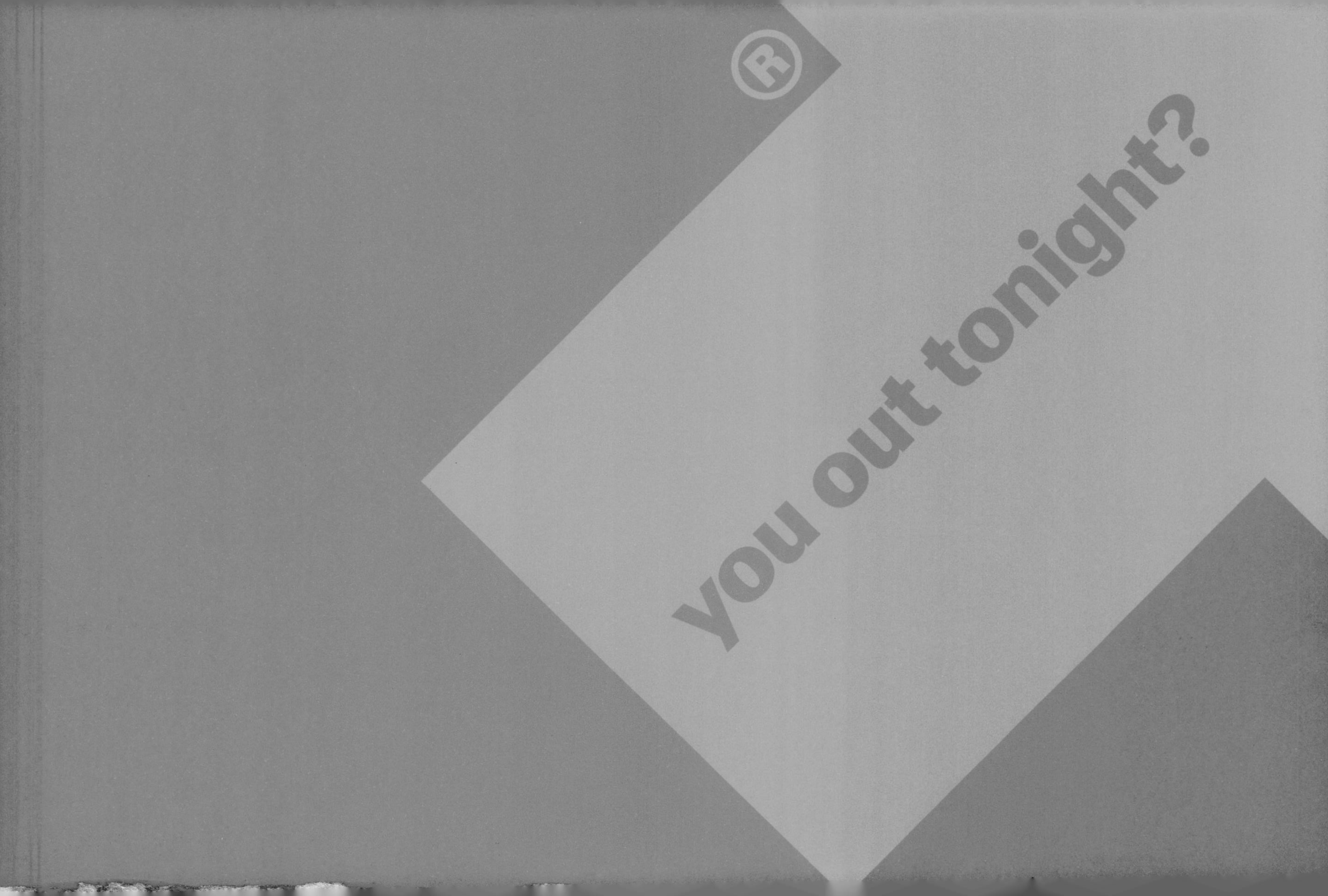

you out tonight?
®

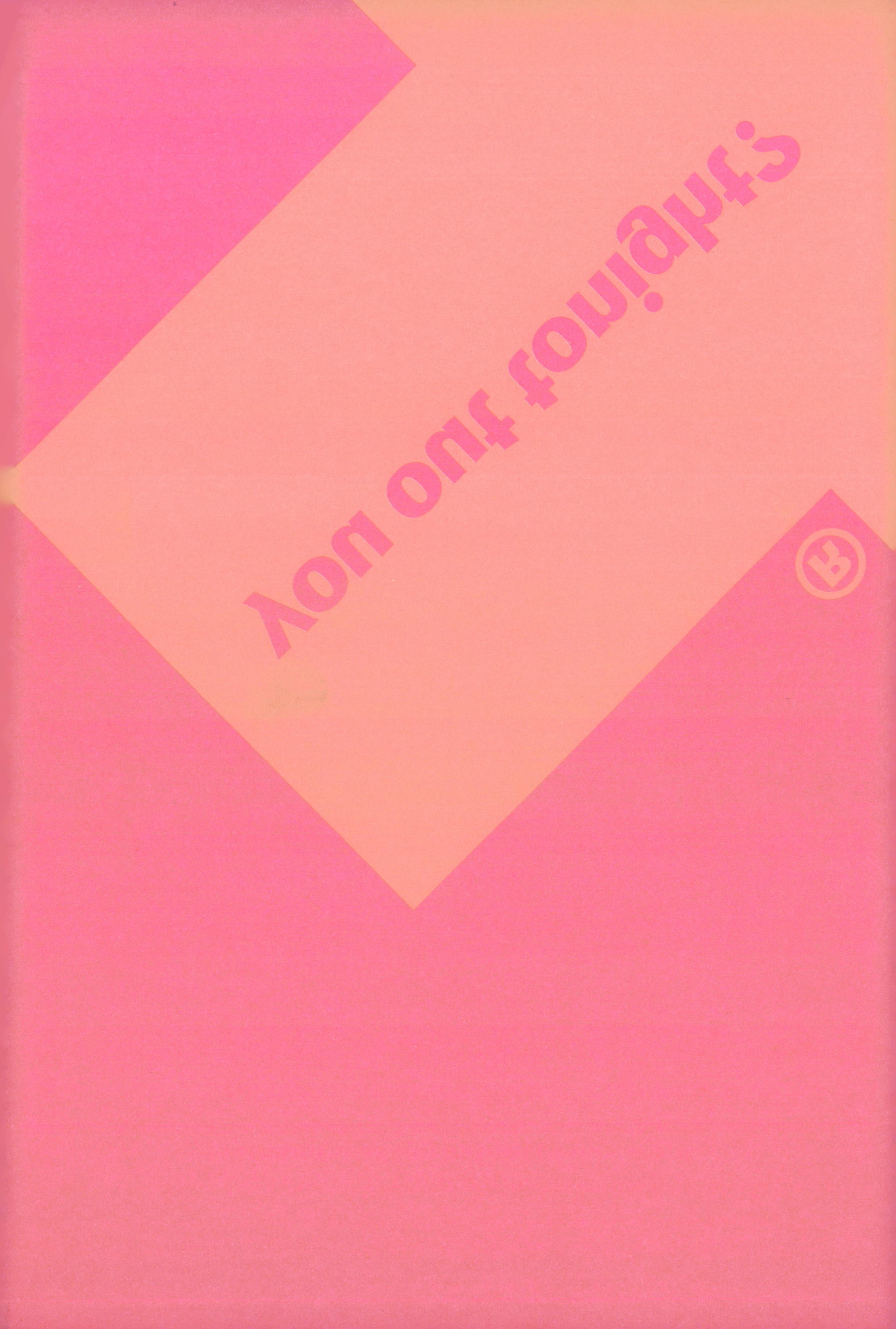
You out tonight?

Design by Alfie Allen & Max Marshall

ISBN: 9781913231606

Acknowledgements
Aaron Wyld, Alfred Golding, Alice Palm, Amelia Valentiner, Bruna Blumenberg, Daniel Fennessy, Azel and Tom from Distorted, Edward Pascall, Max McDonald, Peter Aallyn, Mara, Franka & Annemoon from Roffa Archive, Selina Paton, Tara Sammouri, Tia Payne, Ellie, Mark, Michelle, Maddie, Elliott.

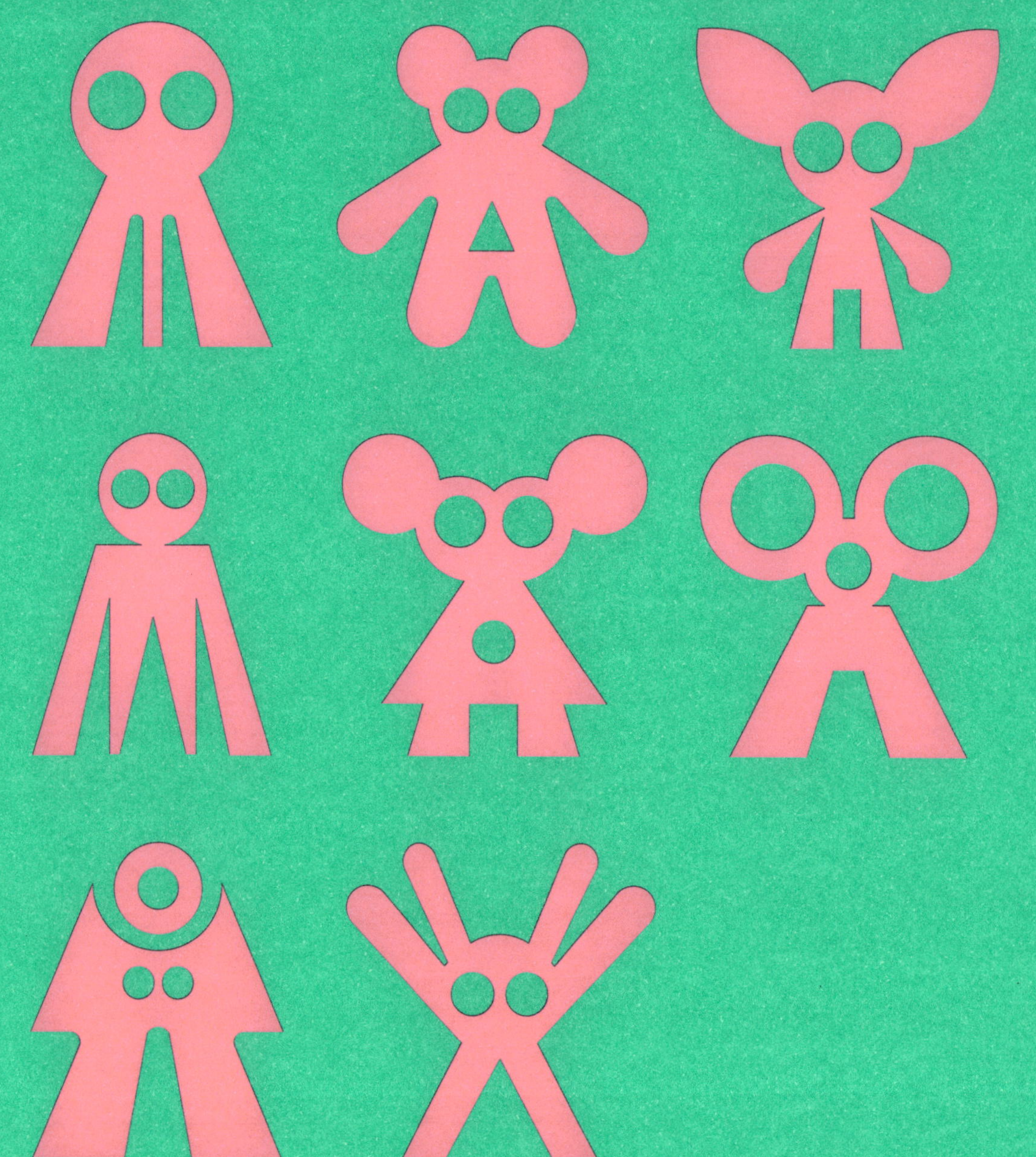

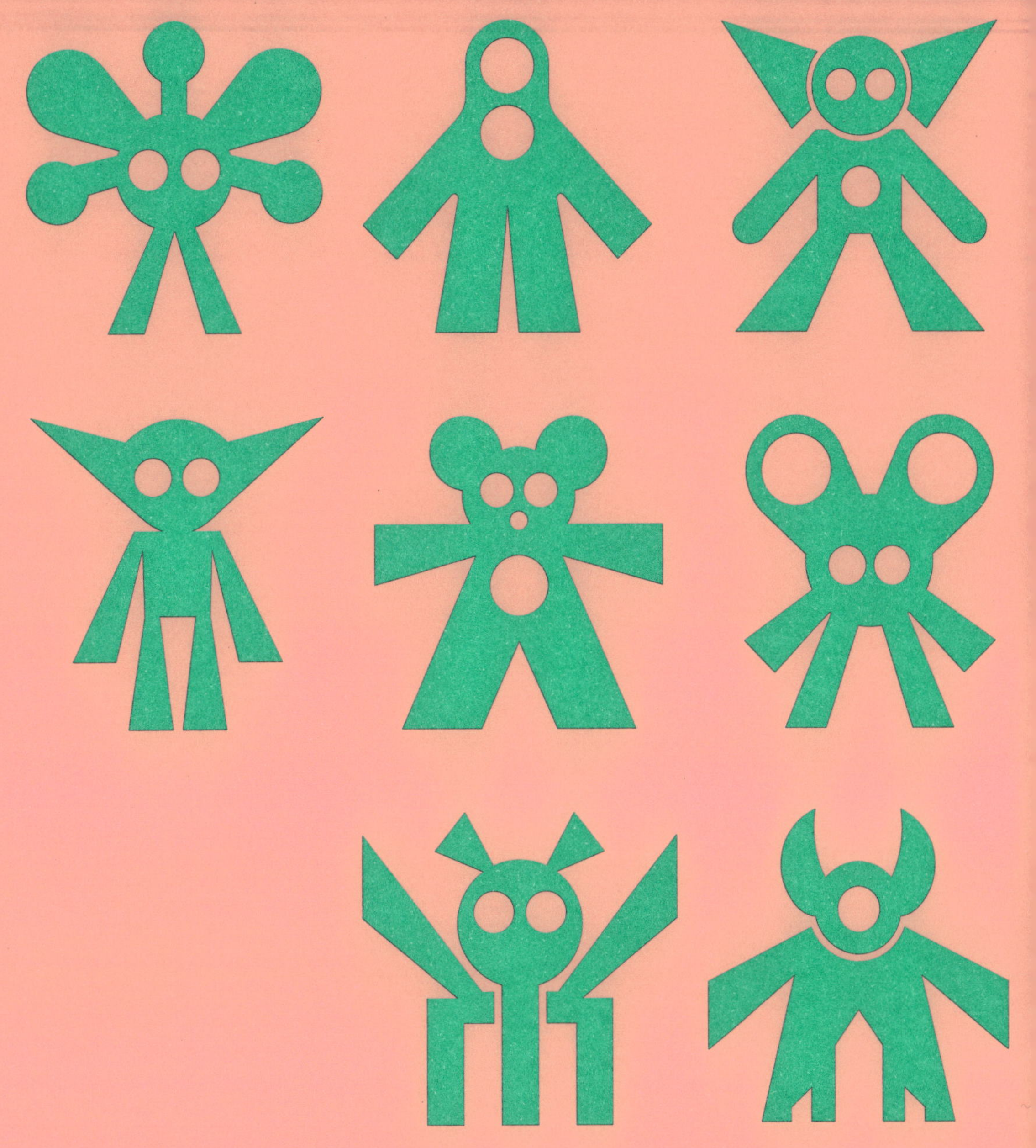